ernment

Early Victorian Government

1830—1870

OLIVER MACDONAGH

Weidenfeld and Nicolson
London

Copyright © 1977 by Oliver MacDonagh

Weidenfeld and Nicolson
11 St John's Hill, London SW11

ISBN 0 297 77250 3 cased
ISBN 0 297 77301 1 paperback

Printed in Great Britain by
Willmer Brothers Limited Birkenhead

For my sons,
Oliver, Francis and John

Contents

Preface

I wrote this book for what the Victorians called the plain reader. If he will not think it impertinent after such an opening, the figure whom I saw across the desk while I was writing was the sober first- or second-year undergraduate. Of course, an author's bounding hope sometimes flanked him on the one hand with fellow professionals, and on the other with gentlemen seeking a gentleman's knowledge – or for that matter, ladies seeking a lady's.

It is then meant to be a general book, related to political and social history courses. For this reason the topics chosen for particular examination are those which seemed largest, and were most public and controverted, in Victorian England and Wales. Moreover, the chosen scale and scope implied omissions, both of necessity and of choice. Education and housing, for example, were certainly burning social questions of the day. But, late and largely local developers, they lie outside the main pattern of growth which I have selected for examination. Scots as well as Irish were governed in the middle quarters of the nineteenth century. But the Scottish administrative and legal structures were much more alien than Ireland's, and the administrative history of Scotland is still more *terra incognita* – at any rate, to me. For some the Hegelian synthesis (or should it be the British *mélange*?) which followed the nineteenth-century struggles would have formed the diamond point of their inquiry. But I preferred the simple categories of the Victorians themselves, 'over-government' and 'centralization'. For some the engrossing questions would have been whether, say, Ashley worked in factory reform to prepare the way for the evangelical conversion of England, or whether Kingsley worked in the sanitary movement because of some obsession with lustration, or whether Chadwick or Trevelyan worked for mastery from megalomania. But each labour had in any case a face value which in itself seemed a fair, full and proper subject for inquiry. Some might say police reform is the elaboration of social controls and treasury reform the capture of commanding heights by the bourgeoisie. But even if one agreed, this exhausts neither their history nor their interest. The controversy on the revolution in government in the nineteenth century is not canvassed here. It began (so far as I am concerned) with a proferred tool for historical investigation, a razor for Occam's hand; and the method in question involves microscopic work, the examination (in Professor Dyos' phrase) of the development of coral reefs – my earlier book, *A pattern of government growth 1800–60*, being a case in point. Neither the tool nor the method is appropriate to a general survey. Perhaps I should add that I intend to return to both in a more fitting context.

The title 'Early Victorian Government' also needs some explanation. For this book retreats in places to the 1780s and advances elsewhere even to 1936; several of its major topics had their clear beginnings before 1837; and *central* government alone is dealt with. I can only plead a certain succinctness, euphony and span of ethos to justify my selection of the label. In fact the book is concerned with the wave of overt and controverted governmental change which began its breaking in the 1830s and reached its final limit on the strand some forty years later, no matter when its various parts began to gather force or how long their final seething lasted.

My special debts are twofold. First I have drawn heavily on certain works, A. V. Dicey, *Law and public opinion in England in the nineteenth century*; S. E. Finer, *The life and times of Sir Edwin Chadwick*; M. W. Thomas, *The early factory acts*; R. J. Lambert, *Sir John Simon*; R. B. McDowell, *The Irish administration, 1801–1914*; D. Fraser, *The evolution of the British welfare state*; E. Hughes, 'Sir Charles Trevelyan and civil service reform, 1853–5' in *English Historical Review*, vol. 64;

and my own paper 'Coal mines regulation: the first decade 1842–52' in R. Robson, ed., *Ideas and institutions of Victorian Britain*. Of course I am indebted to many more scholarly works than this short list would suggest. But these represent my principal academic obligations. Secondly I owe more than I can well repay to my colleagues in the Research School of Social Sciences. Dr F. B. Smith, Dr A. W. Martin, Dr D. K. Schreuder and Mr Derek Abbott have provided solace, quotations and phrases, and stylistic and grammatical chastisement over the past six months. As for Mrs Lois Simms who typed and corrected version after version of my chapters, the length and sweetness of her temper has equalled even the merit of her performance. But my outstanding creditor is, as always, my wife.

Finally I should like to think that my late friend Dr G. S. R. Kitson Clark, who first – and often – told me to write this book, would have liked it after all.

Canberra, 1976

ONE

The favouring and resisting forces

I propose first to sketch in a very general way the context and background of the revolution in social administration in the middle quarters of the nineteenth century which transformed a loose old-fashioned polity with few central functions and little central power into a much more actively and nationally regulated society. What I hope especially to show and explain is that this transformation was not a simple and direct progression but one marked by successive gains and losses and by conflicts of interests and ideas, both diverted and extended by extraneous issues and taking its permanent shape and nature in many instances from the peculiar contemporary conditions. To a considerable extent the quasi-collectivist state of the early twentieth century is the product of these nineteenth-century circumstances, attitudes and ideas.

I think that this may best be shown by examining in turn the main forces tending to promote and the main forces tending to retard centralization and the extension of state power. As to the former, pride of place must of course be given to the changes in the size, distribution and economic functions of the population occasioned by the agrarian and industrial changes of the eighteenth and early nineteenth centuries. In 1801 the population of England and Wales numbered some eight million; in 1893 it was thirteen. It was increasing by between fifteen and twenty per cent every decade. Further, it was the industrial working classes who accounted for the bulk of the increase and the manufacturing towns which gained most rapidly. Between 1801 and 1831 many Yorkshire and

Lancashire towns, for example, grew two- or three- or even four-fold: Leeds grew almost five-fold. These thirty years moreover marked a vital change in the nature of the industrial revolution, for which the introduction of steam was primarily responsible. It was steam which lay behind the transference of much of the textile industry from villages with water power to the largest towns. This in its turn destroyed anything in the nature of the quasi-paternalistic relationship between masters and workmen which had survived to some degree so long as industries were placed in a generally conservative countryside and the working body was relatively small and stable. 'This is now quite changed,' wrote Sir Walter Scott in 1820,

> the manufacturers are transferred to great towns, where a man may assemble five hundred workmen one week and dismiss them next, without having any further connexion with them than to receive a week's work for a week's wages, nor any further solicitude about their future fate than if they were so many old shuttles.[1]

Thus the modern problems of an industrial proletariat and of urban aggregation were already set. The wages contract was substituted for more complex and intra-personal relationships; and as the towns became more and more densely packed there was progressive deterioration in living and sanitary standards, further hastened by the presence of manufacture with its smoke, dirt, trade refuse and polluted water. Of course this thrusting of a vast and growing body of the population into an economic battleground, this destruction of all vestigial remains of traditional securities and protective devices and this deadly concentration of ill-fed and ill-housed people had great consequences in political and working class history. But they had also great consequences in the history of the state. For it was these which set the problem – or at least rendered more manifest a version of the problem – for which more collectivized and more centralized social organization and state regulation had ultimately to provide the answers. They furnished the raw material, the opportunity and the stimulus for radical, tory and humanitarian collectivists alike – at any rate for those

2

whose actions led inexorably towards collectivism, however little they appreciated or intended this themselves.

In some respects agrarian England also contributed its share to the accumulation of raw material for collectivism; indeed down to 1835 it largely engrossed the attention of contemporaries, and its problems inspired the most important single social measure of the century, the poor law of 1834. Though this can easily be pressed too far, agriculture presented many of the same features as industrialism : the extension of capitalism and the profit motive, the destruction of status and securities and their replacement by wage or dole, a fatally ill-adjusted labour market and supply, and slums and disease, mitigated only (if mitigation it was) by the open sky.

So far in our sketch of the prime cause or precondition of the administrative changes we have been regarding the great social and economic upheavals in Great Britain and Ireland as setting new sorts of problems which demanded new types of remedy. Both in their scale and nature these problems were quite unprecedented. But the social upheavals which set the problems also ultimately helped to produce the answers. It may perhaps be clearest to divide this aspect of the matter into three : the technical, the political and (what we may call for want of better words) the theoretical and sentimental. In one respect the industrial revolution may be regarded as primarily a revolution in engineering and mechanical science. Each advance in the machines used for manufacture was conducted on a broad front and preceded by a lengthy period of trials and failures by many individuals. The harnessing of steam was a step forward of another order. It not only transformed the organization and the scale of industry but also brought into being a new system of communications and a new profession.

By 1850 we find the emergence of cheap mass production; of a cheap, rapid national system of transportation; of a specifically engineering and mechanical industry; of a tried and (to some degree) proved body of civil and mechanical engineers, bound closely into a profession; and not least important, of a growing habit of experimentation in engineering and mechanics and a growing belief that no engineering or mechanical problem was ultimately irresolvable. All this meant, for example, that when arterial drainage was called for, the newly invented glazed and earthenware pipes could be produced and transported cheaply and in great numbers almost overnight. It meant that when novel ventilation or sanitary appliances were called for, there were men with some measure of exact knowledge who could and would eagerly take up the challenge. At the same time a corresponding development was taking place in medicine, although this was both much less advanced and much less directly related to the social and economic change. Here again, the most important steps were those taken in method and in professional status. The rejection of *a priori* assumptions, empirical investigation, the building up of a corps of trained, examined and tried men – these were the necessary pre-conditions for a material growth in knowledge.

It is true that by modern standards the state of both engineering and medicine in the 1840s (and particularly the latter) seems absurdly backward. But seen against the background of the eighteenth century the progress between 1800 and 1850 had been prodigious. Without it the contemporary measures of state interference in public health would have been unthinkable. But of still greater importance was its promise for the future. In the long run what was really vital was that there had come into being bodies of professionals who were beginning to apply the correct method of investigation and who were convinced from their earlier successes that for almost every problem there was a solution which experiment would sooner or later reveal. Thus in every technical difficulty the administration had men to turn to; for every technical measure of regulation and control they had men to call on to enforce it. The competence and expertise of such men was rapidly increasing by 1850.

It had also a system of communications which made centralization practicable; and both large scale and specialized industries which could produce the tools for social amelioration rapidly in large quantities and – perhaps most important of all in the circumstances of Victorian England – cheaply. The administration also inherited two material legacies from the revolutionary and Napoleonic wars. One was a considerable mass of statistical and social data, and still more the skills and casts of mind which had been developed in these inquiries.

4

The other was a great body of officer-veterans. These supplied a high proportion of the new officials of 1815–40; and their experience of working within a vast hierarchical and central-ized organization patently prepared them for the new field work and the new form of executive corps. All these were obviously factors of immense importance in the development of a new species of government.

The second assisting force I have loosely called the political. One aspect of this is so obvious and familiar that it needs no elaboration. The reform act of 1832 shifted the balance of political power in society; and, especially in the years 1833–49, the beneficiaries (for whom, despite all that has come and gone, the loose term 'middle classes' is perhaps still the least misleading categorization) secured or were provided with a body of remedial legislation, some of which promoted im-portant administrative change. For the most part it did so negatively, by attacking the inherited tangle of administrative abuses and irrationalities; but there was also a more positive contribution through the middle class desire to cheapen govern-ment and to make it comprehensible and workable.

Below the surface however there was a less obvious political change which had perhaps more far-reaching consequences for our purpose. During the decade 1825–35 the nature of parlia-mentary government was being transformed. The older notions that the business of government was essentially executive, and that whatever general measures of social policy were needed were properly the concern of parliament as a whole, and should normally be introduced not by the government but by private members, were dying. As late as 1836 Mel-bourne still proclaimed the eighteenth-century view that 'the duty of a Government is not to pass legislation but to rule', and traces of this survived to 1850 and beyond. But it was being steadily pressed out by the exigencies of the time. Such a system was obviously too haphazard and ineffectual to satisfy the needs of early Victorian Britain. What was required and what developed with extraordinary rapidity was a deliberate legislative policy continued from session to session. The modern speech from the throne, the lengthening of sessions, the drastic reduction of private members' time and the con-stant increase in government's all date from these few years.

In a word legislation became both the business of the ministry, and systematic and continuous. From our point of view what was especially significant in this was that such a legislative policy necessitated a government instrument to execute and maintain it – commissioners, inspectorates and executive officers. Thus it carried within itself the seed of the modern concept of the public service. But still further, such a government instrument in its turn implied a government or state policy, something continuous and constant and apart from and above the alternating ministries.

There is moreover another aspect to the manner. The new type of planned cabinet legislation dealing with novel and unprecedented social problems required exact knowledge before remedial action could be taken. Hence the simultaneous development of investigating instruments by parliament. The select committee had been used before 1820 but only intermittently, and the royal commission was still more rare. After that date, and more particularly after 1830, both were used with a regularity and a purpose quite without precedent. It is difficult to over-estimate the importance of this development. Through session after session, through hundreds of inquiries and the examination of many thousands of witnesses a vast mass of information and statistics was being assembled. Even where (as was not uncommonly the case) the official inquiry was in the hands of unscrupulous partisans, a sort of informal adversary system usually led to the enlargement of true knowledge in the end. A session or two later the counter-partisans would secure a counter-exposition of their own. All this enabled the administration to act with a confidence, a perspective and a breadth of vision which had never hitherto existed. It had also a profound secular effect upon public opinion generally and upon parliamentary public opinion in particular. For the exposure of the actual state of things in particular fields was in the long run probably the most fruitful source of reform in nineteenth-century England. The bare facts of the extent of suffering, waste, dirt or disease when made known corroded the opposition to reform, whether that opposition was grounded in doctrine, self-interest or inertia. Often the process was dual. The initial 'revelation' excited 'something of that mingled novelty and horror with which a culti-

vated audience listens to the description of the barbarous customs of a recently discovered tribe of aborigines'.[2] Later came
the 'trickling increment' of discoveries that the roots of evils
ran far back, were intertwined and could resist almost indefinitely the repeated efforts to eradicate them.

The third major factor, associated with the social upheavals,
which contributed to administrative change was the 'sentimental and theoretical'. Here the force of prime importance
was humanitarianism. Humanitarianism has been often treated
as a derivative of other forces, such as the two particularly
distinguished by Dicey, Benthamism and evangelicalism. It is
certainly true that the Benthamite emphasis upon the diminution of pain and the increase in pleasure and the evangelical
insistence upon good works and the value of the individual
personality gave both these creeds a humanitarian bias. But
it is also true that each contained elements tending in an opposite direction and that practical humanitarianism was by no
means confined to such relatively narrow circles. We must cast
our net much wider and go back further in time to gauge this
influence. By a relatively early stage in the nineteenth century
humanitarian sentiment prevailed in public attitudes whatever
private conduct or personal motivation may have been; and
when the 'climate of opinion' was predominantly humanitarian, when that opinion was reflected even obliquely in parliament and legislation and when the true circumstances of many
branches of society and the economy were being laid bare,
the road was open for a transformation in the nature of the
state.

But quite apart from their humanitarian and anti-humanitarian elements such overlapping but essentially exogenous
forces as evangelicalism and Benthamism had something
further to contribute to this change. In a variety of ways the
general revival in religion and personal piety which marked
the first half of the nineteenth century promoted new social
attitudes. For example one of its fruits was a novel and intense
concern for sexual morality and 'decent' standards of behaviour. This was often to produce social reforms of a general
character not confined to moral considerations. To take one
instance, as Halevy points out when discussing the effect of
the report of the children's employment commission on mines

7

in 1842, the public conscience was even more stirred by the potential sexual licence than by the cruelty of the system.³ Yet it was this very stirring which led ultimately to the introduction of a new principle to English law, namely the exclusion of women from a particular kind of labour. Again, it was no coincidence that the Oxford Movement (itself deeply indebted to evangelicalism) should have been an ancestor of Christian socialism. For the tractarians the church was first and last a society, if not indeed society itself in its religious aspect. It was a short step from such a concern with the community or group to a concern for general as opposed to particular welfare, and to radical theorizing on social justice. Again in the general religious assault upon the traditional hedonism, intemperance and licence, it was a short step from denunciation to procuring legislation to restrain them, and a very short step from restraining legislation to the setting up of administrative machinery to enforce the restraints. Even these three random examples should make clear the variety of ways in which the nationwide revival of religion and earnestness might affect the nature and attitude of government.

As to Benthamism I shall do no more at present than draw attention to three aspects of the doctrine which were of critical importance for this purpose. First it was a programme for reforming laws by applying the devastating test of utility to every branch of government. Secondly it was extraordinarily inventive in devising universal administrative schemes to replace the existing inefficiencies. Lastly it depended upon men behaving rationally and was faced everywhere by their patent irrationality – hence the development of its manipulative or tutelary aspect, the elaboration of systems of reward and punishment which would induce men to behave in especial fashions for the general good. Such concepts opened the door wide to central control and regulatory administration.

The exclusive concern so far with the factors favouring administrative change may have given the impression that this change was irresistible and unresisted, and that it was recognized by the body of contemporaries to be a patent necessity and eagerly promoted by them. In fact nothing could be farther from the truth. Both centralization and collectivism were altogether alien to the prevailing climate of opinion. Broadly speaking where they made headway they did so surreptitiously and circuitously. Where the matter at issue was openly debated they had to be explained away as exceptions, as unusual necessities or even on occasions as subtle applications of the principle of individualism. When the American political boss Huey Long was asked whether fascism could ever come to the United States, he replied (so the story goes) with the serpent's wisdom, 'Yes, it could, provided it calls itself anti-fascism'. Much the same was true of some important collectivist measures of the early nineteenth century. Moreover we must remember that a large body if not an actual majority of such measures received little or no public attention or examination; or if they did, that their collectivist implications went unrecognized.

In short the age of which we speak, c.1830–70, was one of positive and aggressive individualism; and if during this period the foundations of the modern state were laid, it happened only because of the immense pressure from beneath of the promoting factors, only because of the great difficulty of measuring particular actions of government and particular statutes against the uncertain yardstick of individualism, and only because a large number of the measures (and especially of the Irish measures) slipped through unnoticed. The power of the opposition to collectivism and centralization is further demonstrated by the fact that in several instances in the 1830s, 1840s and 1850s, there was an immediate reaction against collectivist and centralizing measures which had been passed and a very considerable loss of ground; and also by the fact that, taking a broad view of the period as a whole, we find that the initial waves of centralizing and administrative bustle in 1830–50 are followed by two decades of relative indifference and inaction.

Having rid ourselves of one possible misconception, namely that the administrative revolution was achieved painlessly and without resistance, we must now in these preliminary remarks guard ourselves against another, the whig interpretation, a fallacy to which administrative history is peculiarly prone. We must not suppose that the only effect of the opposition, resistance, and confusion in thinking about the nature of the state was to hold up artificially and for a few years an inevitable process; in other words we must not suppose that the only effect of these was to make the administrative revolution happen slightly later in time. This would be wrong for two reasons. First it mattered a very great deal to people living at the time whether something were carried out thirty years sooner or later, and what actually happened to these people is our primary concern; secondly the 'process' (if it may so be called) was not fixed or inevitable at all. It was continuously taking and changing shape. Whether a 'reform' were carried in 1835 or 1895 often made a vital difference to the very nature of the measure, and thereby (in many instances) to the sort of institutions and practice that we have today. These institutions are not a whole, are not uniform, are not without theoretical and normative contradictions and anomalies; and such differences frequently arose from the social atmosphere, the circumstances and the personalities of the participants at the moment when the measures in question were initiated.

A glance at the history of, say, education or police or local government in the nineteenth century will confirm this fully. Dicey, writing on the changes that took place in the climate of law-making opinion in the nineteenth century, makes the general point well.

Ancient toryism died hard. It lived long enough to leave time for the rise of a new toryism in which democratic sentiment deeply tinged with socialism, blends with that faith in the paternal despotism of the State which formed part of the old Tory creed. Liberalism itself has at last learned to place no small confidence in the beneficent effects of state control; but this trust, whether well founded or not, is utterly foreign to the liberalism of 1832.

The assertion that to delay the action of a political creed may introduce into it essential modification, is opposed to the superstition, propagated by many eminent writers, that reformers, though baffled during their lifetime by the opposition of ignorance, prejudice, or selfishness, may count on their efforts being crowned by success in some subsequent age. ... But history lends no countenance to the optimism which it is alleged to encourage. Neither the democratic toryism nor the socialistic liberalism of today is the philosophical radicalism of Bentham. ... The strong counter-current of ancient toryism has, by delaying their action, modified all the political beliefs of 1832.[4]

So much for the notion that a rising force in history, however resisted, will sooner or later win through absolutely unaltered and intact.

Having established these general points we can now analyse more effectively the forces which hindered administrative change and the extremely complicated course which it followed down to 1870. This analysis will form in some repects the converse of the first. Here the physical factors (so to speak) need not detain us long. Obviously the frontier of discovery, or invention, or technique, in medicine or the applied sciences at any particular moment limited the sphere of possible administrative action, or at any rate the sphere of effective administrative action. Obviously the extent of useful knowledge on particular social problems at particular times, the want of a modern science of economic measurement, the deficiencies in statistics and similar limitations in communications had a corresponding tendency. But all this had best be dealt with stage by stage when we come to examine the administrative changes in some detail and more or less in chronological order. The factors which we must consider now are the factors which were most powerful in postponing change – contemporary social and economic assumptions, contemporary political conventions and contemporary vested and class interest.

What is very remarkable in the history of nineteenth-century administration and what makes it so difficult a subject to reduce to order is the fact that, though it is largely concerned with the growth of collectivism, practical collectivism came into existence piecemeal and long before any coherent theory of the sort. Collectivism was never a doctrine in nineteenth-century England, never formulated by a thinker of commanding ability, never applied deliberately and consciously to law. One important facet of all this was that there was no group or body in early Victorian England consciously and single-mindedly promoting collectivism; indeed, no group or body had a clear understanding of its implications or extent, or perhaps even of its existence. Some favouring factors such as humanitarianism were of course more or less common to all sections. But other favouring factors were shared out indiscriminately amongst them. To continue with Dicey's crude, old-fashioned but still indispensable stereotypes of old toryism, middle class liberalism and working class radicalism, each contained elements peculiar to itself which assisted the development of collectivism. The old toryism was paternalistic, inclined towards a powerful state and infused with images of communal responsibility. Middle class liberalism demanded the abolition of exclusively aristocratic and extravagant government; and this demand led to the destruction of many inefficient, venal and irrational institutions. The collectivist bias of much working class radicalism, once its preliminary objective of political power was attained, needs no demonstration. Yet each contained equally important elements antagonistic to the development of collectivism. This was no less true of working class radicalism than the other two on such issues as children's labour or safety regulation.

Toryism was of course predominantly agrarian, but we must extend the term to cover all those who wished to conserve the law and institutions of England intact, that is the main body of lawyers and churchmen, certain of the older trade interests such as sugar and shipping and many others who believed that they gained from or were most comfortable within the existing arrangements of society. I shall not attempt here to analyse the old or 'eighteenth-century' polity. It is sufficient for our purposes to note that it was a system of remarkably weak central control, remarkably autonomous local bodies, and remarkably small units of local government. Thus power in local matters (the power which affected men most immediately in the nineteenth century) rested to an extraordinary degree upon the unreformed corporations, parish vestries and justices of the peace – upon small town merchants, farmers and the gentry and parochial clergy. There were some 25,000 petty instruments of government largely independent of each other and of the central authority in England and Wales. When, as in the boroughs particularly, they proved grossly incapable of performing necessary tasks they were not abolished. Instead new *ad hoc* bodies were set up by private acts of parliament and added to the administrative constellation to revolve for ever. This system of local government had immense prescriptive right: it had grown up over several centuries, it had survived intact innumerable constitutional and political changes, it had come to seem, particularly for those who manipulated it, part of the natural and eternal order of things. It was also deeply embedded in the old system of politics through patronage.

A corresponding development had taken place in the established church and in law, particularly in the latter. Law had long been growing more technical and specialized: even recent reforms and extensions of principle had increased this tendency for there were few repeals and no reversal of decisions. Reform was commonly achieved by the creation of long and complex legal fictions. Otherwise it was impossible to break out of the thick web which generations of lawyers had spun and were still spinning. Equity had long surrendered its original mobility and creativeness and was now even more precedent-chained than the common law which it had once set out to release. Procedure was in chaos, jurisdiction often concurrent and ambiguous. The general effect of the tropical luxuriance of this growth was that no one knew his way about the whole. Instead lawyers worked in ever narrowing fields and the number of vested legal interests, the number who lived by the extreme technicality of the various courts and divisions of the law, gradually multiplied.

These two prime examples of the *ancien régime*, local government and law, make clear at once the great difficulty of effecting any alteration. It was not merely a matter of long established personal interests. Equally important, they had grown into the state so that they seemed almost indivisible from government itself while their age, complexity and technicality blinded men to the possibility of change.

All this serves to demonstrate how powerful was the modifying force wielded by radical ideas and middle class political pressures during the administrations of Grey and Melbourne in the 1830s. But though we recognize that the force which accomplished so much in so short a time must have been extraordinarily powerful, we must also recognize that the eighteenth-century system of government was but partially destroyed. The survival of patronage (even after its political *raison d'être* had disappeared) had the profoundest effects on the very engine of administration, the civil service. Not until 1870 were competition and open examination generally and seriously applied. Lord Stamp has said that a country cannot legislate beyond the capacity of its administrators to execute; and all testimony goes to show that very many of the civil servants of the old order were incompetent, sickly, idle or mischievous. Some may have been all four. There was a long series of particular reforms of law from 1820 onwards. But the central problem, that of organization and jurisdiction, was not tackled head-on until the judicature act of 1873. No doubt the justices of the peace were shorn of much power during the 1830s, and no doubt they had to share much of the remainder with elected representatives. But much of their power still survived and the institution came through intact. The parish system of government was dealt a seeming death blow by the poor law amendment act of 1834. But it did not die. During the late 1830s and the early 1840s the parishes gradually crept back. The municipal reform act of 1835 swept away the bad old corporations. But the municipal electorate was still left smaller than the parliamentary, the new corporations were given inadequate powers and scope, and (as the history of the next decade shows) they were only too often prone to substitute a new set of self-interests for the old. In short the apparently clean sweep of the 1830s should not be taken at face value. Though its achievements were prodigious it was at least half a failure. Much of the old habit of reforming by tacking new institutions on to old survived. Now this was important not merely because part of the older system lingered long enough to be subsumed in a new and more deliberate wave of collectivism in the 1870s, but was also important in explaining the course of events in the 1840s and 1850s, and through them also the shape of the state today. For during this middle period the survival of the *local* tradition of government and of a vast range of local vested interests, new and old, did much to halt a vital movement towards centralization at a decisive stage.

Equally, the opponents of toryism provided a block to centralization and collectivism. During their struggle for political powers those of them who were clients and beneficiaries of the industrial revolution had come to adopt an extreme, often fundamentalist, form of *laissez faire*. In many cases they had fought their way to the top and for the most part they regarded the system which had borne them to success as the natural economic dispensation which must sooner or later produce the utmost general prosperity. The truth seemed self-evident. They had merely to count their achievements, the intoxicating increase in production, machinery, wealth and power, to feel that the system had been fully justified. They were moreover powerfully reinforced in this faith by the findings of the new study of economics. More than a generation before, Adam Smith had elaborated the classical doctrine of free trade, and in 1817 Ricardo had practically founded a school of political economy devoted to the same principle. Though the school was minute and initially obscure its influence was by now overwhelming. The political economists believed that they had discovered a new science which would explain society and they spoke with all the authority of scientific discoverers. As Finer puts it, 'Compared with the Cabinets they not infrequently advised, they were authorities.'[5]

It is true that they did not speak with one voice. Yet all were at least supposed to agree on these broad propositions: that there was a natural harmony of economic interests, that interference by the state with the free play of these interests was injurious, and that consequently (with the relatively minor exception of what patently belonged to the category of public undertakings) a condition of uncluttered enterprise and unfettered competition should be immediately established. Thus the conclusions of the social scientists coincided, generally speaking, with the instincts and interests of the mill owners, cotton manufacturers, bankers, middlemen and iron founders who now wielded an increasing political power, and the effect of the alliance was overwhelming. This was all the more true because the authority was moral as well as intellectual. To empathize truly with the righteous assurance of Victorian mill owners in for example their resistance to 'interference' with the working hours or working habits of their men, we must remember that they were 'a people of the Book' and that the *Wealth of Nations* had asserted:

The patrimony of a poor man lies in the strength and dexterity of his hands; and to hinder him from employing this strength and dexterity in whatever manner he thinks proper without injury to his neighbour, is a plain violation of this most sacred property. It is a manifest encroachment upon the just liberty both of the workman, and of those who might be disposed to employ him.[6]

Clearly this bred an atmosphere hostile to collectivism and centralization alike. It is true that the new liberals demanded and secured reform. But for them reform consisted essentially in removing obstacles and repealing existing legislation. They looked on contemporary society as a vehicle braked by archaic commercial restraints and loaded down with a dead weight of aristocratic and agricultural privilege. Of course it still ran despite these handicaps, but how much more freely and swiftly would it travel if the checks were to be taken off and the unnecessary burdens discarded. Their view of reform was negative and finite. After the corn and navigation laws had been repealed in 1846 and 1849 respectively, the feeling was widespread that there were really no more legislative worlds to conquer. It is also true that they desired a rationalization and a simplification of law and were in this respect at one with Bentham. As men of business they were maddened by the delays, complications, expense and mystery of the existing legal system. It hurt both their pockets and their habits. But here again their concept was negative and self-interested. Their great legal object was security for property, for the 'freedom' of contracts and for the rights and possessions of the individual – *contra mundum*. If this was to be the achievement of a simpler and more effective law, of what value was it to the millions of the property-less or the millions without bargaining powers when they came to sell their labour?

Thus the type of society at which, to speak in general terms, both the new manufacturing and commercial classes and the political economists aimed was in many ways the antithesis of our present aspirations. A free economy was, literally, its object. Competition, individual self-interest and the profit motive were to be given as open a field for action as was compatible with indispensable social bonds. If combinations of individuals (whether masters or workmen) were contrary to the natural order, *a fortiori* since state action could effect infinitely more, state interference could be infinitely more deleterious.

Moreover, the liberal distrust of state action was re-emphasized by two other forces. First was the common tendency amongst these classes to associate *all* central government activity with the sort of government activity to which they were accustomed. Here the absence of a reform of the administration and the continuance of many of the eighteenth-century political conventions told heavily. Whenever it was now proposed that the central power should act in a new field it was widely assumed that it would act as it had always done – corruptly, wastefully and by multiplying sinecures for aristocratic drones. Second, and related to the first, there was a widespread feeling amongst the business classes that their own methods were the only ones which worked. Private enterprise and the competitive principle were daily proving themselves capable of meeting every need where the state was failing lamentably. Indeed as to efficiency they stood at opposite poles. If there was inefficiency in private enterprise it could not long survive: but in state management there was no incentive to efficiency whatever. Hence the common belief that what we now regard as public services would come into being and operate more efficiently through the desire for profit on the part of private individuals and private companies. No field seemed too large or complex for the competitive principle.

We have still not reached the bottom of the liberal opposition to collectivism and centralization. Perhaps the most powerful and persistent of middle class demands was that for financial economy. Private and personal thrift had become almost a religious duty. No item of domestic spending was too small to escape its superintendence. The same principle was applied to public spending. To such an attitude successive chancellors of the exchequer, at any rate from the 1820s onwards, were converted. There was never so complete a convert as Gladstone. It was his life-long conviction, as he said,

that all excess in the public expenditure ... is not only a pecuniary waste but a great political, and above all, a great moral evil. It is a characteristic of the mischiefs that arise from financial prodigality that they creep onwards with a

noiseless and stealthy step; that they commonly remain un-
seen and unfelt, until they have reached a magnitude absolutely overwhelming.[7]

It is true that such a conviction and climate of thought led
incidentally to the hacking away of many anomalies and administrative incubi. But once again its primary tendency was
negative. Its object was limited to the reduction of the expenses of existing government institutions, either by operating them more efficiently or by abolishing or conflating offices.
Fresh sources of government expenditure were anathema, and
it was impossible to extend the sphere of state action without
increasing this expenditure. Thus right through the nineteenth
century the prevailing attitude towards taxation jealously restricted state activity, and it was to have particularly important
influence in delaying the development of collectivism after
1870.

Finally, the liberal opposition was not entirely general,
speculative or the consequence of their business habits. There
was also a hard core of class and personal interest. This was
so because the most obvious fields for collectivist legislation
and regulation in the 1830s and 1840s were often their own
immediate concern, the mills and factories, the pollution, the
hours of labour, the conditions of work, the fencing of
machinery, the employment of children and women and the
contract between master and workman. By and large and as a
group the manufacturers and business interests fought each
attempt at interference as if it were a matter of life and death.
So indeed they persuaded themselves it was. It was no caricature when their opponents depicted them as arguing that
no profit whatever was made except in the last hour of work,
or that the prosperity of England rested upon the labours of
half a million little children.[8] These were the very things said,
backed in many instances by the statistics and laborious calculations of economists. The authority with which they spoke
and the body of learned opinion they could muster shook successive governments at critical stages of factory and similar
restrictive legislation. They could also throw into the scales
their considerable political power as a pressure group in parlia-

ment and their capacity for rigging select committees and side-tracking royal commissions.

This authorized self-interest provided an important check to centralization no less than to collectivism. The municipal reform act of 1835 was a revolutionary measure, but the powers which it gave to the new corporations were quite inadequate for modern urban society. Once again this was largely due to men's experience of the *ancien régime*. Powers were jealously restricted because there was a corresponding tendency to identify all town government with corrupt and futile town government. One consequence of the act was therefore that many of the services which we should regard as automatically municipal – the supply of water is an obvious example – fell into or remained in the hands of private companies or individuals. The rise of new towns and the rapid expansion of old demanded immediate action, and in default of municipal action private enterprises stepped in. This meant that when the movement towards centralization and uniformity in public health (the obvious method of reform) developed, it found itself confronted, often with fatal consequences, by a new layer of vested interests which possessed considerable parliamentary power. A second effect of the municipal reform act was that in the considerable majority of cases it placed the government of the towns in the hands of the new middle classes without sweeping away the old divisions and subsidiary authorities in the boroughs. Like all parvenus, the new local governors were intensely proud of their domains. They resented any attempts at central direction and any efforts to impose a national local government board or even *local* uniformity. This had grave consequences in the many large cities, most of all in London, where the independence of the multitude of local bodies made it impossible to plan for the metropolis as a whole.

Even this short survey of liberal ideas and interests should have indicated clearly enough the essential facts: that they threw an immense weight against the development of the modern type of regulatory state and that they created a climate of thought decidedly hostile to both collectivism and centralization.

We must now attempt in however summary a fashion to strike a balance. First it is clear that the administrative revolutions (for generally speaking there were flows and ebbs as with an incoming tide) were neither irresistible nor unresisted. In fact for almost the entire length of the mid-nineteenth century both collectivism and centralization were totally opposed by the dominant philosophies of the day. As we have seen, one immediate and significant consequence was that down to 1870 each advance of *étatisme* was succeeded by a reaction and a very considerable loss of ground, and the relatively creative decades of the 1830s and 1840s were followed by decades of relative indifference and inaction. Generally the compromises and retreats, the delays and time lapses were not of nineteenth-century significance only. They have left deep and permanent impressions upon even the administration of today. As I have said at the outset, the administrative revolutions did not merely happen in spite of the forces of resistance; they were also in part the products of the fact that such resistance had to be overcome, circumvented or compromised with. Even so, the relative success of collectivism and centralization calls for some explanation. How was such headway made in the teeth of a head-on gale?

There are, I think, three major reasons. The first is the irreducible brute matter of the new and unprecedented social problems. Whatever was said and done individual exertion and private enterprise did not and could not resolve them – and resolved they had to be. The accumulation of knowledge both statistical and scientific had corresponding effect. If it was demonstrated that ventilation mechanisms saved miners' lives or that water sanitation drastically reduced the death rate, it was practically speaking impossible to resist the state interference implied in insisting upon these precautions, the state being the only agency which could insist and enforce effectively.

The second reason was the fact that issues were rarely presented in terms of collectivism versus anti-collectivism, or even of state action versus private action. Many of the implicitly collectivist pieces of legislation or decrees received little publicity; many of the others involved extraneous elements and conflicts of class or sectional interest which obscured the centralizing or collectivist implications. Generally indeed it was of prime importance that individualism, however powerful and widespread a sentiment, was difficult to use as a yardstick for particular statutes; and equally that there was no coherent party or theory of collectivism until long after it had entered deeply if quietly into the system of state. It was a creeping enemy and one without head or brain. To repeat a point made earlier, on the relatively rare occasions when it was openly debated, the matter could be (and was usually) explained away as an exception or an unusual necessity. Thus the wooden horse entered the gates of Troy, sometimes pulled by those who most loudly denounced the evil.

Thirdly, only the anarchic aspects of individualism and liberalism have been stressed, and these were indeed the aspects stressed by and large in the nineteenth century. But they too were subtle and creeping things, for they contained within themselves the seeds of a very different concept of society from that proclaimed: they contained the seeds of egalitarian democracy.

B

TWO

Early factory legislation

The first factory legislation was the health and morals act of 1802,[1] introduced by Sir Robert Peel, the father of the prime minister. This was a plainly humanitarian and evangelical measure, and altogether *ad hoc*. It was occasioned in general by a variety of factors: by the wartime pressure to produce more cotton goods; by the fact that most cotton manufacture, relying on water power, was located in isolated parts of the countryside; by the shortage of indigenous child labour in such places, and thus by the consequent importation of orphaned or abandoned children to work in the mills. In particular it was occasioned by epidemics in the late 1790s among the factory children which first set off a process of inquiry and report. In this way the deplorable conditions of labour and life of these children attracted the attention of and were 'exposed' by a philanthropic Manchester physican, Perceval, and a self-appointed 'board of health'. Perceval eventually got the ear of Peel. The upshot was the health and morals bill, presented as a peculiar and exceptional measure. Its proclaimed objective was to place the factory orphans on the same footing, so far as possible, as ordinary children with homes and families; although in fact (whether by accident or design) its ultimate scope was larger.

The act, which slipped through parliament quietly, attempted reform in three main areas. Firstly it limited the hours of work for children of seven years and upwards to twelve hours per day and seventy-two per week in all, and forbade them to work at night. Secondly it laid down regulations for the area and circumstances of accommodation. The emphasis on ventilation, the whitewashing of walls and sleeping room represented the 'health' element of the bill's title. Finally, the 'morals' element of the title was reflected in the clause enjoining compulsory education, partly to dispel ignorance and partly to occupy the children's 'leisure' virtuously. All three were, in principle, radical innovations. But in practice the act was feeble. The penalty for a breach was a mere £5, and it was left to the local justices of the peace, who might be ignorant, lazy, cowardly or self-interested, to carry it into effect. It is true however that the seed of the notion of inspection was sown. One clause required the magistrates to appoint two 'visitors' annually, who were to be invested with 'full power and authority from time to time throughout the year to enter into and inspect any such mill or factory at any time of the day or during the hours of employment'.[2] Moreover such comparative subtleties as a compulsory register for mills and a compulsory display of the act where workers might read it indicate a true – and for the time striking – attempt to visualize how the measure might be executed. Nevertheless the machinery provided by the act was much too rudimentary to effect any change in practice. Where they occurred the 'visitations' were a mere matter of form. Generally they were neglected. Soon the magisterial responsibilities dropped completely out of sight. The fundamental weakness was the fact that the bill had been sponsored by a private member and not by the Government. No government department had prepared it and no government department was responsible for its later fate. This made it certain that it would not be regularly – or perhaps ever – enforced. For the crucial defect in almost all social legislation before 1830, and the sharpest divide between the old regulative order and the new, was the absence of any direct state involvement in the drafting, management and execution of such measures.

Yet it would be wrong to leave the 1802 act in ultimately negative terms. It was a landmark not only because (even if only in theory) it excluded infant labour, restricted children's working hours, rendered school attendance obligatory and prescribed certain living conditions, but also because it set afloat and sanctioned three important general ideas. Whereas, say, the early chimney sweepers act of 1788 and even the subsequent coalwhippers act of 1808 dealt in a simple and direct fashion with a specific class of persons assumed to be abused, the health and morals act (certain provisions of which applied even to adults) endorsed the notion that, while in general industry should be free of state interference, extraordinary circumstances might require a special intervention in a class of places. The nineteenth-century image of 'rule and exception' in this field was taking shape. Then also a link between education and the protection of particular persons had been forged. Finally the state was regarded as the natural or at any rate inevitable supplier of a domestic and private deficiency.

When the issue next arose, immediately after the conclusion of the Napoleonic wars, it was in the context of changes in the textile industries whereby steam power was replacing water and urban location of mills replacing rural. Child labour of the ordinary kind was now available, and with its use came pressure for a lateral extension of the 1802 act. The evils of gross overwork, physical deformity, disease and high juvenile mortality were as apparent in the children of the factory towns as in the orphans in the scattered early mills. The original justification for intervention, to put the indentured orphans on a par with children protected by families, was replaced by the argument that children with parents be put on a par with the orphans in terms of statutory protection.

The elder Peel was again the figurehead and the parliamentary manager in the second agitation for reform in 1815–18. Although the campaign began as a simple demand for the extension of the act to 'free' child labour in the cotton industry, it was (almost inevitably) inflated and re-directed once the new factors of a superior working model and of a parliamentary select committee of inquiry were added. The select committee, henceforth to be employed increasingly to scrutinize proposed social reform, proved, as has been said, a powerful promoter and shaper of change in many instances. Relatively speaking – and the qualifying 'relatively' must be heavily underlined – the select committee and its stable companion, the royal commission, provided more information, were more accurate, were less partial and more authoritative than the pressure group or 'pressure individual'. More important still they furnished wider publicity of the evils, and often efficiently connected inquiry, the drafting of proposals and the legislative process.

In this particular instance the house of commons committee of 1816 acted as a loud hailer for Robert Owen, who was the key witness as well as the creator of the working model. Owen was immensely respected at this time, not as a philanthropist but as a prodigiously successful cotton spinner, the Henry Ford of the day, successful not merely in producing efficiently and very profitably but also in handling his work force and organizing their labour. In his large factory in New Lanark on the falls of Clyde, Owen had set the minimum age for child employment at ten years, established a twelve-hour day (including one and a half hours for meals) for all between the ages of ten and eighteen, and set up schools, working to an 'enlightened' syllabus for children of three and upwards. Peel was apparently so impressed by Owen's arrangements that he repeated them in substance in his original amendment bill,[3] which forbade the employment of children under ten in textile mills, limited the working day of those under eighteen to ten and a half hours, and required a half hour's instruction in a factory school, to be set up and paid for by the mill owner, for the first four years after a child was admitted as a worker. Amongst the few deviations from pure Owenism was the omission of music and dancing from the factory school syllabus. Although the evidence was presented by an enemy of factory reform, there is a ring of truth about the assertion that girls leaving New Lanark attributed their departure to the 'number of dancing masters ... drills and exercises ... they were more fatigued than if they were working'![4]

Apart from furnishing a model, Owen in his evidence before the select committee anticipated by many years three critical elements in later factory reform. He recommended a ten-hour working day for all operatives, a relay system for children so that their hours could be further reduced without bringing production to a halt and what amounted to a paid, permanent and qualified inspectorate. It is possible though not certain that it was Owen's thinking on this last issue which was responsible for the most remarkable clause in Peel's bill – that which proposed that in future magistrates should appoint a properly qualified person and pay him 'a full and adequate compensation' from the county rates to look to the enforcement of the statutes.[5] In any case, in combination with the powers granted the 'visitor' under the 1802 act, this provision was a further step towards the concept of a professional, national inspectorate.

In its lengthy and meandering passage through both houses of parliament, the bill was amended at almost every point through the exertions of the manufacturers' lobby.[6] The minimum age of employment was reduced from ten to nine years, the age at which protection ceased from eighteen to sixteen. The permitted hours of work for children was raised to twelve, the new education clauses were lost, and the entire measure confined to cotton mills and factories. Most significant of all, the inspectorial proposals were dropped altogether. Enforcement was still left to local justices of the peace – with such assistance as they might hope for from the promise of £10 to a successful informer.

Without any improvement in the machinery for its execution the 1819 act appears to have been practically inoperative. Certainly children as young as six years old still worked, unchallenged, in the cotton industry; and the hours of child labourers were quite commonly sixteen or seventeen in a day and over ninety in a week.[7] Nevertheless this measure also has some significance in marking the track of government growth. An inspectorate had been firmly delineated and the great process of augmentation by enlargement of the excepted category had begun – in fact, in two directions, as ordinary children were given the rights of orphans and seven- to nine-year-olds the rights of those under six.

The remaining pieces of factory legislation of the unreformed parliament are more difficult to classify. John Cam Hobhouse, who was responsible for both the act of 1825 and that of 1831,[8] presented them as humanitarian extensions of protection and as attempts to render enforceable what had already been enacted. In his speech of introduction in 1825 he nobly declaimed that it were better to abandon cottons altogether than amass money from the blood and bone of children, and pointed out that only two convictions had ever taken place under the 1819 legislation.[9] But his bills were scarcely worthy of such sentiments. It is true that between them they embodied three small extensions of protection. Children were to work only nine hours on Saturdays, their upper limit of 'age' for purposes of the acts was raised from sixteen to eighteen years, and no person under twenty-one was permitted to be employed for more than sixty-nine hours a week. Thus the sixty-nine hour week was formally established for all minors, and the twelve-hour day for all below nineteen years. On the other hand the acts made two major concessions to the mill owners which were to create endless opportunities for evasion. One provided for 'lost time', occasioned by variations in the supply of water or by certain mechanical failures, to be made up outside the permitted hours of work; the other shifted the responsibility for guaranteeing the ages of children and young persons from the factory proprietors to the parents.

It seems unlikely that Hobhouse was covertly in collusion with the proprietors and if in fact the concessions emanated from them, Hobhouse probably accepted them innocently as matters of petty detail and mere mechanics. The manufacturers abused him roundly during the passage of the 1831 act, and one observed, doubtless correctly, that he betrayed 'a sad want of acquaintance with the subject on which he undertakes to legislate'.[10] On the other hand Hobhouse was a doctrinaire radical, and the ultra-democrats very soon reached the limit of what they accepted as tolerable 'interference'. Moreover he was to be counted amongst the 'deserters' in the factory reform crisis of 1836.[11] At any rate the 1825–31 sequence provided early warnings (for those who could read them) of the prodigious difficulties of enforcement and of the dangers of losing ground.

The third reform campaign had, then, no immediate effect. But we should note that within it an important new note had been struck and take this as a starting point for a brief consideration of the factor now pushing into prominence – the contest for popular opinion. The working conditions, treatment and general circumstances of factory children were compared unfavourably with those of negro slaves. This was becoming a commonplace in humanitarian reform movements of the day. The carriage of the passenger act of 1828, for instance, was facilitated by the contrast drawn between the shipboard life of the ordinary 'free', fare-paying emigrant and the allegedly superior food, sanitation and accommodation of the slaver.[12] Slavery was of course a particularly emotive matter and decades of effective agitation had broadcast the idea that it was an absolute anathema, over-riding all prudential or economic counter-arguments in its favour; hence the force of any demonstration (more exactly, perhaps, assertion) that things were still more inhumane elsewhere. As early as 1825 Sir Francis Burdett (another radical, to be fair) had exclaimed: 'We hear of slavery abroad but, good God, have we ever heard of any such instance of overworking as has been published with respect to the labour of children in cotton manufactories?'[13] When agitation was renewed in 1830 in the cause of the factory children it was based on precisely this antithesis. The new leader, Richard Oastler, entitled the famous letter in the *Leeds Mercury* which opened the campaign 'Child Slavery in Yorkshire'.

Oastler's letter coincided with the beginning of a long period of labour unrest and attempts to develop a trade union movement. It also coincided with the beginning of a protracted tory counter-attack upon the victorious manufacturing classes and middle class doctrinaires. The upshot was an immediate, belligerent and widespread agitation for a ten-hour working day for children and adolescents under eighteen years. The trade committees rapidly organized propaganda, demonstrations and petitions; and within a year the issue became the predominant one throughout the north of England. It also won general support from humanitarians and reactionary tories, the latter being partly though by no means exclusively motivated by their animus against the whole manufacturing system and its representatives. The working class agitation was not altogether disinterested. Under the existing factory conditions the machines could not operate without child labour. A ten-hour day for children meant a ten-hour day for all – and this was the real objective for many, perhaps for most. No doubt those who were constantly employed would lose some wages; but what the factory hands wanted at this time was a more even spread of employment, some degree of job security and shorter hours. They could scarcely secure these ends directly, when the general opinion was rigidly opposed to any regulation of adult labour. But by making the issue one of child labour, by appealing to humane feelings and decent shame, they attacked the manufacturers at their weakest point.

The opposition to reform was, however, powerful dialectically in terms of the contemporary obeisance to political economy and the work ethic; and a speech of Hope's against the ten-hour bill of the next session sets out all the five major lines of argument employed by the manufacturers. Naturally the first was the stock denunciation of interference with freedom of contract and of labour. To this was added interference with the rights of parents, with the rider, 'If natural ties are unavailing, legislative action will prove still more useless.' Thirdly Hope argued that such reforms injured the working classes by disrupting family budgets: true humanity required the security, not the withdrawal of child earnings. Next, play was made of the threat to production, all the more grave because of growing foreign (in particular, American) competition. The notorious claim that profit rested upon the last hour of factory work, and infant labour, was very shortly to be made. Finally, it was necessary to put the hardships into perspective. Children worked still longer hours in still worse conditions in other industries. In calico-printing they regularly worked sixteen hours per day; in earthenware and porcelain manufacture fifteen; in the armaments industry fourteen. The physical surroundings of employment were more deleterious to children and the bodily strains greater in industries such as building or mining.[14] Some of this was true, more of it plausible, all of it persuasive to a generation reared to a gradgrindian worship of 'fact' and a fundamentalist belief in 'social science'. But it could not hold the line against such simple but deadly testimony as that delivered to the select committee of 1832. A middle class clothier, Whitehead, who had lived for twenty years with thirty or forty Yorkshire woollen mills nearby, told the committee that the children, some of them as young as six years

> are generally cruelly treated; so cruelly treated, that they dare not hardly for their lives be too late at their work in a morning. When I have been at the mill in the season, when

the children are at work in the evening, the very first thing they inquire is, 'What o'clock is it?' if I should answer 'Seven', they say, 'Only seven! it is a great while to 10, but we must not give up till 10 o'clock or past.' They look so anxious to know what o'clock it is that I am convinced the children are fatigued, and think that even at seven they have worked too long. My heart has been ready to bleed for them when I have seen them so fatigued, for they appear in such a state of apathy and insensibility as really not to know whether they are doing their work or not . . . the errors they make when thus fatigued are, that instead of placing the cording in this way (describing it), they are apt to place them obliquely, and that causes a flying, which makes bad yarn; and when the billy-spinner sees that, he takes his strap or the billy-roller, and says, 'Damn thee, close it – little devil, close it' – and they smite the child with the strap or the billy-roller.[15]

One of the later witnesses was an overseer who had been named in earlier evidence as one cruel to the child workers:

Have you had much experience regarding the working of children in factories? – Yes, about twenty-seven years.
Have you a family? – Yes, eight children.
Have any of them gone to factories? – All.
At what age? – The first went at 6 years of age.
To whose mill? – To Mr Halliley's to piece for myself.
What hours did you work at that mill? – We have wrought from 4 to 9, from 4 to 10, and from 5 to 9, and from 5 to 10.
What sort of mill was it? – It was a blanket mill; we sometimes altered the time, according as the days increased and decreased . . .
Were your children working under you then? – Yes, two of them.
State the effect upon your children? – Of a morning when they had to get up, they have been so fast asleep that I have had to go up stairs and lift them out of bed, and have heard their crying with feelings of a parent; I have been much affected by it.
Were not they much fatigued at the termination of such a

day's labour as that? – Yes, many times I have seen their
hands moving while they have been nodding, almost asleep;
they have been doing their business almost mechanically.
While they have been almost asleep, they have attempted
to work? – Yes, and they have missed the carding and spoiled
the thread, when we have had to beat them for it.
Could they have done their work towards the termination
of such a long day's labour, if they had not been chastised
to it? – No.
You do not think they could have kept awake or up to their
work till the seventeenth hour, without being chastised? –
No.
Will you state what effect it had upon your children at the
end of their day's work? – At the end of their day's work
when they have come home, instead of taking their victuals,
they have dropped asleep with the victuals in their hands;
and sometimes when we have sent them to bed with a little
bread or something to eat in their hand, I found it in their
bed the next morning.[16]

These samples of evidence have been quoted extensively
because in no other way could their impact upon opinion be
adequately conveyed. It was alleged at the time and has been
alleged since that this evidence was pre-arranged and coached
beforehand, and that it gave a most unrepresentative picture
of conditions in the industry. The hostile royal commission
of 1833 claimed (though with something of *suggestio falsi*
surely) that 'the greatest number of bad cases occur in small
obscure mills . . .[that] the bad treatment is inflicted by violent
and dissipated workmen . . .' and that extreme 'severity' was
really a thing of the preceding generation 'when coercion was
far more resorted to even in public schools than now'.[17] None
of these charges need be disputed if our concern is the impression which the evidence made upon the public. Simply it
seemed apparent at once to the world at large that such things
were intolerable and that 'intolerability' should out-trump any
or all of the cards in the hands of the economists or the social
'scientists' or the entrepreneurs. In fact, however staged the
performance and however leading the questions, the evidence
as a whole merely described what had actually happened – at

least in some places and at some times – and the presentation was far from sensational. The sensation came with the sudden flood of horror, in auditors and readers, as they learned that all this had commonly occurred and was perhaps, somewhere or other, actually occurring in their own land at that very hour.

Possibly Hobhouse's act of 1831, or at least that part of it which extended the provisions of the 1802 act to all 'children' under eighteen, was a first fruit of the Oastler campaign as well as a second fruit of 'vertical' extension. It was however a change of degree at most. The hours of child labour were still left at twelve, and the measure was anyhow ineffective in operation. So the popular campaign and the parliamentary pressure mounted; and in 1832, another tory radical, Michael Sadler, MP for Newark, introduced a ten-hour bill. By now the manufacturers had organized a powerful parliamentary interest and they succeeded in staving off the measure by setting up a select committee on child labour in textiles. They were, however, hoist with their own petard. When the select committee published the evidence before it – some of which we have just quoted – at the end of 1832, it depicted so dreadful a system of abuses that some action, some very strong and far-reaching action, seemed inevitable.

At this point, the ten-hours movement received yet another stimulus. Sadler was defeated at the general election of 1832, and Lord Ashley, yet another tory MP, agreed to take over the management of his bill. It is difficult to over-estimate the importance of the involvement of Ashley (later to become Lord Shaftesbury). His motives were purely, or at the very least evangelically, humanitarian. To the pitch that any such claim ever can be made, he was moved simply by sympathy and a plain hatred of pain and suffering. In other things he was a narrow, bigoted, protestant aristocrat. But his failings were almost as valuable to the factory movement as his disinterested charity. As Dicey notes, the story that Melbourne jokingly introduced him to Queen Victoria as the greatest jacobin in her dominions has its point. The fact that Ashley's left hand did not know what his right was doing, the fact that he failed entirely to recognize the revolutionary and collectivist implications of his own measures but saw them in elementary terms as reducing the sum of human pain, brutishness and sin, was of considerable importance. It provided him with strength and directness of purpose and reassured public opinion: surely nothing radical and injurious to fundamental English institutions could emanate from so stern and unbending a tory and so pious and unpopish a protestant.

At the beginning of 1833, Ashley reintroduced the ten-hours bill[18] amidst general and even parliamentary enthusiasm and excitement. The new bill provided that those between the ages of nine and eighteen should work only ten hours daily and eight hours on Saturdays, and that these regulations be enforced by compelling factory managers to keep time books. For the moment it seemed as if the agitation must carry the day. But a new opposition rapidly developed. The textile interest had increased its influence in the house of commons in the general election which had followed the reform act; and it possessed a powerful lever in the whig cabinet: leading ministers like Russell, Brougham, Durham and Graham were all more or less inclined to the new political economy and philosophical radicalism. The manufacturers could moreover present two strong counter-arguments to the humanitarian appeal of the supporters of the bill: one, that the factory movement was really the work of professional agitators who desired not the relief of children but the overthrow of public order; the other, that the political economists, the experts, had already demonstrated that the ten-hours bill would ruin British industry by depriving it of profits. They could also have shown with ease, had they thought it prudent to do so, that Ashley's bill was in certain respects a retrograde proposal. It placed nine-year-olds, in effect, on a par with grown men and women, and virtually ignored enforcement; even the rudimentary attempts to grapple with this problem embodied in the 1802 and 1819 acts were not repeated, let alone improved on. All reliance was placed on a horrific scale of penalties, as if the bill were an expression of abhorrence and desire rather than an instrument of change.

Anyway, by wielding all its political influence and persuading moderate parliamentary men to hesitate before taking so momentous a step, the textile interest did secure the post-

ponement of Ashley's bill and the setting up of a royal commission to institute a fresh investigation. The master manufacturers association was convinced that the new commission
would discredit and contradict the earlier select committee,
and with the assistance of their cabinet supporters they took
good care to load the dice. Edwin Chadwick was appointed
one of the central commissioners, with his 'seconds-in-com-
mand' (as in effect they were), Thomas Tooke and Southwood
Smith. All three were, in some sense or other, 'Benthamites'.

Here we must interrupt our narrative to consider carefully
Chadwick, and through him the impact of Benthamism on
administrative change. For Chadwick is the grey eminence of
our subject. From 1832 to 1854 he lurked behind an extraordinary number of the pieces of the revolutionary social
legislation, and he personally shaped in no small degree three
of the most important measures of the time, the factory act of
1833, the poor law amendment act of 1834 and the public
health act of 1848. He was the complete bureaucrat, perhaps
the first of his race, and a true republican in the antique sense
of the term. It was the *res publica*, the public thing, the common good as he saw it, which was his passion. It was a horror
of waste, dirt, disease and inefficiency rather than a personal
sympathy for any suffering person or group of persons which
drove him forward. He was, or at least posed as, a calculator
without compassion, one who insisted on examining all evidence before reaching his conclusion. But he was also one who,
having reached his conclusion, closed his mind fiercely to any
other argument and imputed stupidity and self-interest to all
who challenged it. Last, and indeed first, last and always if
anyone deserves the label, he was a Benthamite. In his closing
years Bentham himself had selected the young Chadwick as
his literary secretary and marked him out as his favourite and
most promising disciple. Chadwick returned the compliment
by a lifelong veneration of Bentham's memory and by becoming perhaps the sole exponent of the pure word of administrative Benthamism in the middle and late nineteenth century. Significantly enough, however, Chadwick never openly
acknowledged a debt to Bentham; and this reveals one of the
problems in coming to grips with Benthamism in action in the

second quarter of the nineteenth century. Those whom the historians speak of so readily as Benthamites did not often speak of themselves in such terms or attribute their ideas or devices to the great man. The only open avowal of total liege-dom which the present author has encountered came from (of all people) O'Connell and at (of all places) the polls at Ennis, co. Clare, in 1829: 'I avowed myself on the hustings today to be a Benthamite, and explained the leading principles of your disciples – the greatest happiness principle – *our* sect will prosper. ... You have now one Member of Parliament of *your own*.'[19] Of course much of this must be set off as character-istic blarney.

Nonetheless, the influence of Bentham upon Chadwick's thought is unmistakable in certain areas, and in particular on administrative organization. What were the administrative implications of Benthamism which Chadwick so fully repre-sented? This involves a partial sketch of Bentham's doctrine. It was, as has been said above, primarily a legal philosophy and a programme for reforming laws. Bentham had grown up as a lawyer in the world of eighteenth-century rationalism. This meant that he had a thorough grasp of the law which he desired to reform and full knowledge of its inability to release itself from its own complexity and obscurity. It also meant that he accepted the current dogma of the rationalists that a rational reform of laws was practicable and would tend towards the happiness of society.[20] His legal philosophy was therefore based on three fundamental principles: first that the reform of laws must be carried through by parliament and not the courts; secondly that legislation was a science, a branch of exact know-ledge; and thirdly that the test of all legislation was the test of utility – did it promote or otherwise the greatest happiness of the greatest number? As Bentham developed and applied them these last two principles formed his master stroke. He was rejecting all gradualism, all feeling for tradition and the rights of prescription, all legal 'mysticalism', so to speak. In-stead, he called upon every law to justify itself and provided a simple and universal method of adjudication. The test of utility in terms of pleasure and pain was, as has been said, peculiarly suitable for legislation, though peculiarly inappro-priate in two other fields where Bentham also applied it, namely the fields of morals and psychology.[21] But where, as with law, external conduct and the common welfare of the community were the sole considerations, it provided (to all appearances) a rational, sensible, direct, equitable and universal criterion.

There is however one important point to be noted with respect to this aspect of Benthamism, namely that by and large it was the common property of the enlightenment. It is true that few of the philosophers recognized as clearly as Bentham the importance of legal reform and that none saw so clearly the value of a measuring device such as the pleasure-pain criterion. But broadly his thought was in line with theirs. Now the latter, though liberal and progressive to a degree, was fundamentally undemocratic in tendency. The philosophers believed that the body of men were (albeit through no fault of their own) sunk in ignorance and incapable of raising themselves by their own exertions. Consequently reform must come from above and come from the enlightened few who had by experiment and study uncovered the basic laws upon which all societies should operate. The proximity of such opinions to benevolent despotism, to bureaucracy or government by the expert who knows better than the citizen what is best for him, is obvious. Equally obvious is the fact that the natural bias of Benthamite legal reform lies in the same direction. Where should power reside if not with the man or men who make the great calculation of pleasures and pains which decides the course of legislation, and who can these men be if not experts trained in such calculations and possessed of a vast body of exact knowledge acquired by empirical investigation? It was no coincidence that Bentham should have been initially a tory or that he should have looked first to a strong and (as he mistakenly expected) enlightened central government to execute his reforming measures.

This bureaucratic tendency was further reinforced by Bentham's lifelong passion for penal and criminal law and by his genius as a political inventor. Concerning the latter Dicey goes so far as to say that it was this which set him head and shoulders above all earlier and subsequent utilitarians.[22] Here again he may fruitfully be seen as a creature of his time. It was no accident that Bentham was the contemporary of Arkwright and Crompton. He formed their near counterpart in the field of administration: in effect he invented the mechanics of government. Devices of central control and inspection, of audit and statistical inquiry flowed from his ingenious imagination. All pointed in the same direction – centralization and uniformity. Reflection and common sense soon taught him that these were the most rational, economical and effective modes of administration, if not indeed the only ones which could secure Benthamic objectives. Centralization in its turn implied power for the central body, initiating power on the one hand to frame rules and orders, and controlling power on the other to see that they were enforced equally, persistently and ubiquitously, without hindrance from local or vested interests.

The last touch was supplied by Bentham's concern for penal and criminal law, for this led him to develop the 'preventive' or 'tutelary' aspect of legislation. What struck Bentham most in this field was the fact that every crime committed was a denial of his principle that there was a natural harmony and identity of human interests. When A stole from B, what A believed to be his interest was obviously in conflict with B's. It was not enough merely to punish A. A's interests went into the common pool of interests as well as B's. What was needed was to change A's interests to bring them into conformity with the interest of the whole. How was this to be done? Once again by laws, by the interference of the central power. As Halevy puts it,

> legislation is the science of intimidation; the general utility is its *raison d'être*, and punishment is the sanction of the obligations which it imposes. . . . The leglislator is the great dispenser of pleasures and pains in society. It is he who creates the moral order. Society is the work of his artifices. In this way is applied . . . the artificial indentification of interests.[23]

Clearly such a conception of the state's functions is not far removed from the collectivist's. Once it is granted that the state may know better than the individual what his interests are and may set up a scale of artificial rewards, punishments and inducements to get him to behave as it wishes, the way lies open to paternal government. It is significant that no branch of Bentham's teaching appealed more to Chadwick, or was more eagerly developed by him, than this concept of the state's duty to devise legislation which would force private interests into conformity with public.[24]

So far Benthamism has been regarded as essentially implying a modern notion of the state and modern machinery of administration; and this seems to me to be the most fundamental, as well as the earliest tendency of Bentham's thought. But there is of course an opposite aspect to the matter. Benthamism is often described as an individualistic political philosophy. How is the contradiction to be explained? It is to be explained, I think, in historical terms. Benthamism contained from the beginning some individualistic elements – after all, the isolated human atom was the basic material of almost all eighteenth-century thought. Gradually, and particularly after 1800, more and more were added, because atomism was the prevailing temper of Bentham's time and class. He had sprung from the middle classes and accepted uncritically the findings of Adam Smith and the political economists. This meant the acceptance of the principles that there was a natural harmony of economic interests, that the economy must be freed of all practicable restraints and left to work out its own salvation, and that state interference in economic matters was, in general, anathema. It is true that Smith's reservation that the public might legitimately undertake whatever social works were, because of their magnitude or cost, beyond the resources or capacity of private persons, could be extended almost indefinitely. Later political economists were doubtless to bless its elasticity. But in the salad days it was little regarded. The emphases were firmly upon the ultimate harmony of the unchecked, the liberation of commerce and the almost limitless potentialities for good of a host of individual strivings. It was obviously difficult to reconcile such a body of *laissez faire* principles with legal and administrative principles tending ultimately in an opposite direction. But the reconciliation was made, or at least the difficulties went unrecognized. Philosophical radicals succeeded in becoming Occamists in the matter, and keeping the truth of one sphere quite separate from the truths of another.

A corresponding development took place with respect to political democracy. Here two forces operating at the turn

of the eighteenth century drove Bentham from, at best, indifference in the matter to a whole-hearted acceptance of the
representative principle in politics. The first was his failure
to persuade the government to adopt his 'Panopticon' or model
prison: he finally abandoned his endeavours in 1811. This
failure convinced him that it was impossible to force rational
reforms through a parliament composed of men with vested
and selfish interests in the abuses. To strike at the abuses it
was first necessary to reform parliament. It may moreover
have helped to generate in his followers, if not in himself, a
certain contempt for and fear of the entire contemporary
parliamentary process, for what Leslie Stephen has named the
'combination of an absolute centralization of legislative power
with an utter absence of administrative centralization'.[25] The
second factor was Bentham's meeting with James Mill in 1808.
From then on Mill acted as Bentham's promoter and manager
and was largely responsible for the development of a school
of utilitarians. Now Mill had, as his son John Stuart put it, 'an
almost unbounded confidence in the efficacy of two things;
representative government, and complete freedom of discussion',[26] and much of this he conveyed to Bentham. The general
effect of these two influences in the first decade of the nineteenth century was to produce in Bentham a radical individualism. Each man was declared to be the best judge of his own
self-interest, and parliaments were to be made frequent and
universally representative so that the self-interest of the legis-
lators would become subordinate to the self-interest of the
electors. As for the ignorance of the great majority of men,
Mill's complete faith in the possibilities of education and free
discussion carried the day.

Obviously this ran quite counter to the implications of Bentham's legal philosophy and projected mechanics of government, which were marked by a deep distrust of the unenlight-
ened multitude, a total reliance upon omniscient experts and
the necessary counter-principle that every man was not the
best judge of his own interest. Moreover the latter seems to
represent the more fundamental element in Bentham's thought
and the former the more temporary and expedient. Though
both lived, apparently amicably, side by side in the minds of
the later Bentham and his first 'disciples' (and for the sake of

flow in argument let us henceforth waive the questions of what exactly constituted a disciple and what exactly a Benthamite) it is significant that the second generation of Benthamites, including Chadwick, had by and large little real interest or trust in democracy. When the second reform bill of 1867 was being discussed, the opposition was led by the 'Benthamite' Robert Lowe and he was supported by several others including Bowring and John Austin. But though many recognized instinctively the difficulty of reconciling wise and efficient utilitarian government with a mass electorate and tight control over parliament, no Benthamite of standing repudiated the dogmas of individualistic political economy and economic *laissez faire*. This is as true of Chadwick as any other. When in the later 1860s utilitarians began to question them fundamentally, the old creed was a dying thing: the hole had become so large that the sock was ceasing to exist.

Herein lies the explanation of the paradoxes and contradictions of the philosophy in action in the mid-century. On the one hand it pulled towards the artificial manipulation of and interference with private interests by the state – towards powerful and centralized government by experts and professionals. On the other it pulled towards economic licence, the abolition of state regulation of manufacture, commerce and the conditions of employment and absolute freedom of contract. In the short run it seemed possible to reconcile the two. During the 1830s and 1840s the interference of the state and its attempts to make private and public interest identical by artificial legislation were admitted on the ground that the state was merely bringing about the conditions in which a free economy would work. This done, it was to fold its hands and gracefully retire. But of course in the long run the tacit admission that there was not a natural harmony of human interests, that the state must act as adjudicator in these matters and that the state could only act on expert knowledge and through effective and centralized machinery of government – such a tacit admission was, as events amply proved, fatal to the ideas of anarchic individualism.

This sketch of Benthamism is, with the solitary difference of emphasis on democracy which we noted, also substantially a sketch of Chadwick's thought, which, formed early in life, remained unchanged throughout his administrative career. These were the principles which informed his first major legislative work in 1833.

THREE

The factory act
of 1833

The royal commission of 1833 had been appointed in haste and political expediency demanded that it would act in haste, for Ashley's bill was due for a second reading on 17 July 1833, and the cabinet had to have its alternative prepared by then. This left a mere nine weeks to investigate and report. As if this were not bad enough, the commissioners were not allowed to choose their own assistants: these were appointed by the government in the old political way and they were for the most part quite inexperienced in the new administrative technique of investigation in the field, by questionnaire and similar modes of inquiry. The first obstacle was the opposition of the working classes, who boycotted the assistant commissioners and demonstrated before them in almost every manufacturing town.[1] This opposition was due partly to suspicion of the police methods of the investigators, but mostly to a shrewd realization that the commission was rigged against them and directed by anti-humanitarians who would certainly declare against the ten-hour bill. All these difficulties and the popular excitement were however of relatively small importance as Chadwick, who dominated the commission, had come to the subject with a fairly closed mind. The lines which he laid down for the investigation and his selection and arrangement of witnesses all fit in with his final recommendations. Indeed most of these were correctly prophesied by radical leaders before the report was even written. Chadwick's acceptance of *laissez faire* economics and the findings of the political economists made it inevitable that he would resist any attempt

at regulating the working hours of adult labour. He adhered
to the 'cheerful' as opposed to the 'dismal' school of the new
science, and believed that the current economic troubles could
be solved – but only by more and more production. This in
turn demanded the maximum working hours, the maximum
profits for industrialists (since more capital equipment depended upon these) and complete freedom of contract between
employers and employed. But it also demanded child labour:
without it, he was assured, factories could not work at all, let
alone work to full capacity. On the other hand it could not be
denied that small children were incapable of working even the
legal twelve hours, let alone the more common sixteen or so
per day without damage to their health; and a rising generation
of defectives was obviously uneconomic.

At this point Chadwick adopted the so-called 'alternative
plan' of the master manufacturers association. This was their
last line of defence. It proposed that children under twelve or
thirteen years should work short hours in double shifts, but
that the adult day should be altogether unregulated. Chadwick
fixed on eight hours a day for children under thirteen years
and no restraints whatever for those over thirteen as the essence
of the economic aspect of his recommendations. This proposal
was greeted with enthusiasm by all who had no special interest
in the matter. The average man had been torn between humanitarian compunction and fear that the economists' predictions
of the ruin of the industry would be fulfilled. In humanitarianism, Chadwick had outstripped the agitators by reducing
children's hours from ten to eight and at the same time had
enabled textile mills to work as long, or perhaps even longer
hours through the principle of the double shift. The textile
workers were of course opposed – their supreme object was the
reduction of their own working day; but this opposition merely
seemed to confirm Chadwick's insinuation that they were in
the hands of unscrupulous professional agitators who cared
nothing for the children themselves but merely used them as
a stalking horse. The smaller country mills were also in opposition. The association's plan had in their eyes the cunning
secondary purpose of forwarding large scale, steam driven
urban industry at the expense of rural water powered mills.
There were not enough children in the country districts to

work the relay system. But it was the master manufacturers who had an interest in the cabinet and it was they who carried the day. Thus Chadwick's economic proposal, serving or seeming to serve both humanitarianism and the sacred principle of the free contract for 'adults', was a general success. True, this involved the abrupt declaration of 'adulthood' at the end of thirteen years. But the commission blustered its way through the difficulty by pronouncing the fourteenth year to be the end of childhood, the confirmation of puberty and the point at which the physical frame can endure protracted labour, parents are set aside and contracts may be entered into responsibly.[2]

All this was one facet of administrative Benthamism. The other was 'tutelary' and regulatory. All factory legislation up to 1833 was in effect an expression of humanitarian principle or feeling rather than law which could be actually applied. No adequate provision for its enforcement had been made. Even Ashley's ten-hour bill relied entirely for its effectiveness upon a minatory scale of fines and the distant and uncertain threat of imprisonment for a third offence. Again, all earlier factory legislation was negative in tendency. Practically speaking, little thought had been given to improving the children's minds and conditions beyond releasing them for a time from the machine. It is true that the 1802 act had contained an education clause and that this had not been repealed by Hobhouse's measures of 1825 and 1831. But, again, it was practically unenforceable; it was vague, merely enjoining the inculcation of reading, writing and arithmetic without clearly specifying place, time or any other of the particulars of instruction; and in any event the pauper apprentices who were to be its beneficiaries had long been supplanted by ordinary child labour. Chadwick's study of penal law, French jurisprudence and the artificial reconciliation of private interests by the state led him to try to supply these deficiencies.

The two pillars of his 'ameliorative system' were the inspectorate and education. The notion of state officials entering private premises and regulating the relations of employers and employed was still a staggering novelty in 1833. Yet it was one that Chadwick recognized as essential for the enforcement of social legislation. He could not afford an inspectorate on the modern scale: he was as inhibited as most other creatures of the age by the prevailing passion for economy in the public service. Sixteen years later Gladstone wrote, 'The undue augmentation of fiscal burdens at home is our great evil.' Nor could Chadwick afford, he believed, to ignore local feeling. He therefore compromised by proposing a concurrent system of justices of the peace and central inspectors who would visit the factories in turn. If either party, employer or employed, distrusted the JPs, they could wait for the central inspector to put their point of view. Beneath the inspectorate proper a class of sub-inspectors (called 'superintendents' in the event) was to be appointed by their superiors, and all were to lie under the control of a central board subject to the home office. The chief inspectors were to be granted immense, indeed arbitrary, powers of interference and regulation. They might enter any factory, inspect any children, 'decide' their ages, order machinery to be boxed off, impose fines – and most vital of all, they were to supervise education. The other pillar of Chadwick's scheme was that all children, whose day was limited to eight working hours, should spend two further hours at school. This had for him a dual purpose. It would keep the children off the streets and free from idleness and corruption, and it would improve them morally and mentally by indoctrination. Here again the strong and arbitrary arm of the chief inspector was looked to for the execution of the proposal. It was he who was to examine the children and decide whether their schools and schooling were adequate. And if he were dissatisfied with the schools or standard he might set one up himself compulsorily, and (where the factory children's penny per week was insufficient) levy a local rate to pay for it. Here again revolutionary principles of administration and state action were being unfurled.

The inspectors and compulsory education were the core of Chadwick's administrative provisions but he added other schemes of considerable ingenuity and far-sightedness. Some factory machinery could not be boxed off, and Chadwick attempted to force the employer's interest to coincide with that of the workers in this matter by making him financially liable for accidents. He proposed a species of insurance and compensation for industrial injuries, the cost of which was to be borne by the employers. Again he concentrated his attention on the most critical difficulty of all in enforcing the early legislation, the determination of age in a period without compulsory birth registration, and in a case where to all the parties concerned – masters, workmen, parents and children – deceit appeared to be in their self-interest, Chadwick decided on the use of medical evidence, requiring surgeon's certificates counter-signed by magistrates or inspectors. At the same time the fact that this was a desperate and imprecise expedient may well have started the train of thought which led him to propose the compulsory registration of births in 1836.[3]

What a multitude of modern devices and concepts, then, did Chadwick's first proposal cover! In its system of central control, of a professional inspectorate with the widest discretionary powers of arbitration and regulation, and in its implied idea of a beneficent omnicompetent and omniscient state, it set down basic principles on which much of twentieth-century government is conducted – or meant to be conducted. Compulsory education, or at least compulsory rating for education, was not achieved until the 1870s. Compulsory registration of births, insofar as the prime duty was laid on parents, had to wait until 1874; effective compensation for industrial accidents was not secured until the employers' liability act of 1880; and so on. The hard, clear and brilliant mind of Chadwick so grasped the tutelary and inventive side of Benthamism that the very first measure he devised as a very young man contained the substance of its centralizing and collectivist implications.

The first measure he devised – but not the first of his measures that was carried. The force of opposition of the factors which have been discussed above was so powerful that the measure reached the statute book maimed and lopped. At first all seemed straightforward. The cabinet accepted his report more or less as it stood and was prepared to put it forward as the alternative to Ashley's ten-hour bill, and the drafting of the new measure[4] was left largely to Chadwick himself. The most significant change was to reduce the age of the children who were to be protected to twelve years, and this anti-humanitarian concession was not really material to the general design. But pressure was soon brought to bear from either side. The ten-hour committees redoubled their efforts when the worst was known, and the north remained in a state of excitement and disturbance. They continued to play their strongest card, the appeal to compassionate sentiment, and focused their agitation upon the fact that children (in particular, girls) over twelve years now received no protection whatsoever. They were aided by the fact that Hobhouse's act of 1831 had extended the age of protection to eighteen – a good example of Dicey's thesis that every statute, however ineffective, contains a principle which influences the course of future legislation. On the other side the manufacturers redoubled their gloomy prognostications that such an extension would ruin British industry, but now Melbourne refused to listen. He had no intention of risking the opposition of the humanitarians and great middle range of the public generally for the sake of appeasing the *nouveau riche*. Thus the great individualist principle of non-intervention in 'adult' labour was broken, much to Chadwick's horror: children between thirteen and eighteen years were to work only twelve hours per day. This was the first retreat. It was followed by a concession to the defeated party: the dropping of the employers' liability clause.

So far nothing essential had been lost; in fact, even the miserable concession to the elder children was to be regarded as a gain. But as the bill was being debated in both houses most of its idiosyncratic and novel features were ripped away, for good and ill. The whole machinery of regulation and control was badly damaged. It had few friends. The manufacturers opposed it for the obvious reason that it threatened to make the act work and would impose an indefinite number of obligations and restraints upon their conduct. As the first historian of the factory movement put it, 'In the estimation of these mill owners, the beginning and the end of the duties of a government consisted in protecting their property and allowing them to treat all those under their control as to themselves seemed best.'[5] The ten-hour committees opposed the executive clauses for less substantial but no less powerful reasons. The working classes regarded anything from Chadwick as a Greek gift. The operation of the royal commission and their own long experience had taught them to believe that the inspectors would be hand-in-glove with the employers and merely new instruments of oppression for the workers. The state would always favour the employing class and the moneyed interest. As things turned out they were eventually though not immediately mistaken. But it was not only natural but perhaps also inevitable and right that they should have suspected Chadwick's authoritarian scheme. Apart from the reaction of the interested parties there was a widespread instinctive distrust of such arbitrary and novel powers and a violent dislike of even the possibility of compulsory rating for education.

Under such pressures Chadwick's measure began to disintegrate. The education clause was retained but robbed of all effectiveness. The inspector's powers to examine children, to set up his own school or to saddle the rates with educational expenditure were dropped; and without them the section was but a scarecrow. The two hours of daily education could not be enforced and the 'ameliorative' and tutelary aspects of the measure collapsed with it. The government itself was responsible for various alterations in the other pillar of Chadwick's administrative scheme, the inspectorate. It abandoned his proposals for a central board to which the inspectors should be responsible and for a species of dual regulation by the inspectors and justices of the peace. It arbitrarily decided that four inspectors would suffice for the entire United Kingdom. This meant that it was impossible for some even to see every factory in their area once a year.[6] Next, the appointment of inspectors was made a matter of political patronage. This meant that they were drawn from the whig faction, the 'Cousinhood' and its hangers-on. One ten-hour committee, that of Birstall, was able to greet the first nominations, with some colour of justice, as 'a briefless barrister – a broken-down Merchant, a poor Aristocrat – and an intimate friend of Lieut. Drummond'.[7] Still more important was the fact that jobbery descended to the ranks of the superintendents and that their salaries were set very low, £250 per annum with no allowances for travelling. With the minute number of chief inspectors the actual tasks of investigation and control largely and unexpectedly devolved on them. These miserably paid officials had neither the independence nor the rank to enforce what regulations there remained after depredations of the interested parties, and they were stultified by being forbidden the access to mills which had been awarded to their superiors.

Thus the factory act of 1833 was in many respects a failure. It rejected the ten-hour day for adults and lost much of the compensating and ingeniously devised executive machinery. Yet even in defeat something had been accomplished. The principle of state responsibility for children under thirteen years and of some degree of responsibility for those under eighteen had been very firmly established. So had the principle that this responsibility included, in however small a degree, the positive duty of education. It is true that in one light these may be regarded as mere reaffirmations of principles embodied in earlier legislation. But the vast publicity and noise which had attended the 1833 measure and the apparent reality of the determination that it should be acted on placed the 1833 act in a different category from the earlier statutes. On the other side something of Chadwick's administrative scheme still survived. The main concept of a central inspectorate was incorporated into the English system of government, and this was in itself an occurrence of profound significance. Again it was not so much that the thing itself was new. Earlier factory reform and reformers had, as we have seen, approached the idea quite closely and inspectorates had taken root elsewhere in the national administration long before. But Chadwick's version was idiosyncratic and more deliberate and thoroughly considered than any of its predecessors, and more important still it had been imposed (so to speak) in open day, a blaze of controversy and a field central to the British manufacturing economy. Thirdly the 1833 act, although largely, was not wholly ineffective. Successful prosecutions under it were few but some there were. Moreover it had important oblique effects. Large numbers of children were in fact dismissed rather than illegally employed and large numbers underwent some charade or other of schooling instead of being left to their own or their parents' devices – even though evasion of either requirement was very easy. The mere existence of an inspectorate, the mere raising of the original public outcry and the mere jealousy of those few manufacturers who sought to remain within the law acted as sufficient deterrents to ensure a partial obedience despite the ineffectuality of the enforcement clauses. Finally and most significant of all perhaps, the whole sweep and notion of the tutelary state had come before the public on a large and dramatic issue and in a tangible form. It had even been proposed by the government when they first put their factory bill – still substantially unaltered – before the house of commons.

The act of 1833 and its background have been described in some detail because it shows the operation of almost all the factors which promoted and retarded the development of the early twentieth-century state. The very first encounter is in many respects the microcosm of the whole. In it we see bureaucratic Benthamism as a Janus-like influence, looking both backward and ahead as it was continuously to do. We see on the one hand the titanic power of the surges of humanitarian sentiment, on the other the depth of the entrenchment of dogmas of political economy. The latter halt, but not entirely, the attempt to interfere with the so-called 'natural' economy, with the so-called liberty of contract and the conditions of adult labour. Also evident was the force of sectional interests and of the political pressures they could bring to bear, whether on the cabinet, in the houses of parliament or through select committees and commissions. In the degree of influence which they could wield these interests were to some extent new; they belong to the post-reform act politics, to a political system in which parties were more concerned to appease electorates, and behind them 'opinion'. This was true in particular of the early whig governments. Grey's ministry demonstrates as well the barrier to administrative reform which the persistence of the old notions of patronage and jobbery represented, and this in turn explains much of the general hostility to state action which the factory act controversy brought to light. It was not, as has been seen, confined to the mill owners, who had much to fear: it also extended to the 'neutrals' and to the working classes, both of whom saw in any extension of state action an extension of the old type of administration – of jobs, of inefficiency, of extravagance and expense. Above all it is apparent that men generally failed to understand the principles and issue at stake, a factor which, so to speak, worked both ways. If they failed to appreciate the significance or importance of Chadwick's administrative machine they also failed to see the significance of even the meagre precedents in state regulation which had been created. These failures were in turn two-faced. They meant compromises and concessions which made the immediate factory act to a considerable extent ineffectual and aimless. But they also meant the unwitting acceptance of revolutionary principles which would almost certainly have been rejected had their nature and implications been thoroughly understood.

However, these observations must be balanced by a consideration of the precedents for Chadwick's administrative system and of its various defects and insufficiencies. The royal commission's proposals of 1833 (in effect, Chadwick's) were a landmark because they were much more widely publicized and debated than any earlier schemes or measures of the kind, and because the mechanics of government and the philosophy of executing laws had never hitherto received such deliberate or powerful consideration. But much of their substance was commonplace in what had been the sister kingdom until 1801 and was now part of the same constitutional entity as Great Britain. The Irish prison inspectorate, for example, had been organized on a national and centralized basis since 1786. The Irish inspectors-general of prisons had by the 1820s powers of examination and enforcement, of expenditure and action not unlike (though less coercive or clearly outlined than) those propounded by Chadwick. In various other fields of Irish government similar developments had taken place in the very late eighteenth and early nineteenth centuries. Moreover the Irish experience of English politicians may have contributed to the importation of Irish administrative models into Great Britain. Peel's share in the metropolitan police act of 1829 appears, as we shall see,[8] to have owed much to his work in setting up the Irish peace preservation corps, which was structually similar as a constabulary, fourteen years before. More exactly to the point, E. G. Stanley may well have drawn on his very recent years as Irish chief secretary when instituting the inspectorate of emigration in May 1833 shortly before Chadwick's scheme was devised. Thus not only were there examples of the key elements of the 'new government' close at hand, there were also bees for pollen-carrying.

Moreover, even in the field of factory reform itself, some of Chadwick's work had been foreshadowed. In the elder Peel's factory bill of 1815 (a modified form of Owen's original draft) one and a half of the twelve hours of the statutory working day for those between ten and eighteen years were to be set aside for 'meals and instruction'; and schooling was required for the first four years of factory life, that is, to the age of fourteen years at least. Another clause in the same bill had stipulated that factory inspectors should be appointed and paid by the local magistrates. In each case part of the road to Chadwick's proposals had been travelled, and it was again traversed in suggestions put forward in various quarters, and particularly by some of the more humane manufacturers, in 1832.

A further qualification upon any claims which might be made for Chadwick as 'onlie begetter' of the inspectorate and related administrative devices and procedures is that his projected inspectors deviated in several significant respects from the original and the later established British pattern. They were in fact hybrids: in part executive officers, in part independent magistrates and in part virtually autonomous dispensers of a species of industrial martial law. Doubtless the explanation of this curious amalgam of functions was the Benthamite stress (reinforced by Chadwick's own temper) upon the expert as regulator and adjuster of relations between contending interests. Something may also be attributed perhaps to Chadwick's failure to recognize or distinguish the various constitutional functions. Thus in one aspect Chadwick seems to be plucking the JP off the bench, dressing him in official uniform, paying him a state salary and calling him 'inspector'. At any rate it is only to a limited extent that Chadwick is anticipating future developments in this field in his blueprint of 1833.

Finally, Chadwick's original scheme was faulty even where it should have been strongest – in its administrative machinery. In 1840 Leonard Horner, the ablest of the factory inspectors, observed of the 1833 act:

There was this further source of error, that it was in some degree legislating in the dark; a great part of the mechanism adopted was entirely of a novel description, of a kind that had never been tried in former factory acts; and after it was set to work, much of it was found to have been ill contrived, and some positively so bad that it obstructed, and to a great degree prevented, the attainment of the object.[9]

By no means all the defects to which Horner referred were to be laid 'to the charge of the original framers of the Bill';[10] and it is also true that Chadwick is entitled to all the indulgence owing an early cartographer of an ill-known continent. Nonetheless the fact that almost all his administrative proposals, regarded in detail as working arrangements, were defective, is suggestive. For it draws attention to three characteristics common to 'social science' in early Victorian England which Chadwick was here exhibiting in a highly developed form. First he was propounding general solutions from a sketchy and hastily worked-up knowledge of, at most, the exterior of the great and complex business with which he dealt. Secondly from a very early stage in his undertaking, if not actually from the beginning, his method ceased to be inductive and slid silently into the *a priori*. Thirdly he gave free rein to the contemporary passion – nowhere more evident than in philosophical radicalism – for the fully rounded scheme: the loose end was abhorrent, no element should be left to dangle or remain apart, all were to be fitted into a single interacting whole, if possible, self-adjusting.

We are now better placed to measure Chadwick's achievement of 1833. It is probably fruitless to ask and impossible to answer the questions of what he owed to earlier measures and schemes (other than Bentham's), and what the agitation of the 1830s would have issued in without his intervention. The case for his making a significant contribution to the administrative revolution at this juncture – and *mutatis mutandis* much the same is true of his later career – seems to rest upon three specific grounds. First in the initial stages of his intervention at least he was a gifted conciliator. With his self-image of a dispassionate social scientist, his genuine freedom from attachment to current practices and institutions and his ingenuity in drafting, he was well equipped to devise 'solutions' which appeared to marry opposing contentions and opposite frames of mind. Secondly Chadwick had proved as administratively inventive as his master and was perhaps his superior in governmental engineering. His design for the 1833 act, given both his own purposes and the concessions which he thought politically inescapable, is an object lesson in making and fitting together the pieces of an administrative machine – speaking of course in the 'pure' and not the 'applied' sense of governmental engineering. Thirdly both of these qualities are related to his major strength, his possession of a coherent and comprehensive philosophy of public action. Administrative Benthamism served him as a type of blinkers. It narrowed his view cruelly and was largely responsible for the *bêtises*, angularities and unassimilable elements in his plans, and for many of the misfortunes and anomalies in his own career. Like the racehorse he was given a clear view of his goal while his fellows and his surroundings alike were blotted out.

FOUR

Later factory reform

The early history of the factory act of 1833 is epitomized in three passages from the correspondence and reports of the first factory inspectors. Very shortly after his appointment, Horner wrote to his daughter:

> They [the mill owners] naturally dislike the Act, like any other interference, but they say that as they were to have one, that which has been passed was very little open to objection, and they see no difficulty in carrying it into effect. ... Nothing would be kinder than the way they have received me, and one of them, Mr Lepper, has placed his little carriage at my disposal, and I am to dine with him today.[1]

On 30 July 1839 another of the inspectors addressed the following confidential letter to one of his superintendents:

> I have to acquaint you, for your own information alone, that I am especially instructed to watch and take measures for obtaining information as to any proceedings in any district relative to assemblages of work-people, or Chartists, or circumstances calculated to disturb the public peace. You will, therefore, be so good as to make me weekly a confidential report on this subject. The newspapers from different parts of your district will generally point out to you any places requiring particularly to be noticed, but take care at Dundee and elsewhere to act with secrecy and pru-

dence, so that you may escape observation, and not be suspected of giving information.

I am, dear Sir,

Yours truly,

James Stuart.[2]

Nine years later a third inspector, Thomas Howell, looked back in these terms upon the first phase of the new factory regulation:

> At that period I had no practical experience of the factory system, or of the working of the Act of Parliament, which did not come into full operation till 1836, inasmuch as under our instructions we were at that period in communication exclusively with the employers, with the view of making the law acceptable to them, and from some of whom we unwarily adopted suggestions which appeared plausible enough on paper at the time, but which a very short practical acquaintance with the factory system in the cotton districts, when the law was afterwards fairly launched, caused me to repent, and which I gladly seize the present opportunity to repudiate.[3]

If the first factory inspectors did not deserve the Birstall committee's opprobrious specification of their backgrounds it is nonetheless true that they were political appointees, whig-liberal rolling stones who had failed in or become bored by or retired from various past occupations. More important still, none but Horner knew anything whatever of mills or the textile industries, and his experience was confined to a brief period of service with the royal commission of 1833.[4] Their subordinates were equally ignorant, and sometimes pluralists or corrupt into the bargain. Thus the factory inspectorate differed significantly from such near-contemporary foundations as the emigration officers or the inspectors of the Irish board of works. In these last cases, the naval officers and civil engineers concerned were at least quasi-experts with a fair body of relevant technical experience and competence, a tolerably specific brief and no political directions. It took the factory inspectors practically a decade to attain an equivalent position.

As Howell admitted, for the first three years of their operations the inspectors worked with and through the employers, and substantially, although innocently, served their interest; and they so acted at the government's behest. This is not to say that nothing was achieved. Fines were occasionally imposed, gross malefactors occasionally exposed or arraigned; and the mere existence of invigilation and the very fact that there was now a law to which some manufacturers conformed, consequently complaining of the unfair advantages enjoyed by the majority who did not, produced some measure of general improvement. But overall it would be misleading to suggest that any comprehensive and sustained effort was made in 1833–6 to enforce the 1833 act, or that the inspectors themselves behaved as neutrals.

In order to ease its passage and render the changes in the textile industry less abrupt, the 1833 act had contained a clause allowing for the progressive application of the age restriction over two and a half years, with the thirteen-year-old limit coming into force only in March 1836. So effective were the representations and claims of the mill owners upon them that as early as July 1834 the inspectors jointly reported that the act should be amended to allow twelve-year-olds to work up to sixty-nine hours a week: two of them in fact advocated the same even for children of eleven. Their subservience to the manufacturing interest may be gauged from this justification of their recommendation:

> ... it will be found extremely difficult in practice, if not wholly impossible, to limit the labour of children, who are 12 years of age, to 48 hours in the week, without serious injury to the masters and work-people; as in many situations it will not be possible to find a sufficient supply of children to work by relays: and unless that plan of working be adopted, adult labour must necessarily be interfered with.[5]

Their views were evidently unchanged in March 1836 when Poulett Thomson, who as president of the board of trade had factory legislation in his charge at this particular juncture,[6] introduced an amending bill to reduce the age of full protection from thirteen to twelve years. Simultaneously, the ten-hour men introduced a counter-measure to impose a ten-hour day on all. In retrospect all this appears as nothing less than a deplorable contest in inhumanity. The new ten-hour bill implied the raising of children's hours from forty-eight to fifty-eight in the week; by the abandonment of any attempt to provide checks upon age, it opened the door wide to the employment of children under nine; and it totally ignored education, safety and welfare. As to the government's measure, *The Times* was not far from the truth when it observed that the mill owners had 'found in Mr P. Thomson a ready tool to their cupidity, and the right hon. gentleman, on looking at his primer, found that "the less labour is interfered with the better". ... The pretence that the law cannot be enforced is sheer nonsense'.[7]

Thomson's bill was carried on the second reading, but only by a majority of two in a vote of 354 – practically speaking, a defeat. The proposal was dropped immediately; the chastened government pledged itself to enforce the 1833 act seriously, and the ten-hour bill also was abandoned.

Thus in mid-1836 we enter a second phase in which the official view of the existing statute and of the duty of the inspectorate undergoes a turnabout, and there is now a third school of factory 'reform' alongside the workers and the masters, who were roughly conterminous, respectively, with the humanitarians and the political economists. The object of the third school was, in the first instance at least, simply to carry the existing legislation into effect. Its essential members were the inspectors, now committed to such a course, not only *ex officio* but also to avenge their humiliation and revealed gullibility. Ostensibly Melbourne's government belonged to the same camp. But in reality, as the course of events in and after 1833 had shown, they were ambivalent. From 1832 on, the mill owners and the textile constituencies formed a considerably larger and more powerful element in the liberal party, and this was reflected by the ministry's behaviour.

The inspectors rapidly discovered when they attempted to carry the 1833 act into full effect that various errors and omissions in drafting and in the administrative arrangements, and the framers' ignorance of the real workings of the industry, had rendered it largely unenforceable. Nor were their powers to issue regulations a satisfactory corrective. In the majority of cases where they tried to supply the deficiencies of the statute by composing local rules, the crown's law officers found their proposals *ultra vires*. An amendment act was the only true resource. Their pressure upon the home office led to the governments's acquiescence in this course as early as January 1837, and within a week the inspectors had the substance of a draft bill before Fox Maule, the under-secretary to the home office.[8] But now began the parliamentary minuet of (in the classic phrase) 'those slippery whigs, whom it is impossible either to differ from or to work with'. First the bill was postponed for fifteen months until 9 April 1838. Then, having introduce it, the government afforded no opportunities for carrying it forward, and more than three months later Ashley himself, in despair, moved the second reading. The ministry, with Russell and Thomson now arguing that the very importance of the measure demanded caution and exhaustive exploration of opinion, urged instead the continued postponement of its own measure; and with the whips on carried the day, though barely. When Ashley returned to the charge on 12 July, the house was counted out and the government widely suspected of having engineered his second failure. Eight days later Ashley moved yet again, this time with a resolution virtually condemning the administration for refusing, under the influence of the manufacturers, to do what its inspectors declared to be indispensable – so to amend the 1833 act as to make it work. Again he was defeated, but the vote was close and the effort not in vain, for the government realized that they dared not simply drop the whole affair.

In effect the next three sessions followed the same course as 1833 had done. In 1839 the government, believing that an amending act could no longer be staved off, attempted to reach a compromise with the mill owners behind the scenes. Both while the bill was being re-drafted and during its progress through the house of commons, the inspectors, gathered in London, were locked in feverish negotiations wih the manufacturers' representatives. But at 1.30 am on 27 July Russell announced abruptly that the government would withdraw the measure.[9] In justification he pleaded an earlier amendment which had been carried against him in favour of extending the factory legislation to the silk and lace industries. But almost certainly the whigs had given way yet again because of the strength of the textile interest and, behind them, the pens of the economists.

At last despairing of Melbourne's government ever acting without the application of additional pressure, Ashley proposed the appointment of a select committee to inquire into the operation of the 1833 act when parliament re-assembled in 1840.[10] The ministry, now tottering, gladly closed with this offer in return for a year's relief in the house of commons. Of course, the committee, which reported on 18 February 1841, rehearsed the old story of the ineffectuality of the factory act, long familiar from the published reports of the inspectorate and the incessant commons' debates; and of course it endorsed the inspectors' successive proposals for making the 1833 act really work. What was needed was not a new law, 'but the fulfilment of the intention of the existing law'.[11] Thereupon, for the second time Fox Maule introduced a major amending bill substantially along the lines of its predecessors. But there was no true prospect of its passage. The whigs were on the point of throwing up the parliamentary sponge. Within a month Horner was told that the measure would be 'suspended indefinitely'. 'Suspended, forsooth!', Ashley wrote bitterly in his diary, 'and thus another year is added to the period over which wrong and violence are to reign without control!'[12]

Thus the factory act of 1833 was followed by eight years of liberal paralysis. The statute itself had proved so difficult to frame and carry that the whig governments were anxious to let the issue sleep as long as possible; and on the four occasions on which they were driven to rouse it with amendment bills, hostile interests had forced them to desist. Moreover, the individualist reaction against regulation and state intervention had been very violent and powerful; trade was precarious; and the working classes had been largely diverted to other types of agitation, political and trade union, the poor law and the charter. Meanwhile, however, the annual reports of the inspectorate were steadily teaching public and parliamentary opinion the actualities of factory life. The opposition was being gradually eroded.

But this was not all. During 1836–9 the inspectors became as disenchanted with the politicians as they had become with the mill owners after their experiences of 1833–6. The public revelation in 1840 that they were, at the government's instructions, acting as its political spies[13] was perhaps the last straw. Increasingly they behaved as a separate interest. The reports became tarter. Horner attempted to mobilize public support with a fiery pamphlet. The 1840 select committee was used as a vent for all the inspectors' accumulated knowledge and impatience. Such a course was possible both psychologically and professionally, because the inspectors saw themselves as promoting (to repeat the committee's phrase) not new law, but the fulfilment of the intentions of the old. In reality, however, the interior momentum of government was carrying them steadily beyond the limits of 1833. First, each amendment bill which they drafted proposed somewhere or other more stringent regulation than its predecessor. Little by little age limits were being raised, working hours reduced, holidays specified, 'lost time' cut and so on. Secondly and more important still, they were being led by an ever deeper understanding of the character of the evils and the difficulties of enforcement to break into altogether new regions of governmental control. For example, just as Chadwick was probably driven to conclude that compulsory registration of births was the only certain basis for enforcing the age requirement, so Horner was certainly driven to conclude that a compulsory national system of schools was the only certain basis for the education of factory children.[14] Similarly the inspectors moved step by step from the concept of medical evidence of age to the concepts of medical certification of physique, of the appointment of factory physicians by the state and of official concern with the health and well-being of the work force generally.

Apart from administrative innovation through increased stringency and universal designs, a third development was also becoming evident. In 1840 Ashley secured committees of inquiry not only into the operation of the act of 1833 but also into the conditions of trades and industries outside the scope of that measure, which was confined to cotton and woollen manufacture. The first of these extra-textiles inquiries, conducted by the children's employment commission, dealt with the coal-mining industry and proved immediately to be the detonator of a further revolution in this field. The mines act of 1842, its immediate fruit, deserves separate and minute examination. But three of its features, the regulation of the labour of adult women and of adolescents and of the working of machinery, must be noted here because they served as precedents for later factory reform. They formed part of a process for which the much-abused word, 'cross-fertilization', is for once apt. The factory act of 1833 fed the mines act of 1842, and the mines act in turn fed subsequent factory legislation.

Meanwhile the committee of inquiry into the 1833 act included in its report a consideration of the employment of children in the silk and lace industries. The first of these trades was largely, and the second wholly exempt from the factory legislation. The select committee found that the conditions and hours of labour were no better in silk and lace than in the cotton and woollen mills,[15] and the *pari passu* argument for including them in the circle of protected industries was incontrovertible. But Peel prevented Ashley from taking any immediate action. For a variety of reasons, economic and personal, the new prime minister did not wish to disturb the manufacturers; and for one who was (in his own estimation at least) no doctrinaire, his attitude to state intervention was and remained very negative and narrow. In this Peel fitted closely the entire run of politicians directly concerned with factory legislation in the 1830s and 1840s: Hobhouse, Althorp, Russell, Poulett Thomson, Fox Maule, Sir James Graham and Sir George Grey. Only Thomson could fairly be described as a blind devotee of manufacturing industry and political economy alike. 'The human race with such a philosopher are but necessary encumbrances to the spinning jenny',[16] *The Times* observed of him. But this was a difference of degree rather than kind. The 'progressive' men generally began with strong biases in favour of manufacture and the economists.

In 1843 the commission on children's employment issued its reports making the familiar criticisms of, and revealing the familiar abuses in the employment of children in the pottery and metal industries,[17] in calico printing, dyestuffs, bleaching, nail-making, paper-making, munitions, tobacco and a number of other industries. It was clearly established that these were in an essentially similar condition to textiles. The 1843 reports were however caught up in a much wider issue and in a grander approach to the entire question. The extensive and very grave working class disturbances of 1842 had had an important effect upon Peel and Graham, the new home secretary. On the one hand it turned them decisively towards free trade and the economic analysis of the political economists in contradistinction to the paternalist, quasi-collectivist attitude of the old tories, Oastler, Sadler and Ashley. On the other hand it led them to propose a great measure for the moral and intellectual 'elevation' of the working classes. As Halevy puts it, they felt that they were 'running the risk of another French Revolution, and British civilization might be exposed to the ravages of an ignorant and depraved populace'.[18] Here we have a return, a most significant return, to the tutelary idea contained, however ineffectually, in the factory act of 1833. *Laissez faire* and the free contract for adult operatives were to be combined with compulsory indoctrination in modern values and 'realities' for the young.

Accordingly, Graham proposed a new factory-cum-education bill[19] at the beginning of 1843. The state was to set up new schools connected with but not belonging to the workhouses, for the education of both factory children and the children of all factory families not yet employed. Most of the cost of building and equipment was to be met from the central exchequer, with the balance treated as a charge upon the local poor rates. Once set up, their running expenses were to be paid in part by stopping threepence per week from the children's wages and in part from the local rates. But the state was to maintain an interest even after the system was instituted. The inspectors of schools employed already by the privy council committee on education were to ensure that satisfactory standards of teaching and accommodation were maintained. With this went the abolition of factory work for children under eight years and the reduction of the working day for children between eight and thirteen years from eight hours to six and a half; all being obliged to attend the new schools during their free time. The measure, which largely imitated the Irish national schools system initiated by Stanley in 1831,[20] was a considerable advance. It extended Chadwick's plan, by cutting down the hours of labour and increasing the hours of instruction correspondingly, and it restored – or rather vastly improved upon – his machinery for making the clause compulsory and effective.

The bill came to grief, however, on a new and almost incidental stumbling block. In effect it had placed the proposed schools under the control of the established church. A storm of protest immediately blew up, particularly in the north and the midlands. The dissenters, with some catholic assistance, drummed up almost two million signatures for the petitions which opposed it. It was in vain that Graham made concessions to guarantee instruction in religion and the free exercise of religious beliefs. For he still insisted upon an anglican at the head of the governing body in every school. For three reasons this was anathema to the non-conformists. They had only very recently and very painfully won equality for almost all places in the state and local government; anglicanism was particularly obnoxious at that moment because of its tractarian and allegedly popish tendency; and, because the measure was confined to textile factories, anglicans would hold the chief positions in districts and towns where non-conformity predominated both in numbers and in wealth. Not only did the dissenters remain intransigent but Graham's concessions also had the unfortunate effect of arousing opposition amongst churchmen who still thought of the conservative party as their own peculiar possession.

The upshot was the complete withdrawal of the bill. This was not merely a final defeat for the tutelary idea; no subsequent factory legislation attempted in nearly so positive or ambitious a fashion to combine amelioration and instruction; it was also a disastrous defeat for the concept of state or national education, for Graham's bill had contained the germ of this idea. Instead of a first step being taken in such a direction, the ill-starred insistence upon anglican control left a permanent legacy of sectarian mistrust and conflict which might otherwise conceivably have been either avoided or diminished. It produced as well a marked reaction against state intervention in the sphere of education and a hardening of individualist theory upon the point. How often was the pattern of the factory act of 1833 to be repeated: an initial movement towards collectivism under the generous impulse of an informed, or with the defensive lunge of an alarmed, public opinion, followed by a sharp reaction which not only regains some of the ground lost but also makes the opposition more self-conscious, more powerful and more clearly articulated. In this particular instance we can also see how important initial timing might be. Even a decade later the anglican-dissenter conflict had modified its form if not abated its feelings. By then the concept of a version of state education in which the state did not identify itself with the establishment but treated it on a level with the other churches was much more firmly rooted. Graham's proposal might have been very different and the development of English elementary education significantly different had he been composing his measure in 1853. It is also true of course that such *contretemps* as that of 1843 contributed to the changed polemical climate of ten years later. But there is no need for us here to burst into that particular maze of interaction.

In 1844 Graham reintroduced his factory bill shorn of its peculiar educational clauses. The reduction of the working hours of factory children to six and a half was retained, and minor improvements were added. 'Lost time'[21] was practically prohibited; no child might now work until he was nine, instead of eight years of age; and the working day of adult women as well as of those under eighteen was reduced to twelve hours. This meant in effect that a twelve-hour day had been secured for all, as the act insisted that the twelve hours must run continuously and not be broken up, except for meals. It also meant that the precedent of the mines act in putting adult women into the category of protected persons had broken down completely the resistance to this intervention on the grounds of individualist principle. Scarcely a single voice was raised in protest in 1844. A further striking provision of Graham's act made the fencing of certain machinery obligatory. In part the new safety clauses specifically protected children: a prohibition on their cleaning machinery in motion is a case in point. But in part they were general in application and necessarily involved the statutory protection of even adult males. Thus the act produced a number of important and even revolutionary improvements and extensions. But on the key issue of education it faltered. It is true that the worst days of the 'coal-hole school' – what the committee of 1840 had called 'a mere formal compliance with the law, the schooling being a mere mockery of instruction'[22] – were numbered. The 1844 act gave the factory inspectors some supervisory powers (or perhaps, more correctly, rights) in this field: it prescribed three hours daily in school instead of two, and it enjoined that these hours must belong to the half of the factory day not worked by the children. But the critical innovations proposed in 1843 – state involvement, special schools, adequate finance and expert control – had all been lost. Finally, the ten-hour day (by now almost a mystical symbol for the factory workers) was still not achieved. Ashley had insisted upon bringing it before the house once more in 1844, but he had been defeated by 138 votes.

We should note that the 1844 act derived largely from the accumulated evidence and the testimony and teaching of experience contained in the annual reports of the factory inspectors, although it also owed something to the example and precedents of the mines act of 1842. The reduction in children's working hours and the first rudimentary health regulations were altogether the fruit of the inspectors' recommendations. They also played a part in securing the twelve-hour working day for women and 'young persons', and the requirement that all shafts and gears be boxed in. Their findings on the number and nature of fatal and other injuries caused by women's and girls' skirts being caught in the machinery proved particularly compelling in this last regard. Of course the mines act had blazed the trail in the critical matter of protecting adult female labour. This was a very significant extension of the concept that certain classes were not the best judges of their own interests (or, if judicious, in no condition to support their judgment), and that therefore in their own defence the state must curtail their absolute 'liberty' to enter labour contracts. To children, women had now been added, and also adolescents, the attempt to protect whom effectively in the mines act had failed in 1842 but was now two years later succeeding in the adjoining field. The mines act had also blazed the trail in state intervention in the operation of machinery. This too was of first significance as a curtailment of the owner's or manager's absolute 'rights' over the working of his own plant, and the principle of exterior regulation in such a matter was carried much further in the factory act of 1844.

The most striking departure and developments were, however, the new enforcement clauses. At last the realism of an executive corps, concerned not with phrases and gestures but with what could actually be carried out in an imperfect world, was receiving legislative expression. One of the enforcement clauses provided that all protected persons begin work at the same hour. It was recognized, or at any rate expected, that this would limit the daily hours of male adult workers, as well as the rest, to twelve, because it rendered the eight-hour relay system impracticable. The textile manufacturers had angrily pointed this out, but were overridden by the argument that without such a provision the concession to women and 'young persons' could not be enforced. Similarly another clause forbade the commencement of factory work before 5.30 am or its continuance beyond 8.30 pm. Again, it was recognized or at least expected that this would rule out anything in the nature of even a partial relay. The manufacturers' protests were once more rejected, this time upon the ground that the inspectors' day must also be limited. Thus the needs of enforcement were placed firmly above the alleged needs of industry, even though adult male labour was by implication being protected. Correspondingly, the superintendents were raised vastly in status (as expressed by stipend)[23] and given full and free access to mills despite fierce opposition by the manufacturers, allegedly for reasons of trade.[24] Once again it was simply stated that thorough invigilation demanded such a change. The certification of physicians and schoolmasters for factory work by the inspectors was similarly justified by the necessities of enforcement. Finally, experience had shown that the Chadwick-type inspectorate, with a high degree of administrative autonomy and wide magisterial and prefectorial powers, did not necessarily mean strong, swift and effective execution of the law, but rather the reverse. It overloaded the inspectors with duties, confused them as to their functions and left them without firm backing or protection at Westminster or Whitehall. In a word, a French form clogged rather than fitted a British system. Accordingly, the 1844 act drastically revised the character of the inspectorate, removing its judicial and prefectorial parts and placing the rest in a chain of command ending with the home secretary and knotted on the way by a central secretariat in Whitehall. The inspectors became senior executive officers of the familiar kind.

To a considerable extent, the world at large failed to realize at the time the prodigious implications or to guess at the long-term consequences of the amendments of 1844. Attention was rivetted on the ten-hour day, and the measure was generally gauged by its rejection, not least by Ashley. Two years later at the opening of the session of 1846 he tried once more for the great symbol, and this campaign was the beginning of the road to final victory, or near-victory at least. The ultimate success of the ten-hour agitation was due very largely to the repeal of the corn laws, but initially the repeal occasioned the loss of Ashley's seat in the house of commons and his bill had to be entrusted to Fielden, the tory-radical manufacturer. When the division came in April 1846 the measure was lost by only ten votes. The prime reason for the weakening of the opposition to the ten-hour day was Peel's unpopularity. Two-thirds of the protectionists and half the liberals supported Fielden. The whig supporters of the bill included many of the party's intelligentsia. Russell and Macaulay were especially noteworthy new adherents; they had previously followed the lead of the political economists. As Peel moved ever closer to Manchester radicalism, they reacted from it and ostentatiously contrasted their breadth of vision with Peel's narrow dogmatism. The move was shrewd politically and probably contributed something to the whig recovery at the general election of 1846.

The victory of the free traders in 1846 was so brilliant and dramatic that it left an immediate impression, like the reform act of 1832, that the towering issue had been settled once for all. And again like the reform act of 1832, it produced a feeling that, now the decks were cleared at last, parliament could get down to settling the great social questions of the day. The ten-hours act of 1847 and the public health legislation of

1848 were the counterparts of the factory act of 1833 and
the poor law amendment act of 1834. 'We have embarked',
wrote Mill to Comte in 1847,

on a system of charitable government. .... Today all the cry
is to provide the poor not only with money but shorter
hours of work, better sanitation, even education. That is to
say, they are to be governed paternally, a course to which
the Court, the nobility and the wealthy are quite agreeable.
They forget that what is done for people benefits them
only when it assists them in what they do for themselves.[25]

In a certain sense these few years about the middle of the
century represent a false dawn for collectivism. It was no
coincidence that Carlyle's *Latter-day pamphlets* and *Tracts on
Christian Socialism*, both attacks upon *laissez faire*, were published in 1849 and 1850 respectively; or that Kingsley's *Alton
Locke* belongs to 1850; or that Mill's own *Political Economy*,
which struggles to reconcile some working class ideas with
economic orthodoxy, belongs to 1848. It is true that this movement (if it deserves such a title) was neither widespread nor
lasting. There was a sharp reaction towards *laissez faire* and
individualism in the early and mid-1850s. Mill, often a useful
weathercock, produced his classic defence of the latter, the
Essay on Liberty, in 1858: whatever the provenance of the
celebrated disputed chapter, the book bore his name and
imprimatur. But short-lived though it was, the wave which
followed 1846 sufficed to produce the ten-hour day and other
important factory legislation, a new mines act, the public
health agitation, and a modification of the poor law.

The ten-hour day was achieved, at least in principle and
appearance, with comparative ease in May 1847. Fielden reintroduced his bill and although some of the whigs (and
especially Russell) had now second thoughts about letting their
hearts rule their heads, their conduct in the previous year
precluded them from clear-cut opposition. The protectionists
continued to vote for whatever Peel voted against, and the
agitation was further and fortuitously assisted by a current
depression in the textile industry. The fact that most mills
were working less than ten hours a day at that moment drew

much of the sting from the manufacturers' last-ditch prophecies of doom. Thus the great goal had been achieved at last. It was not, as Marx supposed, a victory for chartism. Chartism had little to do with it. It was a victory for the humanitarian lobby facilitated by the earlier nibbling away at 'principle', the effective subordination of adult male to female and child working hours in 1844, the precedents of gradual surrender with which all contemporary parliamentarians were so familiar, and the accidents of the political and economic situation in 1847.

Actually, the new measure[26] did not result, as was expected, either in a ten-hour working day for adult men or ten hours of continuous work (broken only by the statutory one and a half hour meal-break) for the protected persons. For it was still permissible to operate a factory for fifteen hours in a day; the relevant clause in the 1844 act had unfortunately not been modified. Further, bad drafting of the 1847 act had left a loophole by which employers could still use child, adolescent and female labour in a species of bastard relay system. Although the hour of commencement of work for protected persons was specified, the hour of their ceasing work was not. This meant that by giving different gangs of protected persons breaks at different times during the day, the machines could be run for thirteen or fourteen hours in all. The inspectors protested bitterly against this evasion of the legislature's intent. But from the other side the manufacturers reorganized their political pressure upon the government (which had been fatally inoperative during the confusion of 1847). The cabinet was willing to leave matters standing, and Grey, now home secretary, basely threw all responsibility in the end upon the inspectors' shoulders. They, however, proved implacable and insisted upon a test case. When the courts decided in 1850 that the working of the statute permitted the 'evasion',[27] Ashley introduced a final bill to remedy the defect. The manufacturers proposed a compromise. Their parliamentary interest was now once more considerable, and the temper of the time much less favourable to factory legislation than it had been in 1847. Accordingly Ashley compromised. In return for (supposedly) abandoning the relay system, the manufacturers secured a slightly longer day for women and adolescent workers. Where the 1847 act had gained them a fifty-eight hour week they were now to work a sixty hour week. It was assumed however that the factories would now open for only ten and a half working hours all round on weekdays, and only seven and a half on Saturdays.

But in fact Ashley had been duped once more. Only women and adolescents had been absolutely limited to twelve hours (ten and a half hours' work and one hour and a half for meals) in the mills in any single day. Children might still work their six and a half hours at any time during the fifteen-hour period specified in the 1844 act. Grey had promised Ashley that the fault would be repaired; but he reneged when Ashley proposed this as an amendment, and the government's brute votes beat Ashley down. The price of this sharp practice was paid by the men and children over the next three years. With children's labour many factories kept working two and a half hours after the women and adolescents had departed. Even at the height of the manfacturers' Indian summer, however, such an extreme of meanness was insupportable. When the attempt was made to stop the loophole in 1853, the new home secretary, Palmerston, yielded simply and unreservedly to the instincts of decency.

I really think that to have little children from eight to twelve years of age brought out on a drizzling winter's morning at five or half-past five, when they perhaps live three or four miles distant from the place where they work, and then in the evening to have them walking back, perhaps alone, to their homes in the dark, with perhaps snow on the ground, is a practice which must entail such evils that no one can be surprised at the extreme mortality among the children of the factory operatives. To limit the children will be to limit the adults, but all I can say is that I think it is so essential to protect these children from being over-tasked that I cannot consider the results which it may be imagined will flow from it.[28]

So it was, as M. W. Thomas concludes, 'that once again pity for the young and defenceless provided the motive force'.[29] The amending statute laid down 6 am to 6 pm as the only permissible weekday period of operation for textile mills and the sixty-hour week and 'the normal day' were entirely safe at last. There was no longer any ambiguity. Adult men had secured the limitation of the working day to ten hours and a half, and the now compulsory half-holiday, although there remained grievous dissatisfaction that the sacred ten-hour principle had been lost.

The year 1850 (with the plumbers called back in 1853) marked the limit of the advance of factory regulation for a generation. The extensions over the next twenty years were lateral, deriving from the principle of comparability. The gains of cotton and woollens spread quietly from one field to another. But 1850 remained the legislative high water mark. The process of enlarging the circle of protected industries began with Ashley's act of 1845[30] extending the 1844 legislation to calico-printing. The first phase of expansion naturally, if somewhat illogically, centred on the hitherto excluded textile industries and their satellites, such as bleaching and dyeing. Next the great range of other child-employing industries where working conditions and arrangements were essentially similar to those in cotton manufacture came under review. These included pottery, the metal trades, paper-making, chemicals, glassworks and printing. Thirdly the principle of comparability was applied to the unit of production, whatever its size. 'Child slavery' might as well – and as ill – be practised in a machine shop with half a dozen hands, or in a tiny bespoke tailoring attic as in a factory covering several acres. The apotheosis of all these came with the appointment at Ashley's urging (he was now Lord Shaftesbury) of another royal commission on children's employment in 1862 and the enactment of its major recommendations five years later. The factory act extension act of 1867 and the hours of labour regulation act of 1867 in effect subjected almost all factories and workshops employing children to the 1844–53 protective legislation, and women and 'young persons' working in these places rode into the stockade on the children's backs. As usual there was fatal executive weakness in the initial legislation. The second measure, which covered workshops, was left to the local authorities instead of the factory inspectors to enforce, and they proved a broken reed. The remedy, to extend the inspectors' jurisdiction to cover the handicrafts, had to await an amending statute eleven years later.

By the later 1860s then, over a wide range of industry the abolition of infant labour, the reduction of the hours of child labour to six and a half, the principle of 'protected classes' in the mills and workshops, the sixty-hour week all round, compulsory education over the age of eight and rudimentary forms of the modern working week and of factory safety and health codes had been achieved. Specific failures included the ten-hour day, Chadwick's tutelary idea (perhaps a pyrrhic loss) and his scheme of industrial insurance. More generally, there had been no break-through to universal industrial protection. Although the circle of 'exceptions' was ever-widening, a circle it remained. Outside its limits, state regulation ceased. This meant continued gross abuses of infant, child, adolescent and female labour elsewhere – to say nothing of adult males.

The next decade saw the final rounding off and consolidation of early Victorian factory reform. Aptly enough perhaps, it was carried through by a tory-paternalist rather than a radical-liberal government. It was, however, also a tory-political government. The electoral consequences of the reform act of 1867 were felt much more powerfully in the general election of 1874 than in that of 1868, and amongst them was the hard-pressing of labour issues upon the candidates in industrial cities. When Disraeli's ministry pushed through the factory acts of 1874 and 1878, as when they pushed through the trade union and the conspiracy and protection of property acts of 1875 and the repeal of the remaining master and servant legislation, they were redeeming pledges given in return for working class votes. The 1874 act met the promise (so far as the factories and workshops embraced in the 1867 legislation were concerned) to establish the ten-hour day, the historic working class goal. It also carried forward for the first time in a quarter of a century the frontier of regulation. The minimum age of employment was raised to ten years and the minimum age of full-time employment to fourteen. Women and adolescents were specifically included in the body of 'protected persons' who were to receive the benefit of the ten-hour day. Men were deliberately excluded: they gained it not in their own right but through the accident of working side by side with the protected persons. There followed a third royal commission in 1876 and a second major statute in 1878 which consolidated, repaired and co-ordinated the legislation of the preceding thirty-five years.

This seems precisely the right note on which to end. For the legislation of the later 1870s represented the consummation of the early Victorian endeavour. In so far as that endeavour was originally cast into shape by Chadwick, it had been wrenched into different forms long before. The inspectorate and the entire administrative climbing frame had been changed, in some respects even reversed. The tutelary concept had withered. The emphases upon efficiency and production were but a memory. 'Protection' was an unchallenged principle, the debate now confined to its proper limits and nature. But all this had been implicit in the factory reform movement from the beginning. It was a simple response to an apparently simple need. That the governmental arrangements for securing enforcement should alter, or that the degree and area of coercion should grow after trial and error, or that the screw should be tightened ring by ring with hours reduced or ages raised or corresponding classes added, was in the very nature of mid-nineteenth-century movements of this kind. So too was the narrow pursuit of a single object: however it might ramify the extensions were but branches of the original trunk, and the concept of final triumph, to be expressed in one grand act of parliament.

The extent to which the combatants of 1833 soon found common ground was perhaps best expressed in J. S. Mill's canvass of 'freedom of contract' in *Principles of political economy*. Mill adhered to the accepted formulation of a general rule modified by 'exceptions'. He showed considerable obfuscating ingenuity, however, in defining where and why the overriding proposition that every individual was the best judge of his own interests and should be at liberty to pursue them was in turn to be overridden by other considerations; or more precisely perhaps, in defining where and why the overriding proposition justified state intervention. Of course children and 'young persons' could not be the best judges of their interest: for them 'freedom of contract' was often 'but another name

for freedom of coercion'. Secondly, in such an affair as education, since good judgment itself might depend upon being
subjected to it, compulsion was justifiable. Finally there were
'matters in which the interference of law was required, not to
overrule the judgment of individuals respecting their own
interests, but to give effect to that judgment'. If (to turn Mill's
example, which referred to operatives, on its head) some employers wished to establish a ten-hour day, they might be re-
strained from pursuing what they conceived to be in their own
best interests because their rivals resisted the innovation. Here
all would have to be coerced if 'the judgment of individuals
respecting their own interests' were to be given effect.[31]

In much of this there are characteristic ambiguities and
dangling ends. The third 'exception' might be either narrowly
confined or indefinitely extended, and it is left an open question whether (to maintain our example) the 'good' manufacturers are favoured because of their higher morality or because
of superior (or for that matter inferior) numbers. Again,
although this was written six years after women had first been
included in the circle of 'protected' persons, it is difficult to
see how they might enter it by any of Mill's three back doors.
In fact Mill seems to argue that they should not enter at all.[32]
Doubtless the explanation of his curious tentativeness and
opacity here is that to classify women with those of imperfect
judgment was to imply their inferiority to men, while to
classify them with men was to imply that they should receive
no statutory protection. For cardinal to Mill's entire position
was the principle that full persons should be contractually
liberated, altogether 'free' to pursue their interest, as they
themselves judged it, in selling their time and labour.

Here as so often the mid-century Mill truly reveals the early
Victorian mind. This was the eventual or mature image of
the time on the subject of factory reform. 'Interference' was
rapidly accepted or acquiesced in on all sides but only as an
extraordinary suspension of a master principle. The principle
was expressed as freedom of contract and the norm settled as
the adult male. The factory world was envisaged as a sort of
open range dotted with sanctuaries for the weaker animals.
By the 1840s this was the picture of reality for the anti-re-
formers too. They devoted their energies not to destroying the

sanctuaries but to minimizing their size and number and to ensuring that the remainder of the range was really open, except insofar as the protection of the weak necessarily involved a degree of limitation for all. This attitude was epitomized by the national association of factory occupiers, formed in 1853 for resisting future and burking past factory legislation. It did not dare openly to propose any modification of the classes governing protected persons. Instead it stood altogether upon the free contract for men – with, incidentally, such short-term success as a pressure group that the factory act of 1856 rendered it virtually impossible to extend safety regulation, such as by further fencing of machinery, wherever adult males were employed. Conversely, and characteristically, Macaulay profited from his 'conversion' of 1847, and struck the celebratory note of progress which the mass of his educated compatriots wished to hear:

> . . . the practice of setting children prematurely to work, a practice which the state, the legitimate protector of those who cannot protect themselves, has, in our time, wisely and humanely interdicted, prevailed in the seventeenth century to an extent which, which when compared to the extent of the manufacturing system, seems almost incredible. . . . The more carefully we examine the history of the past, the more reason shall we find to dissent from those who imagine that our age has been fruitful of new social evils. The truth is that the evils are, with scarcely an exception, old. That which is new is the intelligence which discerns and the humanity which remedies them.[33]

Such then was the final form of the early Victorian struggle for factory reform; and it is in this context that we can speak of the legislation of 1874 and 1878 as marking the 'victorious' climax of a phase. Meanwhile there were harbingers of a new era. In the early 1870s several bills were introduced in the house of commons proposing a nine-hour day for men as well as for protected persons; and the royal commission of 1876 entered at length into the consideration of both health and hygiene in factories. These were early indicators that the battle was about to move on to fresh ground.

We should not however regard legislation and formal regulation as our only measure in this or in any similar field. The actual change in working people's lives in factories and workshops depended also upon the character and conduct of the executive officers. Persuasion, *exposés* and menaces could all give the inspectors, in favourable conditions, effective power far beyond what the statutes, as such, provided. Some instances of the operation of extra-legal influence will be provided later in our consideration of the coal mines. Factories, being less technical, perilous, autonomous and obscure than mines, were less susceptible than mines to such forms of personal authority. But even they were materially affected by them in some cases. Nor should we suppose that this would work only where the officers were numerous and ubiquitous. On the contrary, their paucity often helps to explain their power. When the 1844 act was being forced through and when the ten-hour day was first 'won' in 1847, the critical argument was, over and over again, the facilitation of inspection. Neither should we suppose that because no master agitator or theoretician was recruited to the service it must lack master bureaucrats. Stuart apart, the first inspectors pursued the simple goals to which their working experience soon converted them with steady, even ruthless, determination. The unsuccessful test-case of 1850 and the ultimate plugging of most of the hole by the amendment act of 1853 were both the fruit of Horner's intransigence and indomitability, in particular. What inspectors might do under an act of parliament was by no means synonymous with what inspectors actually did. Even the terms 'act of parliament' and 'cabinet government' might take on different meanings once an executive corps took root in their field of action.

FIVE

Coal mining

Coal mines[1] and factory regulation were intimately inter-related in the early years, and administrative innovations shuttled regularly from one to the other. But the major re-formatory impulse in mining derived from the horrific, large-scale and well-publicized accidents which occurred more and more commonly in pits in the second quarter of the nineteenth century. The textile industry had no counterparts. On the other hand textiles were a much simpler matter technologically, and to that extent more amenable to the crude forms of regulation then available. Moreover their main lines of political defence against 'interference' lay in the house of commons instead of, as in the case of mines, the house of lords; and the commons was a much easier nut to crack in the 1830s and 1840s than the upper chamber. A great deal of the variety in the developments in the two fields is attributable to these contrasting circumstances.

Safety in coal mines had been the subject of quasi-official inquiry and intermittent public discussion for a generation before a commons select committee was set up in 1835, as a consequence of pit disasters, to explore the possibilities of statutory regulation. The need for regulation was clearly established by the evidence before this committee, but so too were the great difficulties of prohibitions and the utter con-fusion (not to say contradictions) of scientific opinion on safety methods and devices.[2] The select committee shrank from pro-posing legislation. Soon afterwards a voluntary committee was set up in South Shields to review the whole matter more thoroughly and professionally, but this had still not reported when the first mines act was being hammered out.

The 1842 act[3] sprang, instead, from the report of the royal commission on child employment in mining which had been issued earlier in the same year. The commission was concerned essentially with the well-being of children; safety entered the picture only incidentally and almost accidentally because the employment of children in certain tasks endangered their own as well as miners' lives. The additional proposal to exclude women from underground work did not derive directly from child protection. But it was a sort of lateral extension of the 'moral principle' that those who were less than 'full persons' should be especially safeguarded. Additionally useful was the revulsion against the half-nakedness in which many of the women worked and their being used as vile beasts of burden. From first to last the safety of the miners as such was scarcely mentioned. The initial case for intervention was, therefore, made essentially in terms of child welfare. The causes of sexual decency and Christianity provided further arguments; and as with factories in the 1820s, so with coal mines in the 1840s: slavery was also used effectively as a foil. As late as 1849, the question was asked in the house of commons, 'Has she [England] a drop of sympathy for the white slaves at home?'.[4]

The first shot in the 1842 campaign, the Bishop of Norwich's speech in presenting petitions for action upon the commissioners' report, indicated what was to follow. It was on the commissioners' description of women and children, 'chained . . . to their labour of dragging small vehicles loaded with coal through narrow apertures or passages, in which they were obliged to crawl upon their hands and knees, their garments drenched with water', that the Bishop lingered.[5] Ashley, who had been originally responsible for the commissions on child employment and was the natural executor of their recommendations, followed the same path in composing and introducing his bill to terminate the iniquities. He assumed that no one could possibly dispute that such practices were intolerable in a civilized state:

. . . never, I believe, since the first disclosure of the horrors of the African slave-trade, has there existed so universal a feeling on any one subject in this country, as that which now pervades the length and breadth of the land in abhorrence and disgust of this monstrous oppression ... [of] evils that are both disgusting and intolerable – disgusting they would be in a heathen country, and perfectly intolerable they are in one that professes to call itself Christian.[6]

Ashley's speech concluded with a scriptural appeal, 'to break off our sins by righteousness, and our iniquities by showing mercy to the poor ...' Unlike the lords (some of whose mine-owning members were made of sterner stuff), the commons quailed before such a declaration. None in the mining lobby ventured to question Ashley's assumptions, while the non-committed members tumbled over one another in expressing their abhorrence of female and child labour and their veneration of the author of the proposed reform. Graham, the home secretary, postponed a few specific details for further consideration, but otherwise appeared to accept the bill officially. In the name of the cabinet he assured Ashley in the course of the debate that the government 'would render him every assistance in carrying on the measure'.[7]

Red sky at dawning, shepherd's warning: Ashley's early triumph was his last. In both method and fate, his 'compromise' on mining in 1842 was a sort of dress-rehearsal for his 'compromise' on factories in 1850. Centred upon the coal trade office at Newcastle-upon-Tyne, opposition to his bill grew rapidly. This was based – shades of the mill owners' response in 1832! – partly upon a denial of the facts alleged in the commissioners' report, and partly upon an assertion that wholesale changes in the supply of labour would ruin the industry. Ashley attempted to settle once for all with these opponents at a meeting on 20 June in London, when he hammered out a compromise which, he understood, would bring the resistance to an end. He made one very large concession. In place of his original proposal to prohibit the employment of boys under thirteen years, he agreed to lower the age limit to ten years (provided that those between ten and thirteen worked only three, and alternate, days per week). The group whom he had met had included Lord Wharncliffe, who was a member of the cabinet with mining interests; Hedley Lambton, MP for Durham, and John Buddle, the principal agent of the colliery owners of the north-east; so that Ashley had very good reason for his conclusion that he had reached a final agreement with both the government and the trade. The amended bill passed the commons unscathed but the lords at once referred the bill to a select committee, from which it emerged badly mutilated. The restriction of the hours of work of children between ten and thirteen years was altogether abandoned. The apprenticing of pauper children, which Ashley's bill had prohibited – 'here', he had exclaimed, 'you have a number of poor children whose only crime is that they are poor, and who are sent down to these horrid dens, subjected to every privation and every variety of brutal treatment'[8] – was practically re-allowed. The minimum age for tending winding machinery was lowered from twenty-one years to fifteen. Other clauses were emasculated after the second reading.

Ashley at once declared that the amendments both invalidated the general purposes of the bill and rendered what was left unenforceable. Naturally he felt, and said publicly, that he had been sold. But Wharncliffe had told the lords, as soon as the bill came up for their consideration, that 'the Government had taken no part whatever with respect to this bill. The Government intended to remain perfectly passive. . . .'; while Buddle, together with the principal coal owner in the upper house, Lord Londonderry, denied that the meeting on 20 June had reached a binding agreement. What weight precisely to attach to misunderstanding and what to treachery it is difficult to say. Certainly Graham's and Wharncliffe's respective declarations on behalf of the ministry could not be reconciled; and Lambton, another noble coal owner of the northeast, confirmed Ashley's understanding of the compact with the trade – 'It must be self-evident that you would only consent to make these concessions on condition of receiving our support.'[9] At any rate the 1842 act was a sad ghost of the original proposal.

Essentially the shorn measure prohibited the employment of females of all ages, boys under ten years and apprentices over eighteen years in coal mines; and the employment in machine-tending of all persons under fifteen years. Apart from a novel truck clause this was all. It is true, and of first importance that three great principles, two of them new to English law, had been carried. These were the exclusion of adult women from certain employments, the exclusion of certain persons from the management of machinery and the prohibition of child labour in a new field. But almost as much had had to be abandoned, and the executive clauses were defective. Much, however, still depended on how the clause empowering the home secretary to appoint inspectors was interpreted and carried into effect. Here as in its parliamentary vicissitudes the important fact was that the bill originated outside government. Whatever Ashley had had in mind in inserting this provision – probably no more than a vague desire to imitate the factory legislation – Graham was nonplussed. In fact he made but a single appointment, that of H. S. Tremenheere,[10] an assistant poor law commissioner.

Tremenheere, who was to serve for sixteen years without either colleague or successor, was called indifferently in the official papers 'commisioner' and 'inspector'; and this epitomizes the ambiguity of his position. He did undertake some prosecutions under the 1842 act; and he noted its weaknesses, pressed intermittently for their amendment and reported annually. But he regarded the examination of the social problems of the mining districts as his main function. In fact he often wrote as if it were his business to discover and neutralize the causes of dangerous discontent. Set loose with only very general instructions he was practically independent of the home office. His salary, no less than his social standing and his conduct as an administrator, indicated the status of commissioner. So too perhaps did the immediate reason for his appointment : in effect he was kicked upstairs to release the home office from an entanglement with angry dissenters. Yet he contributed more perhaps than any other single person to the first form of the second mining inspectorate, which eventually supplied much of what his regime omitted and superseded even his own work in the end.

Tremenheere pressed for a new form of inspectorate as early as 1845. Having canvassed the subject with mining engineers and managers he was convinced 'that *Inspection* of the mode of Ventilation in each Colliery by a properly qualified Government Officer, *without powers of interference* would tend greatly to diminish the risk'.[11] Tremenheere's conception of the inspector's utility (it matched his view of his own function) was that of teaching by superior knowledge and soft words rather than by coercion. His answer to the problem of explosions was a technically qualified inspectorate, visiting and reporting on the safety precautions in various mines, advising colliery managers and inducing them to emulate each other. But he also asked, as a result of his experiences as inspector, for an amendment of the 1842 act in three particulars: first, that boys under ten years be required to attend school for some specified time; secondly, that magistrates be given power to summon witnesses in prosecutions under the 1842 act; and thirdly, that all explosions involving loss of life should be reported to the home secretary. The absence of the second from the act had been responsible for the failure of many prosecutions in South Wales and the north of England, with the consequence that women and little boys still continued to work in mines in these districts; while the absence of the third meant that the department lacked regular information and the opportunity to conduct regular inquiries.

The response of the new home secretary, Sir George Grey, when these proposals reached him at the end of 1846, 'Is any power required to be given by Act of Parliament for such inspection?', points to one of the mysteries of the business. On the face of it there was no reason why the home secretary should not have appointed the new inspectors straightaway. The act gave him discretion to appoint as many inspectors as he pleased and gave the inspectors powers to examine any machinery or workings; and the only executive functions envisaged by Tremenheere concerned existing legislation: in safety matters the inspector would merely advise and 'diffuse knowledge about ventilation matters'. Yet Tremenheere's recommendations, which were published in his annual report in 1847,[12] were not carried out until 1850, and then only through the medium of a new statute.

Meanwhile the subject of mines inspection was brought forward repeatedly after 1846 and agitation in the house of commons was continuous. No less than four private members' bills, proposing more or less stern intervention by an inquisitorial and repressive inspectorate, were introduced in 1847 and 1849.

The bills mainly derived from, and were mainly supported by radicals, Duncombe, Wakley, Hume, Bright and others. Characteristic of their self-justification was Hume's attempted distinction between legislative interference with wage contracts, which was objectionable, and 'ventilating mines', which was 'another matter'.[13] But the bills were also supported by some members of a very different type, such as the tory Colonel Sibthorp. The cry of class discrimination was raised. Wakley observed that whenever a measure to help the working classes was introduced it was staved off as long as possible. 'Why,' he concluded (perhaps truly), 'if a noble Lord were blown out of a coal mine, there would be legislation on the subject the very next day the Parliament assembled.'[14] Similarly, Duncombe complained that however obdurate the cotton lords had proved, the coal lords promised to be worse.[15] The parliamentary coal interest was blamed for the failure of reform, and it was hinted that Grey himself was influenced by his family connection with mine owners. Grey never opposed the principle of mine inspection outright. Each time he pleaded for postponement – because of the gravity and complexity of the issue, because the mine-owning members had left town, because the recommendations of eminent scientists were awaited, because the session was too late – because of any and every cause he could lay hands on. Occasionally he threw out generalities about vexatious minute interference and the prodigious size of the service which would be required. But since the demand for reform had been first raised in the commons as early as 1844, and since several dramatic explosions took place and hundreds of lives were lost in each succeeding year, his excuses gradually wore thin.

What is the explanation of the protracted failure to act? Six main reasons can be ascribed. First, the coal interest was wealthy, powerful and strategically situated in parliament. In the northeast it was thoroughly organized with a permanent secretariat; in the commons, the cabinet and most of all the lords, it could work for procrastination and the emasculation of bills with devastating effect; and a mere reference to the industry as the commanding height of British manufacture invariably gave pause. Second, the agitation for an inspectorate was originally sustained, at least in part, by the new trade unions, and was sometimes pressed in the idiom of class conflict. This cut both ways. But on balance union support was probably a liability at this stage.

The other four retarding factors were more enduring, being problems of peculiar difficulty, special to the regulation of coal mining. The first was that of scale. There were nearly two thousand collieries scattered throughout Great Britain, many with several pits. All were more or less difficult of access. Some were three thousand feet underground; in others, miles of passageway had to be traversed to reach the working faces. To have each pit inspected thoroughly, say, quarterly, reported on and re-examined where changes in working methods were proposed, would have needed an executive corps running perhaps into hundreds. Where were such immense numbers of qualified men, where was the money to pay their salaries, to come from? Next was the variety of the measures needed. To take the single question of ventilation as an example, the airflow which contemporaries deemed necessary for safety in 'fiery' mines might vary by a factor of ten or even more from case to case; moreover, even these figures depended on the degree to which the current was unobstructed and no one could tell what further allowance should be made for the possible range of changes in barometric pressure. Thus the framing of specific regulations seemed at first sight virtually impossible. Another factor, scientific ignorance, reinforced the last. Exact knowledge of the causes of explosions was, as one inspector later observed, still in its infancy. Educated opinion realized how little had been established so far and at the same time assumed that scientific certainty would eventually be attained. On both counts this operated against immediate statutory intervention. Finally, there was the matter of 'responsibility'. This was a double-edged weapon against the establishment of an inspectorate. On the one hand it was argued that any diminution of the managers' responsibility would weaken the miners' best protection against death and injury; on the other, that inspectors would not assume the burden (which would inevitably attach to them if they could lay down what was to be done) so long as they lacked the power either to make a full assessment of the deficiencies or to ensure that their own recommendations were carried out.

D

These last four difficulties, those of scale, heterogeneity, scientific uncertainty and responsibility without power, would not disappear overnight or even for decades after the establishment of state controls. They were lasting governors of, or at least continuing influences upon the entire question.

But however strong the array of opponents some ostensible reform was unavoidable. Disasters multiplied in 1847–9, attracting more and more newspaper publicity in snowball fashion; memorials and petitions for government action rained in; the ministerial defences for delaying legislation became less plausible with each sterile session. The government's main shield against the assaults was the practice, begun without much forethought, of appointing one or two 'eminent scientific men' to investigate and report upon various mine disasters. Not merely did the inquiries establish the causes of particular disasters (though this never led to further action), they also helped to ward off criticism of the government for doing nothing by suggesting that the whole matter was *sub judice*, and even comment consequently improper. In the long run, however, the effect of the special commissions was to increase the pressure for state action. Though quite closely confined to the matter in hand, the commissioners could not but indicate the appalling general state of ignorance amongst both managers and working miners and the necessity for some form of supervision. By 1849 the need for a fresh statute and a new inspectorate was practically established. Thus the force of scientific authority was now added to the pressures which had first been exerted within the administration (by Tremenheere), by reformers (primarily, the South Shields committee) and through the mining unions several years before. The upshot was the appointment of a lords' select committee of inquiry in the spring of 1849.

The spectrum of the testimony before the committee was not wide. It noted that there had been a remarkable consensus in favour of inspectors with rights not merely to enter and inspect mines but also to call for and examine working plans. The only essential difference of view – although it was a most important one – was whether or not the inspectors should have powers 'to order and to enforce penalties'. The committee endorsed what was undoubtedly the majority opinion, that the inspectors should merely advise, lest managers and owners shuffle off that 'responsibility which naturally belongs to them, and which it is not only desirable not to withdraw, but rather, if possible, to increase'. Sympathy with the working miners' objectives was expressed, but the committee contended that vexation and disappointment could be the only fruits of a coercive executive:

> The cases to be dealt with are too various in their conditions, opinions as to the fittest remedies in each particular instance are occasionally too doubtful, and the difficulty and cost of applying them often too great, to justify the positive enforcement of the views of a Government Officer.[16]

Nonetheless the report came out strongly in favour of some form of inspectorate, however much owners and managers might object to an inquisitor roaming about their workings, questioning their men, scrutinizing their drawings, criticizing their procedures and telling them (and the home secretary) what changes they should make. Nothing should outweigh 'the imperative duty of Parliament and the Executive' to protect the miners' lives, limbs and health, both by inspection and direct enactment so far as practicable.[17]

Though its positive recommendations were few and its analysis of the inspectorial system was superficial, the report at least aired and balanced the best contemporary opinions. The argument on the inspectorate was confused. But this was mainly because the contestants had confined their choice to the somewhat unreal alternatives of advising or coercive officers. The advisory service was in fact a *pis aller*. It tried to reconcile two contrary impulses, hesitation to legislate at all in such a matter at such a stage, and the need at least to appear to take remedial action. The compromise was essentially of the same type as the common practice in the 1830s and 1840s of rendering an initial reforming measure permissive, but not compulsory. If Tremenheere's peculiar view of his functions originated, the scientific commissions spread the idea of regulation by advice; and it happened to fill the immediate need conveniently. The establishment of an arbitrary, despotic service in England in 1849 was inconceivable, nor could it have worked in a legal and political system alien to it at every point. On the other hand, advising officers were anomalous. What no one discussed was the type of inspectorate natural to, and already established in the British environment: an executive corps which saw to it that a law was executed and whose experiences and recommendations helped to shape and re-shape that law. The reason for this omission was, really, the unwillingness of most parties to commit themselves yet to constraining and prohibitory legislation; in this respect the proposed advisory inspectorate was simply the latest in the series of devices to put off the awkward choice.

Even the lords' committee report was not immediately sufficient to produce legislation. While the committee still sat, Grey appointed two scientists, Blackwell and Phillips, from his panel of official 'inquirers' to inquire generally into safety measures, and subsequently argued that legislation should await their recommendations. But when reported at last in May 1850 these substantially repeated the findings of the previous inquiries.[18] The government had now nothing to fall back on and a bill was finally introduced in July. It proposed a mild version of the 'advisory' inspectorate. The home secretary might appoint inspectors, who would be empowered to enter any coal mine, examine its operations and recommend changes where he adjudged existing practices or machinery to be unsafe. If the owner or manager refused to adopt the changes within a reasonable time, the inspector was to report the case to the home secretary – no more. The only other significant provision was that owners or managers were required to report fatal accidents to the home secretary within twenty-four hours, and that coroners were to give the home secretary forty-eight hours' notice before holding an inquest in such a case. The only penalties prescribed were for obstructing inspections and failing to report accidents; and the operation of the act was to be limited to five years. There was still some opposition and a division in both houses, but except for a handful of minor concessions in favour of the coal interest, the bill passed intact and received the royal assent on 14 August.[19] Three months later Grey appointed four inspectors and divided Great Britain into four areas of inspection.

Two of the new inspectors, Blackwell and Dunn, had long

been prominent in the discussion upon an inspectorate; the others were established mining engineers. Blackwell's appointment reinforced the idea (which had also coloured the special 1849–50 inquiry) that the inspectors were more permanent commissioners of inquiry than executive officers. But if so, the salary was not commensurate with the status. Even with travelling expenses, £400 p.a. was less than half the salary of a good mine manager or engineer. This was a source of trouble from the start. Men resigned from the service to take up better posts – Blackwell himself resigned within a year – and for a time some supplemented their incomes by acting as consultants or arbitrators. Even when the salary was raised in 1853 to £600 p.a. the complaints of the inspectors did not cease, presumably adding to the difficulty of recruiting able and energetic men.

If the rewards were much too small, the inspection areas were much too large. Initially each inspector had over four hundred collieries in his district; a single thorough inspection of, and report upon all 'his' pits might have taken a man three or four years to accomplish. Even when the corps was increased in 1855 to twelve,[20] the inspection regions were still too extensive for regular, even annual, visits to every mine.

Despite all these inadequacies, legislative and administrative alike, the first inspectors laid the foundations of a real system of control. It was established almost at once that the inspectors should prosecute for breaches of those clauses of the act to which penalties attached. This was a critical precedent. Neither the act itself nor the preceding arguments had made it clear that the inspectors should act as the executors of the legislation in this sense. The new decision was not immediately important. The subjects on which prosecutions could be undertaken were very few before 1860. But even the amending legislation of the 1850s steadily increased the number of offences – and all this apart, the recognition of his role as enforcement officer specified the inspector's function and secured his standing. Nor was the 'advisory' work necessarily negligible, at any rate where owners had been already cowed by fatal accidents upon their properties. This was particularly the case in the salad days of the new inspectorate when owners did not realize quite how circumscribed the powers of an inspector really were: later they were by no means so sub-missive. Nonetheless there was enough oblique control at every stage to indicate what remarkable things the state might achieve in fields like this, although powerless to inflict a legal penalty.

Next the inspectors provided, almost *de novo*, the statistics of their subject. Hitherto even the mortality from accidents was barely guessed at, and its causes were still less explored. The systematic collection of information gradually made it clear that fatal accidents were much more numerous than had been supposed, that explosions were not in fact the major cause of fatalities, and that occupational diseases killed many more miners than the disasters. The foundation of accurate knowledge, even if still of an elementary kind, was now being laid. The fourth and most important achievement of the early inspectors was to provide a professional and continuous evaluation of the problems of regulation: the various inquiries preceding their appointment had been (as was usual in such cases) irregular and superficial. The first opportunity to turn the new advantage to account came in August 1852 when all the inspectors were asked to comment upon a recent report of a house of commons select committee[21] inquiring into safety in collieries.

By then there were six inspectors, three of whom had served already for twenty months, and two of whom had visited France, Germany and Belgium on a study-tour of the continental systems of control. Before forwarding their individual replies to the home office the inspectors met and discussed the report, a general meeting foreshadowing the later annual and even more frequent gatherings whereby they concerted their power *vis-à-vis* both the home secretary and the collieries. Generally the inspectors in 1852 agreed in both their criticisms of the committee's report and their own recommendations for new legislation. Concerning the latter they were practically unanimous. They agreed that inspectors should be empowered to stop the working of any colliery which they considered to be unsafe and which the owners refused to reform, that the act should cover ironstone mines as well as collieries (the evils being substantially the same in each), and that owners be required, under heavy penalties, to fence off all abandoned workings. Further, they agreed upon, and proposed the amendment of what they regarded as the defects of the existing legislation. They asked for a time limit (with penalties for failure to perform) to be prescribed for the production of maps and plans by mine owners, for sufficient intervals and notice to ensure that inspectors had an opportunity to attend all colliery inquests and adjourned inquests, and for the rectification of other clauses where it had proved impossible to recover the damages specified.[22]

A second achievement of the inspectors was the sweeping away of many of the misconceptions which had characterized the discussion on mining regulations down to that time. The lengthy and detailed reviews by the inspectors of the report of the 1852 select committee furnish an example. First they showed that the committee (like every previous inquiry) had exaggerated greatly the importance of explosions as a cause of mortality amongst miners. In their experience explosions accounted for some 20 per cent of the deaths instead of the 66 per cent asserted by the committee. The committee was equally astray in believing that afterdamp caused 75 per cent of the deaths arising from explosions: 7 per cent was more likely. They pointed out moreover that in concentrating upon 'fiery' mines the committee had ignored over two-thirds of the collieries in Great Britain. This type of basic information, never formulated systematically if indeed known before, made it possible to define the problems with some precision and established valid general perspectives for the first time.

Next the inspectors dissipated myths about the use of science. The committee had misunderstood and wildly exaggerated what science could do at that time to improve mine regulation – here again reflecting a prevalent general error. For instance the committee had assumed (as almost everyone who had spoken or written on the matter hitherto had assumed) that ventilation was the key to safe working, that one or other of the methods of artificial ventilation must be superior to all the rest, and that the minimum velocity of air current necessary for safety could be determined. The inspectors had no difficulty in demolishing these jejune assumptions. One observed that the belief that ventilation was the sole significant factor was in fact the distinguishing error of all 'theorists': in reality ventilation was 'but one item of a catalogue'; the 'best airflow' would be worthless without adequate airways or if some of the underground regions were cut off from the main stream. Similarly it was folly to search for a minimum 'safe' rate of current or a minimum 'safe' sectional area. In some mines 100,000 cubic feet per minute were needed, 5,000 would suffice in others. Again the select committee, after a lengthy and (one might almost say) eager discussion of the merits of the various systems of artificial ventilation, had opted for the steam jet as superior to all the rest, and in particular to that most commonly employed, the coal furnace. The inspectors pointed out that the entire question of ventilation mechanisms was still, scientifically speaking, *sub judice;* and that in any case it could not be sensibly discussed without considering the comparative costs of operating the various systems. The real question was not how a few very large collieries might best increase their ventilation but how the large number (nearly 40 per cent of the whole) which still trusted to the 'caprice of wind' might be induced to adopt *any* form of artificial ventilation.[23]

All this is not meant to suggest a species of 'God said *Let Newton be!* and All was *Light.*' Some of the inspectors' proposals had been put forward already by laymen; others were unlikely to succeed. The next essential reform, the subjection of all collieries to both 'general and special rules' which were to be enacted in the mines act of 1855, was not so much as mentioned in 1852; and this applies to many other subsequent innovations. Improvement, moreover, was to be slow and painful. Although each of the intermediate amending measures, the acts of 1855, 1860 and 1862,[24] added materially to the inspectors' powers and range of work, twenty years were to pass before new legislation established by the mines act of 1872 a largely effective system of control. Almost twenty years were to pass before sufficient data was accumulated to draw firm statistical conclusions. 'Expertise' was a gradual acquisition, the fruit of protracted field work, observation and comparison. If this was what lay ahead, the statutory powers of the inspectors were negligible in 1852. The 1850 act, wrote the best contemporary critic of mines legislation, 'did little more than provide for the appointment of inspectors, who were few in number, and not invested with much authority.

They could do little more than record the number of accidents, and act as assessors to the coroners holding inquests on the victims of accidents.'[25]

Nonetheless by 1852 the inspectors had become in effect a corps, already transforming itself into an executive arm of the ordinary kind. It had begun to concert its activities and to perform creative as well as regulatory work. The publication of regular annual reports, which clarified and determined the inspectors' philosophy of reform and prepared educated opinion for further changes, commenced. Moreover the want of formal powers did not necessarily mean the absence of effective powers. In some cases the inspectors anticipated powers which they were later to enjoy, or more precisely, achieved as much by informal means as they could have done under statutory authority. One of the most vigorous members of the corps, and the main mover in 1852 of the proposal to require all disused workings to be fenced to the inspector's satisfaction, had reported a little earlier that in twenty-two of the twenty-three such cases which he had recently encountered, the owners had complied without demur to his requests.[26] 'Public opinion', suspicious trade unionists, the parliamentary question and a reckless press were useful assistants. Moreover if progress was slow it was also continuous and apparent from the start of the inspectorate. In 1851, 19.35 deaths occurred in collieries per million tons of coal mined; in 1861 the figure was 10.95 and in 1871, 9.15. During the decade 1851–60 the accident mortality amongst miners was 1 per 245 employed; in 1861–70, it was 1 per 300; and in 1871–5, 1 per 430. Moreover the fall in mortality was steepest in those classes of accident which the inspectors could do most to influence. Explosions, for example, accounted for 24 per cent of the accident deaths in 1851–60 but only 17.8 per cent in 1871–5. Conversely, deaths from roof and wall falls, which the inspectors could do least to check, rose from 37.6 to 41 per cent of the totals over the same periods.[27] It is not, of course, suggested that a simple causal relationship between the work of the inspectors and the fall in mortality can be established. Other factors operated on either side. Safety mechanisms improved and scientific knowledge grew throughout these years. But coal mining also became more and more dangerous as work was carried on at ever deeper levels and in less accessible places. But there can be little doubt that the inspectorate contributed substantially to the reduction in the accident rate, even if there is no certainty as to the precise extent of their contribution.

If 1852 did not then represent even the beginning of the end so far as safety in collieries was concerned, it did mark (as the phrase goes) the end of the beginning. After nearly two decades of serious concern and one of formal statutory intervention, the stage had been reached at which at last the interior momentum of government could come significantly into play. Perhaps the most interesting general lesson of the pre-history of this development is its demonstration that inspectorates did not necessarily spring fully grown upon the scene, but might evolve. In this case there were two quite separate forms, one established in 1842 and the other in 1850. For nine years they coincided, until the second took over all the duties of the first which were not quite idiosyncratic to Tremenheere. The first was conceived of initially as an executive rather than an investigative or advisory service. In fact social inquiry of the most general character became almost its sole function. The second was originally conceived of as investigative and advisory rather than executive. Yet it turned at once in the opposite direction. Indeed the second inspectorate set about transforming itself almost from the moment it began. By 1852 the officers were joining together in their demands, and in particular demanding that they be given power to stop workings which were in their opinion dangerous. Of course they did not want absolute powers and with them absolute responsibilities. As one of them observed in 1869,

Much as the question of more inspection ... may be desirable, I have often thought that many of the casualties herein reported might have happened while I was in the mine. Often have I found men working in great danger for want of their places being propped and spragged when props and sprags in abundance were lying out of use within a few yards.[28]

Equally, of course, there was nothing sinister or conspiratorial in their proposals for a change in the formal character of the inspectorate. The advisory service was inherently unstable. There could be no lasting halfway ground between no coercion at all and a statute prohibiting bad practices and providing for its own enforcement.

SIX

The Poor Law

The second great whig measure of social reform was the poor law of 1834, the product of a royal commission of inquiry (one of the first of its kind), appointed by Grey's ministry in 1832. The setting up of the commission, which implied a promise to attempt a comprehensive and final solution to the harassing problem, was the climax of long agitation and conflict. Two major investigations had already taken place since 1815, when deep-set agricultural depression succeeded the comparatively golden years of the revolutionary and Napoleonic wars. But the conclusions of the inquiries had been contradictory and indecisive.[1] Meanwhile the poor rate had continued to grow until by 1830 it amounted to one-fifth of the national expenditure and threatened to crush landed property beneath its weight. The consequences for the fast disappearing independent labourers were indicated in the 'labourers revolt' of 1830, and by the terrifying industrial crises which gripped the country. Matters seemed clearly to be coming to a head; and with a new, reforming party in office after a generation in the wilderness and the paralysing issue of franchise finally decided, bold and grand measures appeared to be the order of the day.

Any attempt to reconstitute the poor law would have to be both bold and grand; for the old poor law, formulated two and a half centuries before, touched almost every aspect of domestic government. It provided the only general social securities and the only general regulation of labour.[2] But its prime characteristic was perhaps the complete absence of either central control or uniform policy.

Was unemployment to be regarded as an offence or a misfortune? There was no clear answer. Was relief to be administered as a deterrent, as a dole or as a livelihood? Again there was no clear answer, or rather there was a multitude of differing answers to the question. The fissiparous tendency of the old Elizabethan statute, which left the fifteen thousand parishes of England and Wales practically autonomous, had come fully into play with the agrarian revolution of the mid- and late eighteenth century. More specialized and capitalistic farming, an endless stream of enclosure acts and the destruction of independent small-holders led to a prodigious increase in the number of agricultural labourers. This increase was accelerated by a rise in the birth rate (or fall in the death rate, or both) among this labouring class, and its ill effects were accentuated by the operation of the antique laws of settlement, which placed responsibility for every pauper at the door of his native parish. Thus the circle was completed. Parishes became clogged with redundant labour, and this local over-population merely produced still greater local over-population and still steeper declines in living standards over time.

The parish vestries reacted variously to the crisis. Some continued a deterrent policy, but the majority adopted a more positive line. Some gave a simple cash dole, some put the paupers to work on local public works such as road making or draining commons. Most followed the Speenhamland system of 1795[3] in one form or another and attempted a paternalistic government of the parish by making payments, not for work done but according to family or personal need. But whether the parish attempted to cut its losses by a cash dole or to get something in return by going into business or developed the quasi-feudal device of the subsistence or living wage, the effect was much the same. The poor rates grew inexorably and the independent labourer was being forced out of existence by the competition of paupers. A new form of serfdom and labour drafts appeared to be developing willy-nilly.

The evils and burdens of the system were still further aggravated by the methods of parish government. Here self- and sinister interest operated almost without restraint. The vestry, or body of the ratepayers who controlled the overseers of the poor, generally fell into the clutches of the middle-sized farmers and village shopkeepers. They usually worked the poor rates to their own advantage at the expense of the large farmers, whom they could out-vote; and their administration was amateur in the extreme, wasteful and often corrupt. The only restraint upon them was the pauper's right to appeal to his justice of the peace. The magistracy on the whole escaped the worst of the poor rate, as this was assessed on the occupation, not the ownership, of land. Thus they could exercise prodigality and paternalism at little real cost to themselves, a very dangerous temptation. As Nassau Senior put it, 'They can indulge their love of power without appeal and their benevolence without expense.'[4] Parish autonomy had a further weakness. The care of the sick, aged, impotent and mad was an important if greatly neglected aspect of the poor law, tithes having long since ceased to perform their original function of carrying a portion of this burden. The small size of the parish unit meant that where the parish could rise to a workhouse or almshouse at all, it could rise to only one for all these varied classes. The condition of two or three dozen persons of all ages and either sex afflicted by misfortunes ranging from idiocy to being an orphan, and from senility to blindness, and subject to the sort of rule which the amateur overseers were likely to provide, must have been pitiful beyond words. This, then, was the old poor law which the royal commission was called upon to tackle: a system of law deeply embedded in the economy and government of England.

Broadly speaking, opinion on the poor laws was divided into three: into those who wished to retain them, those who wished to modify them and those who wished to abolish them. Humanitarians, sentimental radicals and paternalistic tories belonged to the first group. This is not to imply that any, even from these cadres, was perfectly satisfied with the existing poor law: no one could be. But taking it all round, they saw the old poor law as providing a measure of basic security for the labouring poor, and this seemed to them to outweigh its disadvantages. They feared that any reform in the current climate of opinion would deprive a great body of their fellow creatures of even their last defence against absolute want and hunger. The second group, those who wished to retain but modify the poor laws, were to some extent motivated by the same sentiment. But it was counter-balanced by their alarm at the ever mounting expense of the poor rate. They saw a way out in extending everywhere the growing practice of making pauper labour as self-supporting as possible – either by selling it to employers or by setting it to the production of profitable goods or of useful services. Broadly speaking, where the first group was concerned above all with the retention of a subsistence wage, the second was as anxious that this should cost the general public as little as possible and that British agriculture should escape bankruptcy.

The third group was the most influential and powerful if the least numerous. Its guiding lights were political economy and Malthusianism. Apart from its unquestionable abuses and evils and its crippling cost, the old poor law was anathema to most political economists. It was the greatest existing clog to the free working of the economy: it choked the supply of labour and hindered the 'free' contract between employer and employed, and it had led recently to the parish entering more and more the field of private enterprise and acting as an employer in its own right. Malthusianism produced the further and devastating objection that the poor law increased the improvidence of the poor and thereby led to earlier marriages, increased families and ultimately to the population outstripping the means of subsistence. These views were spreading rapidly through the enlightened and political classes, endorsed, as they appeared to be, by the galloping fever of the poor rate; the royal commission of 1832 fully accepted them before it went to work. They seemed to point in one direction only – the total and uncompromising abolition of the poor laws – and it was very probable that this would be the general recommendation of the commissioners.

The royal commission was well weighted with 'progressive' men inclined towards political and economic individualism. Nassau Senior, for example, was a very influential doctrinaire of this school. As things turned out, however, the most important appointment was that of Edwin Chadwick, as yet an obscure and unbriefed young barrister to the world at large, as an assistant commissioner to do the field work about

London.[5] From what we know of Chadwick's frame of mind and the tutelary mode of thought, we can see at once that he could not adopt any of these three approaches. He objected quite as violently as any Malthusian both to the basic security or subsistence wage conception, and to the notion of the parish in business. On the other hand he differed from the Malthusians and anarchic individualists in two important respects. First the idea of cutting the whole business adrift and abandoning any attempt at control was deeply antipathetic to his bureaucratic temperament and his Benthamic training in the artificial harmonizing of conflicting interests. Secondly, he belonged, as has been said, to the optimistic wing of the school of political economy. He therefore repudiated the Malthusian thesis that population must inevitably outrun the means of subsistence and instead asserted that there was no economic problem which greater and freer productivity could not solve. His prime objection to the existing poor law, apart from its administrative chaos and intellectual incoherence, was that it held down productivity in every conceivable way. The cheapness and ubiquity of pauper labour was destroying the independent labourer and forcing him to join its ranks, and pauper labour was clearly without the incentive to produce as much as possible: its basic wage was guaranteed and it gained nothing whatever from greater exertion or skill. Again the allowance system brought the parish into business, and even were the parishes not being run by ignorant, scheming oafs of vestrymen, they could not produce as efficiently as private enterprise. Finally, the laws of settlement[6] immobilized a huge labour force for which the factories were crying out. Thus what Chadwick wanted was to 'de-pauperize' the able-bodied, to force them out from their fatal protective cover, to drive them into the open labour market and to compel them to fight for their living and develop their skills, industry and exertion. In all this Chadwick certainly did not think of himself as being inhumane. In the long run it was not only in the labourer's own interest that the manufacturer should make the last penny of profit out of his labour: it was also essential for his survival in nineteenth-century England. More profits meant more capital and a still sharper appetite for profit-making, and these last were the only means by which industry and productivity could expand fast enough to provide employment.

But how were these ends to be achieved short of abolishing the poor laws? Of course the answer was: through the artificial reconciliation of individual interests by the state. One must render it in the labourer's interest to join the free labour market and work under the unfettered interplay of supply and demand. This was to be achieved by the so-called 'less-eligibility' principle, which meant simply that the poor law should be rendered less attractive to the labourer than going out to fight for his living. Poor relief was to be available only in a workhouse, and within the workhouse to be rendered still more abhorrent by three particular devices: first, the reduction of the pauper's standard of living by such measures as cutting down his rations; secondly, strict discipline and regimentation; and thirdly, compulsory, difficult and unpleasant labour. Chadwick expected that these conjoined devices would induce the great body of able-bodied paupers to refuse poor relief, restore incentives and a superior standard of living to the independent labourer and stigmatize pauperism as disgraceful; last but not least, this system would cut back the poor rates and provide capital for development and productivity. Chadwick's plan was therefore essentially Benthamite in its conception and purpose. The 'less-eligibility' principle was to reconcile artificially the self-interest of the labourer with the common good, and this common good was conceived of as an essentially uncontrolled economy.

But how did this obscure, minor and temporary official come to lay down the principles on which much of the greatest piece of social legislation for two centuries was to be erected? The answer, as Finer says, is in part accident and in part because (like his factory proposal of the same year) his project fitted in exactly with the prevailing mood of the politically powerful.[7] The first step was the conversion of Senior, who had hitherto accepted the Malthusian thesis.[8] Next, and more important, there was a loud demand at the end of 1832, while the field investigations were still in progress, that the royal commission should report immediately. The commission protested, the government temporized and the sop of an interim report from each assistant commissioner was thrown to the noisy public. This was Chadwick's opportunity. Instead of following the example of his fellow assistant commissioners and summarizing his investigations and presenting the preliminary results in as neutral and factual a form as possible, he produced an entire and all-embracing plan, complete with evidence and apologetics, working up to his 'less-eligibility' principle and the administrative machinery for its execution.

It was an amazing *tour de force*; it swept the boards. The blue book which contained Chadwick's report sold everywhere; the press and parliament seized on it with delight. It seemed at the beginning of 1833 to throw light where all had hitherto been darkness, conflict and confusion. It looked forward with all the assurance of social 'science' to a glowing future of manufacturing and agrarian prosperity. It confidently promised an England freed from the haunting fear of bankruptcy through rising rates if the poor law were retained, and from the equal fear of peasant and working class revolution if the poor law were completely swept away. The new *deus ex machina* was acclaimed with wonder and gratitude, no less by the royal commissioners themselves than by the body of propertied opinion throughout the country.

The appeal of Chadwick's poor law proposal in 1833 rested almost entirely upon its promise of an easy way out of economic and political difficulty. While public enthusiasm was focused on the 'less-eligibility' principle, two other features of the scheme, no less important, were either neglected or misunderstood. The first was the tutelary idea. Chadwick had already begun to work upon the non-economic causes of pauperdom, such as sickness, intemperance and bad living conditions; and in this field he was in some degree a pioneer. Benthamism had taught him that every social evil must have a cause which scientific inquiry would discover and scientific administration could remedy or correct. Thus he envisaged from the beginning a body of what he called 'collateral aids' to run side by side with the harsh application of the 'less-eligibility' principle. He intended there to be comprehensive investigations into the circumstances of non-able-bodied pauperdom, into housing and sanitary schemes and workmen's compensation, and into the various modes of segregation of the non-able-bodied paupers into special institutions for each particular category – the orphans, the aged, the sick and the lunatic. But he had deliberately played all this down. As yet Chadwick had very little exact or reliable information on these social questions; he counted on being in charge of the entire operation later on and he deemed it politic to emphasize exclusively the popular elements in his scheme, the saving on rates and the security against mass disorder. For all these reasons he touched only very lightly and generally on the tutelary aspects of the scheme, leaving the impression that they were 'extras' and inessentials.

The second and still more important feature of his project which public opinion misunderstood was the machinery of administration. To secure support Chadwick presented this not, so to speak, in its own right, but as one particular governmental mode of effecting his economic objects. Its three main features were to be the replacement of parish autonomy by an omnipotent central board; the merging of the several parish units into unions of parishes; and the substitution of neutral, paid and professional local officials for the amateur and quasi-political government of vestries and JPs. He argued that the vital 'less-eligibility' principle would *not* be introduced if the parishes retained their independence; that individual parishes could not *afford* to set up the specialized institutions which the new poor law would demand – only a union of thirty or more parishes could meet the cost; and lastly, that amateur parish government would no longer suffice for the running of such poor law unions – amateurs could not devote enough time or afford to travel the increased distance to the union centre. Thus he made it appear that his administrative proposals were designed to meet humdrum, petty, practical problems, mainly of logistics, and that they were much less integral to his whole scheme than was in fact the case. He had displayed them as mere matters of money, convenience and scale, thus opening the door to alternative devices, supported by arguments cast in the same mundane and *ad hoc* terms.

So far Chadwick had himself, his hurry and the fragility of his early situation to blame for the public misunderstanding and the consequent distortion of his plan. The next stage was the cabinet alterations.[9] It is true that, considering the vast scope and the sweep of the measure, Chadwick's draft was accepted to an extraordinary degree. Only four changes of importance were made. But unfortunately for him each of these changes had much more widespread and serious consequences than was anticipated. First, where Chadwick had given his proposed central board power to forbid absolutely the granting of poor relief outside the workhouse, the act merely gave them permission to 'regulate' outdoor relief. This was vague and clearly opened the way for a retreat towards the old allowance system. Secondly, where Chadwick had given the board the powers of a court of record with the capacity to commit offenders for contempt, this was dropped from the bill during the second reading. Thereby the board was stripped of thorough coercive power. Thirdly, where Chadwick had given the board powers to compel the local guardians of the new unions to raise rates for, and to build new workhouses, the act finally limited these coercive powers to maxima of £50 p.a. or one-tenth of the annual rate. Such sums were ludicrously inadequate. They meant in effect that the central board could not force the local unions into action at all. As the 1909 royal commission on the poor law summed it up: while the central board could restrain the local authorities from acting, it was in practice 'powerless to force them to act'.[10] This concession proved fatal to the scheme. If the board could not compel the unions to build workhouses, the 'workhouse test' – the centrepiece of Chadwick's economic scheme – fell to the ground. Finally, Chadwick's proposal that the laws of settlement be abolished was rejected, and this retention of the parish responsibility for native paupers struck another blow at his great objective of freeing or 'uncongealing' the labour market. These alterations crippled the project in many ways. In particular the second and third robbed the central authority of much initiating and discretionary power and left it weak and negative.

As was the case with the factory act, the government followed up its concessions to public opinion while the bill was before parliament by concessions to the old idea of patronage once it had been carried. To Chadwick's own as well as to the general amazement, he was not appointed one of the three central commissioners. Instead, the posts were raised in salary, and by implication in rank, from £1000 to £2000 per annum, and men from the ruling political caste were found to fill them. The enraged Chadwick was eventually persuaded by the whig leader of the house of commons, Lord Althorp, to take the fatal step of accepting a sort of permanent secretaryship to the commission, with the vague understanding that he would be next in line for promotion when a vacancy in the commission occurred.[11] This proved the worst of all possible arrangements. Only one of the commissioners, George Nicholls, even understood, let alone sympathized with Chadwick's measure.[12] In vain did Chadwick appeal against the decisions of the majority. But equally in vain did the majority of the commission demand that they be rid of their turbulent priest. For Chadwick was no ordinary secretary. He was not removable; he was not even a subordinate. He could and did appeal to the cabinet against the commissioners' conduct; occasionally successfully though usually in vain. Hence, the poor law administration was from the beginning divided into two camps. Most of the assistant commissioners (the executive in the field) sided with Chadwick, but they were under the direction and in the power of the anti-Chadwickian commission. Moreover the quarrel was greatly exacerbated by personal antipathy between Chadwick and the Lewises, father and son (the son, Cornewall Lewis, succeeded his father as commissioner in 1839); and jealousy, insult, frustration and rage drove Chadwick into an almost hysterical opposition. From 1837 on, the commission paid no attention whatsoever to Chadwick's advice: indeed it reacted violently against every proposal which he made; and from 1838 on, it practically broke off all relations with him and removed all poor law business from his hands. The deleterious effects of such a contest on the administration of a social service system are obvious. From Chadwick's own point of view he suffered all the more because public opinion believed that it was he who was responsible for the commission's policy. He was blamed in fact for what he himself had fought tooth and nail, and was forced to witness, without being able to protest publicly against the parody of his own principles and projects.

We must recollect throughout, therefore, that although the new poor law turned out to be in many respects blind and cruel, it was (as Finer observes) never Chadwick's measure which was being enforced but a lopsided and distorted version of it.[13] The changes which the government wrought in the bill, and the directing administrators whom it provided, increased, infinitely more than even Chadwick anticipated, the gap between his ideal blueprint and reality. He had not wanted the laws of settlement maintained, and their abolition would have provided some alleviation. He had regarded the reduction of the poor rate as merely incidental to freeing the labour market and was not to blame when boards of guardians treated the reduction as an end in itself and ignored his vital compensating factors. But there is not much else to be said on his behalf.

As we have seen, Chadwick had brought many of his troubles upon his own head. He had tried to play on public opinion in his report; he had failed to protest powerfully against the dropping of the coercive clauses; and he had crowned it all by accepting the anomalous secretaryship. It would moreover be very wrong to imply that Chadwick's only errors were tactical and political. We must also recognize the deficiencies and misconceptions in his own procedures and in his handling of the first and foremost problem of agricultural labour, to say nothing of the industrial worker or the impotent poor. First, Chadwick while proclaiming 'the reign of fact' had either a very imperfect understanding of reality or a reckless disregard for what constituted relevant and proven facts in this particular case. Even on such critical matters as rural wage rates, actual numbers of unemployed or regional variations, very little reliable information had been collected. Instead the report of the royal commission tended to dwell on particular spectacular cases of abuse and to describe and narrate rather than to quantify or compile.[14] Secondly, although the report was for prudential reasons cast in universal terms, it was really based upon one special aspect of the problem, rural pauperdom, and even here the matter was to a considerable degree misconceived. In practice Chadwick's workhouse system compelled the agricultural labourer to accept lower and lower wages, for the cutting out of the allowance system compelled his wife and children to work in order to survive. The general effect was to overcrowd continuously the agricultural labour market and thus to press on wages more and more, and so far from raising, actually to *reduce* the labourer's standard of living. The 'natural' level of wages, which Chadwick automatically assumed to be both precise and discoverable, was merely a political economist's abstraction: it simply did not exist in rural England after 1834. It was the agricultural labourer who paid the price for Chadwick's mistake. Although he had claimed to be scientific and thorough, he had nevertheless proceeded to build an entire system upon an untested, non-empirical and *a priori* assumption, and thus must bear some of the responsibility for the further degradation of the rural poor.

The administrative aspect of his plan also suffered from important weaknesses. The first of these was the independent status of the central board. It is not easy to say what the relationship of such a board to the political power should have been in the 1830s, but it certainly should not have been that which Chadwick brought into being. This is not really a criticism of Chadwick personally: his choice was understandable. With the existing levels of patronage and jobbery it was perhaps to have been expected that he should try to keep his administrative machine clear of parliament. But even if it were true that it was in the circumstances of the time the lesser of two evils (which is probably not the case), total autonomy had nonetheless most unfortunate consequences. An independent board to run museums may proceed quietly enough, but an independent board whose activities touch almost every nerve of social life is bound to produce violent and hostile reactions. In the sort of politics which followed 1832, these criticisms and protests were inevitably voiced and supported in parliament, where the commissioners had no responsible defender. In default of anyone else, the home secretary had to attempt their defence; but since he had no real control over their behaviour, he was regarded merely as their tool. The house of commons came, therefore, to suppose that the only way in which it could discover what the commissioners were really up to was through parliamentary inquiry; and these inquiries were repeatedly set afoot.

Thus total separation from parliament had the opposite effect to that intended. So far from making the commission strong and fearless, it made it weak, confused and extraordinarily subject to political pressures. The commissioners lived in dread of unpopularity and inquisitions, and by the 1840s this low morale had extended even to their executive officers. For the central board soon began to sacrifice those assistant commissioners who took firm action to any noisy and potentially dangerous public demand. Again this was rooted in a fundamental weakness and unreality in administrative Benthamism: its failure to understand the essentials of the political system in which it was to operate, in particular that that system had fundamental laws, amongst them an inherent bias towards a ministerial executive and towards the concentration of political powers. The consequences long outlived Chadwick's association with the poor law and left the poor law administration perhaps the weakest and most timorous of all new branches of government in the nineteenth century.

The second great weakness in Chadwick's scheme was the power still left to the local authority. He had refused to go the full length of centralization for two reasons: in the first place he believed that a national instead of a local poor rate would demand too expensive and vast an administrative machine (here doubtless we see the contemporary obsessions with economy and small units at work once more); and in the second, he expected that the self-interest of the local guardians would operate in the interests of his general plan. Moreover his study of the Napoleonic system in France had led him to believe that the plan would be more effective if it allowed some degree of representation for local taxation.[15] Of course in all of this the fault was not wholly Chadwick's. It was the government which had removed their ultimate coercive powers over the local unions from the hands of the commissioners and thus left the act more a permissive than a compulsory measure. We can therefore only guess how Chadwick's project would have worked in practice in this regard.

But it does not seem unreasonable to envisage difficulties. The poor law was to be administered locally by elected authorities: they were to fix and raise the poor rate. But these authorities had to work through paid professional public servants who were not under their control at all, but under that of the central board. Herein collision was inevitable. Again Chadwick leaned greatly upon the central board's power to persuade the local boards of guardians to take the right line of action. He was still under the influence of the notion that one had only to demonstrate the operation of social laws for all rational men to accept one's indisputable conclusions. Admittedly he backed this up with coercive powers: if at last persuasion failed, then the commissioners might compel the unions to do such-and-such about raising or applying a poor rate. But could he really have got the best of both worlds in practice: could the poor law administration have been representative and dictatorial at once? Was Chadwick not miscalculating gravely the degree of general agreement? How were the commissioners to decide at what precise point to abandon hope of persuasion? Would not the shadow of local power without the substance, and the interval and argument which would presumably precede the central board's application of 'the big stick' merely aggravate the bickering and embitter the relations between the two? In short it seems all too likely that instead of getting the best of both worlds, Chadwick's scheme would have got the worst. The knowledge that an iron fist filled the central board's velvet glove would probably have sharpened the local appetite for power while leaving it unsatisfied. Here again the burden of the criticism is that Chadwick did not understand the facts and the nature of English political power, and he did not allow for them in his blueprint.

It must be emphasized again that the actual poor law of 1834 contained several important changes (some of them, as we have seen, for the worse) from Chadwick's original proposals, and that some of our criticisms of Chadwick's own plan are the criticisms of perfection. It is easy to be wise after the event. Much of Chadwick's work and thought still survived, and in a few instances (notably the retreat towards the allowance system in the north) his gravest errors were corrected in practice. At the same time some of the foundations of modern central government had been laid. It is true that problems were left unresolved : the political status of the new type of central commission, its relationship to representative local institutions, the recruitment of executive officers and central responsibility for the actions of subordinates. It is also true that without coercive powers the central board could not properly or fully discharge its function, and that without being subordinated to the cabinet the board could not properly or fully use coercive powers. But the mechanical deficiencies were largely remedied by the poor law amendment act of 1847; and from the beginning the poor law commissioners possessed or enjoyed command over a corps of professional officers, control over audit, discretionary power to frame orders and regulations and to declare (if not quite to enforce) a uniform policy, a system of regular reports and an ever-growing body of exact knowledge. The substance of centralization had been established and a precedent of great importance carried through. Correspondingly some foundations were also laid for modern local government. The poor law union and board of guardians were *ad hoc* expedients of Chadwick, not very carefully considered: yet they remained the primary unit of local administration throughout the century and were built upon for many other purposes – forever a reminder of the place of accident in the history of administrative growth. Even the underlying economic policy (foreign and deplorable as it all may seem to people of this generation) was not without defence works. In a certain sense Chadwick and the political economists were vindicated by the course of nineteenth-century history. One way of solving the economic crisis of the 1830s *was* greater production. The short-term consequences *were* a gradual improvement in working class levels of real wages and a condition of more or less full employment. Even if this is by no means all the story, even all the short story, it is genuinely a portion of it.

Finally, in terms of historical consequences the important thing about the distorting of Chadwick's plan was the actual and specific distortions. The poor law of 1834 cannot be explained wholly within or wholly without the terms of administrative Benthamism; and the same applies to what derived, in a more or less direct fashion, from the amending act. The year 1834 represented one of the great formative moments in the history of the treatment of the poor by organized society, and some of the disparate elements fused together in the sudden heat of the hour remained inextricable until they were at last abandoned. Moreover the relationship between the bureaucratic-ideologue and the politician was altered from the moment that the former entered office, in place of inveighing against the existence of particular offices or particular forms of office from outside. What followed was by no means a one-way traffic. The politicians were not the only people to be managed. A few lapidary sentences of Salisbury's on quite a different business forty years later makes this very clear:

> ... the essential point is that the language used should be understood by those to whom it is addressed. Now it is our function to address Indian officials[16] – and speaking of the generation now coming into office – their vocabulary is derived with more or less fidelity from the writings of political economists. To the modern Indian statesman the refined distinctions of the economical school are a solid living reality from which he can as little separate his thoughts as from his mother tongue. To us it may seem indifferent whether we call a payment 'revenue' or 'rent', so we get the money; but it is not indifferent by what name we call it in his hearing. If we say that it is 'rent', he will hold the Government in strictness entitled to all that remains after wages and profits have been paid. ... If we persuade him that it is 'revenue', he will note the vast disproportion of its incidence compared to that of other taxes. ... I prefer the latter tendency to the former.[17]

As to the working out of the poor law of 1834, the commissioners began at once to unite parishes and to attempt to establish union workhouses throughout the south and west. In these regions of England they were very soon successful in setting up union administration and ultimately successful in destroying the 'allowance system', though in one form or another it still lingered on in patches down to 1850. However, the central board's inability to force the unions to do anything that they did not wish to was evident from the outset. The board failed completely to secure either 'collateral aids' or specialized workhouses. The guardians, obsessed with reducing the poor rate to the lowest point which would not actually provoke the labourers to servile war, generally adopted the single comprehensive workhouses. In the single workhouse, however, the commissioners' residual power to enforce uniformity of administration with the workhouses (through the paid, permanent masters) interacted with the guardians' desire for economy to the general disadvantage of the inmates. The policy of making the workhouse 'less eligible' than the outside world, which had been originally meant for the able-bodied alone, came to be applied more or less indiscriminately to all. Thus lunatics, the old and orphans were (it is scarcely an exaggeration to say) punished no less than 'the idle'. Again the masters under the control of the central power had little discretion: the minutest regulations were prescribed for one and all. This meant, for example, that the principle of the segregation of the categories of paupers was still continued *within* the single workhouses, with such monstrous consequences as the separation of parents and children and of husband and wife. No doubt the commissioners were foolishly, if not wickedly rigid. But this is not necessarily to say that the principle of uniformity was wrong in itself. However it was applied, it could not work satisfactorily while those applying it were deprived of power over half their field – the raising and spending of rates and the building of workhouses. The familiar stereotype of the Victorian workhouse was mainly the product of leaving the central board without the power to force the localities to *do* anything: with only a vague right to suggest and a sort of negative right to veto. His experiences robbed Chadwick of all faith in democracy: 'the affairs of the parish', he said roundly in 1840, 'are best managed in the absence of its representatives.'[18]

In the north the commissioners met opposition from the start in their efforts to unite parishes. They hesitated during the most favourable years, 1834–6, and when at last they decided to proceed regardless of unpopularity they met the full tide of unemployment and agitation from 1837 onwards. From 1837 to 1842 the north lay in the grasp of hunger and the intermittent collapse of industries. Whole towns went suddenly out of work; hundreds of thousands were suddenly thrown on the point of starvation. The poor law in these circumstances was impossible to operate or institute. One could not place two-thirds of the entire population of a union in workhouses; and even if such fantasy and cruelty were contemplated, where were the workhouses which would hold them to be found? Moreover, the new poor law, the new bastilles, the new commissioners and the perennial Chadwick had become symbols of oppression to the industrial poor. Fanatical opposition to the poor law became a central theme in chartism, which, by means of its threat to public order and its alliance on this issue with the right wing of the tory party, exerted great influence on parliament and produced a ceaseless parliamentary campaign against the commissioners. This proved all the more unnerving because the commission was originally given a five-year lease of life and was due to come up for renewal in 1839, by which time its unpopularity had grown so great that the whigs merely renewed their existence for a single year in 1839, and again in 1840. Here then the full force of their unfortunate political situation came into play. They bowed before the storm and abandoned the 'workhouse test' and with it the 'less-eligibility' principle. The return to 'outdoor relief' in the north was of course good in itself. But it made nonsense of the new poor law, the other elements of which were still enforced despite the abandonment of its central policy; and it was the non-able-bodied rather than the able-bodied paupers who paid the price for this fortuitous dichotomy.

If we are tracing the development of the modern state, the story up to this point is confused. In a sense Chadwick's original measure was anti-collectivist in intention: it was working towards an essentially 'free' economy. But in other respects it tended powerfully in the opposite direction: in its concept of the state as social regulator, in its central administration and in its notion of collateral aids. There followed a reaction against these collectivist tendencies on the part of the propertied and political classes. Coercive power was struck from the hands of the central administration, 'collateral aids' were thrown completely overboard and the counter-concept of local decisions placed against that of the state as social regulator. The consequence was a considerable, though by no means total loss of ground between 1834 and 1844. On the other hand, the working classes, though for very different motives, joined in the attack upon centralization, which they mistakenly conceived as the real author of their current misfortunes. But the obverse side of the working class agitation was actually collectivist, where Chadwick and the propertied men were anti-collectivist. What the operatives demanded was some basic security other than the workhouse prison and the permanent degradation of the new pauperdom in times of distress and unemployment. In all of this we can see substantially the same pattern as in the factory act agitation of 1833, in which the sides do not clearly divide as pro- or anti-, but promote or resist different elements of each simultaneously.

After 1842 the issue changed. The operatives had largely won back 'outdoor relief'[19] and the worst of the economic distress was over; while the commission, given grudgingly and with many warnings a further five years of life, had once and for all lost its nerve and confidence. Now began the humanitarian attack upon the appalling conditions of life in the new workhouses. Like the mining industry and shipping, it gained from a series of catastrophes, epidemics and scandals which provoked public inquiries and ultimately an irresistible public demand for the remedying of the worst abuses. In 1842 came the first of these scandals, and with it, the first humane relaxations of workhouse regulations – the withdrawal of the rule imposing silence at all meals; the bringing together of families hitherto separated into male, female and infant; and the first vague efforts to separate prostitutes, lunatics and infected persons from the general body of paupers. This process continued gradually until 1847, but it was not an unmixed blessing. The scandals, exposures and inquiries of 1842–5 finally destroyed the morale of the administration and led the terrified commissioners to sacrifice their subordinates shamefully. The Andover scandal of 1845–6 was the last straw. Not only did it reveal most horrifying evils in a workhouse – paupers so starved that they fought each other for the rotting bones which it was their labour to crush into manure – but it also led to a 'showdown' in public between the central board on the one hand, and Chadwick and a group of ill-treated assistant commissioners on the other.

Chadwick had much the better of the tussle, but whoever won, the poor law administration (now shown to be riddled by jealousies, spite and cowardice) inevitably lost. When it came up for renewal once more in 1847, it was swept away. The poor law act of 1847[20] set up a new board, which like the

India Board was to consist of a president who would be a member of the ministry in power, and two secretaries, one of whom might be a member of parliament. The new commissioners retained administrative discretions denied to other boards; but, subject to the new conditions, this was accepted without protest. Apart from finally removing the unruly Chadwick from the scene, the new act had two great merits. It remedied the paralysing weakness caused by the old board's so-called independent status: the government was now genuinely responsible (in the constitutional sense of the term) and there was now a proper channel of communication between the board and parliament. Secondly, and partly in consequence of this, the new act stilled the long agitation against the new poor law which had driven the old commissioners into a palsied alternation between blind rigidity and blind surrender. This meant that the new board could undertake a common sense policy of gradual improvement in peace. They were, of course, greatly aided in their work by the fact that the economy, even the agricultural economy to some extent, had righted itself at last, and by the fact that the laws of settlement were also swept away in 1847. No doubt their achievements between 1847 and 1870 were very meagre. But a beginning was made in very many fields. In 1848 the first schools for pauper children were set up; in the 1850s 'outdoor relief' was frankly admitted and regularized; by 1860 the segregation of the different classes of paupers into different quarters of the workhouse was virtually accomplished, and generally the harshness of the old uniform regulations was being softened from year to year. In almost all these fields the English poor law was following in the wake of the Irish, for Ireland was without effective political influence at this time and the central administration there could work 'paternally' in almost complete security. Even in 1870 the English workhouses were still barbarous as places and as a system. But for all that, vital changes had taken place. First, more and more money was being spent upon the poor and unfortunate without protest. Secondly, pauperdom, especially non-able-bodied pauperdom, was at last coming to be regarded by more and more people as a misfortune rather than a crime or cause for segregation. These gradual changes in attitude obviously marked the beginning of a trend towards collectivism in the last fields of poor law activity to hold out uncompromisingly against it. At the outset of our period Cobbett had defined a pauper as nothing more than a very poor man. By its end, this view was starting to battle seriously with the mighty philosophy of disgrace.

In one area, however, the new poor law had almost from the start turned upon its tracks and developed in a fashion alien to its origin and object alike. This was ill-health. Here the rudiments of a free, non-pauperizing national service gradually developed, and did so moreover by a process of undeliberate administrative growth, innocent of both planning and planners. When in 1834 sickness and infirmity had been merged with poverty in general, the 'less-eligibility' principle was meant to apply equally to them. Logically there was no alternative: if the paupers received superior medical attention, accommodation, comforts or supplies to the independent poor man, then wherein lay the incentive to avoid the workhouse when one was ill or physically or mentally incapacitated? But once the world of paper and ink were left and realities encountered, this rule was practically impossible to keep.

In the first place the old poor law had in its muddled, inconsistent and indiscriminate application embraced treatment of the sick independently of pauperism. A *volte face* here would not have been easy either to explain or to enforce. Secondly, if paupers were given any significant measure of medical attention at all, they would be better off than hundreds of thousands of 'independent' men and their families. It is true that since the last quarter of the eighteenth century voluntary hospitals, both general and specialist, had spread and grown, especially in London and the larger provincial cities; and part of their function was to treat the sick poor outside the poor law. There was an equivalent expansion of public dispensaries, which often served in effect as out-patients' departments of the hospitals. But the operation of these 'systems' provided yet another illustration of the fact that for the deprived, early nineteenth-century life was a lottery, a desperate game of chance in which survival, or being lifted from utter misery, depended largely upon the accident of residence or acquaintance. The voluntary hospitals covered effectively only so many tiny circles of surrounding population: there were innumerable tracts of people in between. Moreover they worked largely on a ticket basis, whereby subscribers introduced patients, and 'introduced' patients either engrossed the available beds or were preferred for them. Thus the majority of the destitute lay outside the range of the voluntary institutions.

It is also true that self-helping attempts to bridge the gap by means of medical and sick clubs and provident associations amongst artisans and workers in general were warmly approved and legally facilitated. But these societies were still in an early stage of development in 1840. In any event they were likely to embrace only men in the most secure and highest paid manual and clerkly employment. That they were nonetheless needed by such people in Victorian England is a commentary upon the very high proportion, relative to the probable present-day equivalents, of working class net income which was spent on medicine and physicians. In any case the mutual associations were altogether beyond the reach of the very poor.[21]

A third reason for the failure of the 'principles of 1834' in the field of health was that medical costs, medical confidence and the degrees of medical action were not static but growing rapidly in the middle quarters of the nineteenth century. Thus poor law medicine, like prison or army medicine which were also paid for from public funds, tended to become more and more ambitious year by year. However powerful the economizing forces of the time, they met their match in 'experts' who pronounced what was necessary. It was therefore increasingly difficult for the competing voluntary 'systems' to keep pace with the poor law. Last but far from least, the distinction between pauper sick and the sick 'independent' poor was in the final analysis a misleading one. For sickness was much the most important single cause of pauperization. In fact it was probably responsible for the majority of the declensions from poverty into pauperism in the nineteenth century.

All this explains why neither the 'less-eligibility' principle nor the 'workhouse test' was ever thoroughly enforced so far as health went, and why poor law medicine eventually travelled far from paupers and pauperization. Even at the outset the medical officers appointed under the new poor law treated paupers 'outdoors' wherever such treatment was sanctioned (as it was increasingly) by the relieving officers. Treatment for accidents or maternity does not seem to have involved translation to a workhouse at any stage. Quickly, too, it came to be accepted that inability to pay the necessary doctor's fee or pharmacist's bill sufficed for entitlement to outdoor treatment by the poor law medical officer.[22] In short, virtually from the beginning there were vast exceptions to the deterrence rule.

Of course, the poor law commissioners were concerned at the virtual abandonment of the principles of 1834. In their annual report for 1841 they deplored the superiority of the pauper's condition to that of

> the needy but industrious ratepayer who has neither the money nor the influence to secure equally prompt and careful attention nor any means to provide himself and his family with the more expensive kind of nutriment which his medical superintendent may recommend.[23]

It was in vain. Not only had it proved impracticable either to reduce the level of the pauper's medical treatment below that of the independent labourer or to force everybody claiming poor law medical attention into a workhouse, but also an anti-1834 view of the new poor law had been enshrined in a public health statute in that very year. In 1840 parliament had enacted that smallpox vaccination should be freely available to all upon demand, and that poor law medical officers were to serve as the public vaccinators.[24] A year later a supplementary act made it absolutely clear that acceptance of this service did not pauperize the recipient.[25] Quite as significant as this development itself was the reason for it; namely, that the poor law unions and their physicians constituted the only system operating nationally upon which any item of a universal health service could be provided. As preventive medicine expanded, so too did the tendency to employ this system for ends quite independent of pauperism, or even poverty.

The substitution of the poor law board for the ill-fated commission in 1847 both facilitated and speeded these developments. In 1852 the board formally sanctioned medical relief for all who could not afford private treatment: this was so whether or not the head of the household remained in employment. In 1853 the vaccination service became compulsory for all infants.[26] About the same time poor law unions began to divide their medical functions structurally by appointing separate officers for the outdoor and the indoor work: these were the district and workhouse medical officers respectively. Roughly contemporaneously the unions also began to set up public dispensaries, providing more and more a general rather than a pauper service,[27] and the scale and sophistication of the workhouse hospitals rapidly increased. During the 1850s, too, the division of outdoor and indoor medical care ceased altogether to imply a division between non-pauper (or quasi-pauper, at most) and pauper. Instead those needing intense or prolonged care were sent to workhouse hospitals, and those who did not were treated at home. *Pari passu* the workhouse hospital was tending to become dissociated from the workhouse itself, even if they were physically contiguous or incorporated. The point must not be pressed too far: the 'stigma', though fading, had not disappeared from any aspect of poor law medicine, and of course the stain held fastest to the workhouse hospital. Nevertheless even that was changing, not only in its conduct and arrangements, but also in the estimation of the world at large. More and more was it coming to resemble a public general hospital as we understand the term.[28]

By the 1860s the considerable majority of the hospital beds in England and Wales were provided under the poor law services,[29] with doubtless a corresponding dilution of their pauper connotation; and in the later part of the decade – when early Victorian shibboleths were toppling like scythed poppies – poor law medicine was finally cut away from the repressive elements of 1834. In 1867 Gathorne Hardy, introducing a metropolitan poor bill, categorically rejected any link between sickness and the 'less-eligibility' principle.[30] Whatever the notion of deterrence still applied to, it no longer included illness or infirmity. The measure itself, enacted as the metropolitan poor act of 1867,[31] represented a further stage in the process of divorcing medical relief and pauperism. Each of the poor law districts into which London was divided was to provide a full range of general, specialist, isolation and mental hospitals and ambulances. This represented a halfway house at least in the growth of a 'neutral' public health service, ultimately the responsibility of the state.[32]

Thus when the poor law board was incorporated into the local government board in 1871 it was already furnishing a free general health system for the poor, mainly disentangled from the notions, and even to a certain extent disentangled from the institutions of 1834. Moreover the momentum already acquired carried de-pauperization rapidly forward. The London regional model was widely imitated; the number if not the proportion of poor law hospital beds steadily increased; public dispensaries and infirmaries were henceforth built apart from the workhouses; and fever and isolation hospitals were opened to all, free and as of right, in the metropolis. In 1885 a seal of sorts was set upon the entire liberating movement when the medical relief (disqualifications removal) act[33] declared that use of the poor law medical services did not deprive a man of the franchise: one of the consequences of pauperization had always been electoral disqualification.

We might fairly say that, by the mid-1880s, what Chadwick had originally conceived of as a collateral aid – the separate treatment of sickness and physical or mental incapacity – had come about, although in a form and manner quite alien to his taste and not to be guessed at by him in the heady days of 1832–4. What did evolve haphazardly was probably more humane and durable than anything he was likely to have devised, and it did produce the basis of a system of state medicine. But let us not end on too triumphant a note. The Victorian development was cheap, poor, grudging and wasteful; and the original brand of the broad arrow could never be altogether effaced. The first series of defects could disappear in time (which is far from saying that they did); but the second mark, though ever fainter, was ineradicable so long as the poor kept pride. It would require an altogether new beginning in formal style, and in the rhetoric of right and citizenship, before this wound could heal.

SEVEN

Local Government

We must now turn away from the economic fields, from the efforts to deal with working class and pauper problems, to the civil and domestic reforms of the 1830s and 1840s. Broadly these can be regarded as the follow-through and consequence of the reform act of 1832. But this does not mean that, from our point of view, all tended in the same direction; and several essentially political measures had unexpected administrative consequences of first importance. The new electoral laws themselves, for example, had necessitated a central register and eventually permanent officials to regulate them, while the civil marriages act of 1837, designed to appease non-conformists, ultimately led to a network of local officials under a central board who registered not only marriages but also births and deaths, and even the causes of death, thus paving the way for the later public health campaign and laying the indispensable statistical foundations for modern administration.

The most important field for civil reform was that of local government, and the most important piece of whig legislation within this field, the municipal reform act of 1835.[1] Here we must make two preliminary general observations. First, no Chadwick had a finger in the pie. It may seem absurd to stress the absence of bureaucratic radicals, particularly since the royal commission on municipal government, which the whigs set up in 1833, was well supplied with equally convinced utilitarians who followed the example of the poor law inquiry in rigging the evidence, making it fit in with preconceived conclusions and stampeding the public by a melodramatic and terrifying report. But none belonged to the small section of the Benthamites who grasped and emphasized the tutelary, despotic and mechanical aspects of the creed. The utilitarians on the commission stressed instead the perhaps more superficial, certainly more commonplace feature of democratic individualism.

The stock programme of the democratic radicals for local government reform was threefold: a widespread, but not universal suffrage, sufficiently extensive to break the power of he oligarchs but sufficiently restrictive to withhold power from the mob; equality of suffrage within the privileged circle of the enfranchised; and a delegatory rather than a parliamentary system of representation. The report of the commission, which was inspired from without by the arch-democratic radical Joseph Hume, consequently implied that improvement must derive from two sources – universal and equal suffrage for (but only for) ratepayers, and tight control of the elected by the electorate, by means of annual elections.[2] These were expected to cure all urban evils. The questions which would have engrossed a social or a bureaucratic reformer – what were the new corporations to do, how was their policy to be rendered uniform, how was it to be enforced, how was impartiality to be preserved or rational administration to be secured? – these questions were never asked. Secondly, the municipal reformers failed to touch the counties. The radicals had not succeeded in breaking down the distinction between the borough and county franchises even in the favourable conditions of 1831–2. They despaired completely of achieving much larger amalgamations and interpenetrations in one of the years of reaction which immediately followed the reform act. Thus we must recollect that from their own point of view their measure was but a half-measure – indeed, considerably less than a half-measure, for they were confined to those towns which already possessed a corporation, and this did not cover many of the rising manufacturing areas.

We have already touched a little upon the old form of urban local government. Generally speaking it was, like the old poor law, characterized by want of co-ordination, purpose or policy. The local units were almost entirely autonomous and often the product of historical circumstances which had long since disappeared. For all their variety, however, we can divide them into three main types. Pride of place, if not of performance, must go to the corporations, some 250 in number. About three-quarters of these were closed oligarchies, the remainder being open or elective. The closed corporations were constituted by co-option and characterized by nepotism, and they were exclusively tory and anglican strongholds. Their main function had become the administration of a number of charitable foundations. Though the royal commission of 1833 painted a very lurid picture of their corruption,[3] they were perhaps *en bloc* rather less corrupt and rather more efficient than their open counterparts. This, however, availed them little in the conditions of the early 1830s. It was clear to almost all, apart from their beneficiaries, that they were quite incompetent to provide the sort of urban government which the new circumstances demanded. The whigs hated them as citadels of tory influence, their principle of co-option was anathema to radicals of every colour, and the non-conformists bitterly resented their exclusion. Above all, they could not be defended either rationally or statistically, and the way had been paved for their destruction by the repeal of the test and corporations acts in 1828.[4]

Where no corporations existed, urban government devolved upon the old parish system and the parish vestries. It has been already noted in the discussion of the poor law in the last chapter that even before 1830 the vestries were tending to divide into 'democratic' and closed. Which way they went partly depended upon traditional local practice. Often the business fell into the hands of a small group of the leading ratepayers who met once a year and allotted offices and decided policy: for all practical purposes they formed a continuous oligarchy. Elsewhere the majority of middle-level or poor ratepayers, or their *soi-disant* representatives, held command. The matter had been further complicated by the select vestry act of 1819 which weighted the franchise according to the amount of property one possessed.[5] The statute was, however, discretionary, and in the event the number of English parishes which had adopted this rich-man's system amounted to roughly one-fifth of the whole.

In the country districts the supreme and overriding question for the parish was the poor rate, or, more particularly, whose self-interest was to rule in fixing and administering it – that of the richer or the poorer ratepayers? But in the towns there were other administrative issues of equal importance. The shape and effectiveness of urban local government was, therefore, a matter of much more far-reaching significance. It cannot be said, however, that any particular form of vestry proved itself to be automatically superior to the rest. A few great towns in the north and midlands which were without corporations – Birmingham and Liverpool, for example – threw up small bodies of leading ratepayers who used their power in closed or select vestries intelligently and progressively, applying business methods and employing staffs of permanent local officials in their efforts to solve the novel problems of urbanization. But in London the select vestries were self-interested and corrupt. On the other hand, much the same might have been said of the more 'democratic' vestries in the metropolis. Where open vestries existed in London they had tended to develop a Tammany Hall species of 'democracy'. They were generally more ignorant and less concerned with informed experiment and planning than their closed counterparts in the north.

The third type of instrument of local government was the improvement commission. During the preceding century there had grown up over three hundred of these *ad hoc* bodies, set up by private acts of parliament to deal with specific problems in specific towns. There were improvement commissions to manage lighting, the supply of water, street cleaning and paving, street widening, police, the protection of property and many other matters. They operated in towns with and without corporations alike, for the old corporations, whether closed or open, had usually proved incapable of taking effective action in these fields. Generally the improvement commissions were oligarchic, made up of leading local citizens and magistrates who held office for life. But here, once again, oligarchy was not necessarily synonymous with bad local government. On the contrary some of these commissions were the pioneers of modern local administration, and taken together they provided the bulk of the useful work accomplished before 1830. Where they were most effective (and this again was usually in the new northern and midland towns) they closely resembled the best select vestries. They, too, were impatient of the subdivisions and irrationality of local government and were tempted to move beyond their legal sphere of action. The police commissioners of Manchester provide the classic case of this type of exorbitance. They took over street cleansing, street paving and the supply of gas, and attempted to enforce town planning and to gain a monopoly of the supply of water.

This then, in outline, was the system or lack of system of urban government in 1830. The only bodies in the entire constellation which really grappled with the new difficulties of town management were a handful of select vestries and a certain number of improvement commissions. Even these were not without their defects. They naturally saw towns through upper-middle class eyes and failed to realize the still graver problems in the working class quarters of the cities. They were driven to exceed their proper powers, albeit for the public good. They were virtually irresponsible and uncontrolled, apart from being blown off course occasionally by some sudden radical or demagogic agitation. Finally, they suffered from the complete absence of co-ordination, they overlapped and conflicted, they had no regular or systematic access to experimental knowledge, and they could never in the nature of things rise above the opinions and energy of a score or less of private individuals who had neither training in administration nor technical education, and who lacked the means of ensuring continuity. This, a latter-day form of household government, was the choicest fruit of the haphazard.

The whig reform of local government began with J. C. Hobhouse's vestry act of 1831.[6] This represented the clearest of enunciations of the elective principle in parish government. It provided universal and equal franchise for all ratepayers, women as well as men; annual elections; and the secret ballot. Hobhouse's was, therefore, a doctrinaire radical measure, democratic in the extreme by the criteria of the day. The act was, however, permissive, and not compulsory. Two-thirds of all the ratepayers in a parish had to vote for its adoption before it could come into force; and, in fact, its adoption was largely confined to London, where democratic vestries (usually of the worst type) were already comparatively common. Thus the general situation was practically unchanged when the royal commission of 1833 came to report. The report, as we have seen, followed the lines and breathed the spirit of Hobhouse's act of 1831. Universal ratepayer suffrage and annual elections were conjoined to form the panacea; and, by implication, all the evils and maladministration of the unreformed corporations were attributed to the absence of these beneficent and rational devices.

Inspired by such sentiments, the municipal reform act of 1835 swept away the 178 closed corporations[7] and replaced them by open or elective bodies. Unlike the sphere of action of the old, the competence of these new corporations was narrowly and exactly defined. They lost, moreover, the management of religious trusts; and although they were empowered under the act to take over the duties of the existing improvement commissions, this again was permissive and not compulsory. It is true that the new corporations were given, in addition to the traditional revenues of the old, the right to levy a rate if these proved inadequate. But it was not expected that this right would be widely or extensively used. The emphasis was on spending and doing less, not more. The essential innovation of the act was the local electoral system. The radicals gained the substance of their demands, equal household franchise and annual elections, even if the tory opposition did secure some important modifications during the bill's passage through parliament. A three-years' residence requirement to qualify for the franchise, an income qualification which meant that the local government suffrage was in some respects more restricted than the parliamentary, and a body of aldermen elected by the councils themselves and not the local electors – all represented partial defeats for pure electoral democracy.

What did the reform of local government accomplished by the statutes of 1831 and 1835 amount to? The answer is, a great deal in terms of 'civil and religious liberty' and egalitarian principle, but almost nothing in terms of day-to-day living. In the municipalities the circle of privilege was drawn much wider and the non-conformists had won near equality. This had important political consequences. The whigs greatly extended the basis for their party, and O'Connell's prophecy – and hope – that the new municipal councils would form training grounds for democratic agitation[8] was not entirely unfulfilled. Moreover, Russell's policy of taking the recommendations of the new corporations into account when appointing magistrates resulted in many more manufacturers and dissenters taking their places beside 'gentlemen' on the bench. Melbourne had to stomach his aristocratic prejudice – 'It is certainly true', he once confessed, 'that I always admitted a man's being a Trader to being an objection to his becoming a Magistrate'[9] – for the sake of electoral support. This 'dilution' formed, once again, a major revolution of its kind, and incidentally erected new obstacles to the effective enforcement of factory legislation. But if we regard 'reform' in the sense it is being employed consistently in this book – namely, the introduction of more modern or more efficient government – the whig statutes achieved little. Turning the closed corporations into open ones, permitting but not compelling the new corporations to supersede the improvement commissions, and increasing the number of more democratic vestries, merely widened the area in which the national conflict between whigs and tories, liberals and radicals, could be conducted. It left the basic problems of town management unresolved. Local government was still amateur government, without a coherent policy or expert knowledge. The concepts of the lowest practicable rate and of the minimum of administrative functions for the urban authorities still carried the day, and only a handful of the boroughs took advantage of their power to assume the duties and responsibilities of the improvement commissions. Indeed, it is arguable that the municipal reform act brought about, in the short run at any rate, a decrease rather than an increase in efficient government. Making the corporations so many bear-pits for party struggle tended to obscure still further their administrative functions, and the rising radical and democratic influence produced more powerful assaults upon the most active improvement commissions and select vestries – assaults launched upon the grounds of either the need for economy or closer public scrutiny or open government, or some supposed theoretical objection to public ownership of gas production and waterworks. From all of this it will be apparent why the absence of bureaucratic radicals (perhaps we should say simply *the* bureaucratic radical) from the reform of local government was of critical if negative importance. Had a Chadwick managed the commission and report, other questions would certainly have been asked and other purposes pursued. When a decade later his work on public health led Chadwick into the field of municipal government, a homeric contest followed his inevitable efforts to establish centralization, uniform and rational institutions and a professional administration.[10]

What, meanwhile, of local government in the rural areas? Here, apart from the poor law, both 'efficient' reform and 'democratic' reform failed to make headway. After 1834 the constitution of the country vestries mattered comparatively little, for the parish had ceased to be the unit of administration for most purposes. Instead, the poor law union replaced it in many instances, and the boards of guardians of the unions were elected by ratepayers on a franchise weighted according to property – of which undemocratic system, incidentally, Chadwick heartily approved, believing that government by the rich and wise would better secure his immediate purposes. The parish still retained at least three considerable functions, the collection and distribution of church rates, the normal policing of its area and the management of by-roads. An attempt was made to reform the last in 1835. The whole road system of England and Wales was by then in chaos, with the turnpike trusts commonly bankrupt and everywhere doomed because of the rapid development of the railways. Melbourne's government failed to carry its proposal of 1835 to deal with the main roads by abolishing the turnpike trusts and placing them under the control of a central board and inspectorate. It did, however, pass a highways act[11] to cover roads managed by the parish. This very complicated statute provided for the creation of unions of parishes for road building and road maintenance, and also for the appointment of professional road surveyors. But like so many of the statutes of the 1830s, when it met the opposition of the country party and the house of lords, it was transmuted into a permissive and uncompulsory measure. This meant, it need hardly be remarked, that it was almost valueless and produced no change. Police reform for the parishes followed, as we shall see, an almost identical course, with much the same sad conclusion.

On the more general issue of rural local government, the

radicals continued after 1835 their efforts to reform it after their own fashion. Once again, they concentrated their attack not so much upon the inefficiency of the system as upon its unrepresentative character. In particular they were scandalized by the fact that magistrates, appointed from above and answerable to none, controlled the local finances; and by the fact that the poor law franchise was based on property and not on numbers. On two occasions in the later 1830s Hume proposed bills to extend to the countryside the type of reform bestowed upon the corporate towns by the municipal reform act of 1835. He wanted annual elections, universal and equal franchise for ratepayers, and elected county boards which would manage exclusively all local taxation and expenditure. Despite the countenance of the whig cabinet, both bills failed to pass a second reading in the house of commons. Thus the hereditary system of rural government, as modified by the poor law of 1834, struggled on into the second half of the nineteenth century. More than thirty years later, one critic, Lord Edmond Fitzmaurice, wrote:

> For this system, if system it can be called, while indefensible in theory, is equally so in practice. Under its dispensations the public is daily reminded that what is everybody's business is nobody's business. Union authorities, highway authorities, county authorities, and parochial authorities, are all engaged in trying to drive their coaches through Temple Bar together; and while they are struggling with one another in the foreground of the picture, a host of out-of-door paupers are descried in the distance walking past empty schoolhouses and open drains, down badly-mended roads towards palatial workhouses.[12]

At the mid-century, perhaps the most striking features of the progress of local government reform were how much of the old order had survived and how negative and sterilizing such changes as were made had proved. Amateurism and autonomy were still leading principles in both urban and rural local government; and men's ordinary lives in their homes, workplaces, towns and villages had been little altered. Moreover, the joint result of eighteenth-century survivals and early whig reforms was rapid proliferation and utter medley of authorities. School boards, highway boards, burial boards, constabulary boards and poor law unions now bordered and overlapped vestry, borough and parish, justices of the peace and improvement commissions. As Fitzmaurice justly observed, 'each Act has proceeded on a plan of its own, till an absolute and unrivalled chaos has resulted'.[13] He might have added that the fact that the newest forms were popularly elected, and generally on the most various suffrages, contributed to the confusion and immobility.

Not until the 1870s was large scale reform again attempted. The local government act of 1871 at last reduced the chaos to relative order, establishing a central department of state with general supervision over local government affairs. Some forty years later, the education act of 1902 abolished the separate school boards and brought public education, including technical education, also into the sphere of local government. Between these dates, 1871 and 1902, reform of a certain type, that concerned with uniformity, rationality and representation in the system, was rapid and widespread. In the 1880s and 1890s the map of local government was totally re-drawn to relate it to the changed distribution and structure of the population; and the principles of a more equal and democratic suffrage, and of election instead of appointment to office, were vastly extended. Together four statutes, the municipal corporations act of 1882 and the local government acts of 1888, 1894 and 1899,[14] reorganized borough government and invented and employed new and more fitting local units, the county borough and the administrative county, urban and district councils and (for London) metropolitan borough councils. Together the same acts provided, with various degrees of democracy, new elective systems, and dismantled to some extent the fancy franchises which had hitherto favoured wealth. All this was sensible and necessary reform. But like the changes of the 1830s, it was improvement concerned essentially with forms rather than with substances. It was political, economic and geographical needs which were satisfied, rather than social. Apart from the public utilities of gas, lighting and the supply of water, these reforms did little either to enlarge the area or to deepen the integrity of urban government. In some respects, the initial measure of this phase, the local government act of 1871, was even retrogressive. It tended to re-connect pauperization and qualification for receipt of state assistance; it tended to replace the specialist and expert type of executive officer by the 'general practitioner'; and it re-emphasized the need for economy in expenditure and treasury influence upon policy in general. Moreover it precipitated new, or rather renewed old struggles on behalf of local as against central power, and amateur and elected as against professional and permanent officers.

It is true that the canvas of local government was swelled by side-winds in late Victorian England and Wales; and this was true in particular of the earlier 1870s. The food and drugs act of 1872,[15] although in other respects an unsatisfactory measure, did imply significant new powers and functions for local government. Two pieces of legislation of 1875, fruits of 'Disraelian' reform, were still more important. The artisans' dwelling act[16] enjoined local authorities to appoint medical officers and sanitary inspectors (some had long since done so, but such appointments were now to be general and obligatory) and empowered them to purchase slum property by compulsory order and to re-build upon the cleared sites. The public health act of the same year[17] rendered the powers of local authorities in this field at once more definite and more discretionary; and it specifically obliged them to maintain a water supply, to collect and dispose of refuse, to abate nuisance, to regulate offensive trades, to notify infectious diseases and to condemn and destroy unwholesome food. All this constituted an important reorganization and consolidation of the public health work of central government departments, in so far as it specifically touched local government. But it also, as we shall see, represented the culmination and close of an earlier advance rather than the beginning of a new.

After 1875 we enter another phase of immobility in local government despite (to apply Eileen Power's famous phrase) pockets of progression in a pre-progressive world. It is arguable that this phase lasted for more than forty years, until the winding-up of the local government board and the redistribution of much of its work among new departments in 1919. It is even arguable that it lasted for more than half a century, until the passage of the local government act of 1929. This is not to say that there was no innovation, experiment or creative growth in local government in the last quarter of the nineteenth, or in the first decades of the twentieth century. But this came – somewhat after the fashion of the enlightened improvement commissions and select vestries of two generations earlier – from 'spill-overs' from exogenous social reform, from particular 'advanced' local authorities or state officers or from voluntary associations. The local government reform of the 1870s, like that of the 1830s, was primarily a political change; and in each case the assumption that insurgent democracy implied social amelioraton was scarcely validated by experience.

Of course, man – particularly middle class man – does not live by bread alone. Self-government, open government and cheap government – the catch-cries of the nineteenth-century radicals – were undeniably goods. Perhaps they are more readily accepted as goods today than at any other time since 1914. Moreover, the Victorian decentralizers and village devolutionists, even the Toulmin Smiths and the Peter Rylandses, have been lampooned rather than read by posterity. Their arguments were not always ignorant or absurd, and the centralized bureaucracy which they experienced in mid-nineteenth-century England was sometimes both. Nonetheless, the Victorian obsessions with self-expression, representation and equality of numbers in local government reform had terrible and tragic consequences; and nothing should ever be accepted as outweighing, in the final balance, the mass of avoidable suffering, disease, misery and death for which the failure to order efficiently the relationships and structures of central and local power was indirectly responsible.

EIGHT

Public health and sanitation

The public health and sanitation conflicts from 1842 to 1854 were in many ways the most complex and illuminating of all the phases of administrative reform. While they led to great extensions and elaborations of the new administrative methods, they also produced perhaps the last major victory of individualist over collectivist principle.

The problem of public health, as it was presented by the agitations in this field, was essentially the problem of nineteenth-century urbanization and industrialization. Squalor and disease infested the countryside, too, as they had always done. But the horrific scale and communal consequences of urban squalor forced them more immediately and powerfully upon men's attention. Great Britain was being transformed into a nation of great cities. Further, the transformation was extraordinarily rapid, and it was accompanied by the concentration of manufacture in large urban aggregations. Finally the transformation took place while local and national government was still incompetent to undertake remedial measures, and while engineering and medical science were only beginning to take their modern shape. The size, speed and nature of the growth, and the political, administrative and technological atmosphere in which it happened form the background of the crisis which became manifest in the 1830s.

Between 1831 and 1841 the death rate in the five largest cities in England *rose* from 20 per thousand to 30 per thousand, after it had previously been arrested and driven back: the writing was on the wall. It was not, however, the urban death rate in general, but rather a particular epidemic of cholera in 1831–2, which led to the first administrative action. The panic caused by the first attack of this hitherto unknown and unpredictable oriental disease[1] which carried off some 16,000 persons, led to the compulsory creation of local boards of health, despite the powerful opposition of most ratepayers to the expense. But these were *ad hoc*, emergency devices and very ill-conceived. When the cholera disappeared as mysteriously as it had come, the boards simply faded away without a protest.

A more substantial beginning for reform was the work of a handful of London doctors and philanthropists: Southwood Smith, Arnott, Kay, Belinaye, Slaney and others. Their investigations into the relationship between disease and the living conditions of the poor in the early and middle 1830s had established a body of information, brought the matter to the notice of public and parliament, and apparently bolstered the widely held atmospheric theory of infection.[2] Chadwick, while encouraging these reformers from afar, was at the same time being made forcibly aware, through reports issuing from poor law unions up and down the country, of the need for action to improve public health. From its inception the poor law commission had of necessity to consider questions of public health, both generally through the impact on the poor rates of families deprived of the breadwinner and specifically through attempting to combat disease within the workhouses themselves. The London typhus epidemic of 1838 brought together the reformers and the administrator, Chadwick.[3] The heavy mortality of the epidemic and its concentration in poor districts, particularly the east end, finally convinced Chadwick of the need for preventive administrative action. At his insistence the poor law commission asked Kay, Southwood Smith and Arnott to inquire into the living conditions of the poor and the probable causes of disease, and to propose remedies.

Broadly speaking, their proposed reforms rested upon the improvement of the dwelling house. Certainly, the living conditions of the urban poor were lamentable almost beyond words, and as bad in the new towns as in the crazy, dilapidated, swarming tenements and alleys in the old. Rapid industrialization meant so many opportunities for speculative builders to get rich quick. There were no restraining bylaws or building regulations; instead the unbounded profit motive and a seller's market bore their natural fruit. Drainage and sanitation were commonly omitted; in many industrial areas there was only one privy to every thirty back-to-back dwelling houses; the average for industrial areas as a whole was probably about one privy for every hundred persons.[4] Meanwhile the multiplication of population and the letting and sub-letting steadily continued, until two, three, or four entire families often shared a single room, and child mortality rose to an appalling level. It was not so much this situation as such, however, which prompted the first sanitary reformers to concentrate upon the dwelling house. While the investigators acknowledged the need for more efficient sewers and regular water supplies, their firm belief in foul atmosphere or smell as the main source of all infection focused their attention on overcrowding and the absence of interior sanitation as the primary causes of foul atmosphere. Obviously the way to sweeten and purify the air was to disperse the population and provide modern sanitation for the working class homes.

The report made little impact upon the public or the politicians. The poor law commissioners merely communicated the findings to Russell, the home secretary, who apparently ignored them. A year later, however, after extensive publicity, the question was considered in parliament; and even though little enthusiasm was manifested, the commissioners were instructed to hold their own inquiry into the sanitary conditions of the working classes.[5]

To both the commissioners and Chadwick the proposed inquiry seemed to present a heaven-sent opportunity. The commissioners saw it as a means of diverting their rancorous and brawling secretary to pastures new; while Chadwick embittered by the recent failure of his attempted constabulary reform[6] and by now convinced that sanitation was central to any solution to the problems of the poor, viewed it as an opportunity to produce a comprehensive scheme true to his Benthamic training and his bureaucratic cast of mind. Thus he turned all his energies upon the problem of sanitary reform. For two years he toured London and provincial cities, studied continental practices and read chemistry, engineering and

French and German jurisprudence. In 1842 the fruit of these colossal labours, the *Sanitary report*, was published under Chadwick's own name.[7] It achieved a prodigious and instantaneous success, partly through its intrinsic merits and partly through shrewd promotion: ten thousand copies were distributed free, and the newspapers carefully cultivated.[8] Press, politicians, and fellow civil servants hailed it enthusiastically. Its only critics were the small band of sanitary reformers already in the field; for Chadwick had now come to disagree violently with the dwelling house remedy put forth by the London doctors. He saw their continued influence as a threat to his own scheme; indeed they had nearly forced him to abandon his inquiry in 1841. Normanby, Russell's successor at the home office, had in fact introduced three bills concerned with building improvement and drainage in 1841. Though never passed, they remained as a warning to Chadwick that he might be pre-empted by some unsatisfactory half-measure.

What had brought about his change in attitude? First, the facts that his angle of approach was different and that his range of knowledge and interest was much wider; and secondly, his Benthamic training and truly bureaucratic passion for complete and all-embracing answers. From the beginning Chadwick saw the problem as an administrative and engineering one rather than a medical; and from a very early stage he saw that better house sanitation would not remove, but might even aggravate the evils. In his eyes the fundamental error of the sanitary reformers was their tendency to isolate house sanitation from all other issues. If *per impossibile* every family in every town in England were provided with its own house, and every house were provided with not merely a privy, but even the newly invented and very expensive water closet, what would happen? There might be no place whatever to deposit the contents of the lavatory: many areas in the new towns were without road drains of any description. Even where road drains existed, they usually issued in cesspools, foul accumulations near the dwelling houses which were cleared out by manual labour perhaps once a year. Even where the domestic situation was better and water closets were connected with the large road sewers for draining streets, this merely meant the accumulation of filth and poisonous gases below ground, and ultimately the discharge of whatever the sluggish water could move into the river or stream from which the town's drinking water was drawn. For the old sewers were generally large, square brick tunnels, porous, constructed without any regard to levels and provided with no system of water flushing.

Thus, Chadwick was perfectly right when he claimed that better house sanitation by itself might very well increase the evils which it aimed at curing. Cesspools would merely become larger and fouler, sewer gas back up into the houses and streets and the water supply grow even more tainted than before. He was therefore led to take the revolutionary step – a truly revolutionary step in terms of the science of sanitation of the time – of considering house drainage, street drainage, main drainage, water supply and street cleansing and paving as all necessarily interconnected, indissoluble constituents of one great and general problem. At this point we should recollect that Chadwick still adhered (as indeed he was to do all through his life despite accumulating evidence to the contrary towards its close) to the atmospheric theory of infection. In fact he pursued it more logically and wholeheartedly than its originators among the early sanitary reformers. From his first principle that the real danger lay in the presence and proximity of filth he drew the uncompromising deduction that the filth must be removed as far as possible and as fast as possible. The sanitary reformers had not really thought beyond the physical removal of filth from the four walls of the dwelling house.

Given his objectives and his recognition of the interrelationship of all aspects of sanitation and water supply, it is easy to see why Chadwick's problem narrowed itself to a technical engineering problem and to an administrative one. Engineering alone could solve the difficulties of removing refuse as far and as fast as possible. Effective administration alone could put the engineering solutions into practice and break down the barriers between the multitudinous spheres of town government which this would involve. We have already seen something of the fantastic mixum gatherum of local government which had grown up in eighteenth-century and early nineteenth-century England. First, with a few exceptions such as Winchester, the old corporations ignored sanitation as lying outside their scope: this was, perhaps, just as well. Next, there were two archaic survivals, the courts leet, before which citizens might be summoned for nuisances, and the commissions of sewers. The courts leet were hopelessly entangled in medieval procedures and the commissions were oligarchic, limited in powers and areas of jurisdiction, often corrupt and still more frequently inactive. Generally speaking, both institutions were ineffective and obsolete.[9] There remained the parish vestries and the improvement commissions. As we saw, little could be hoped of the vestries except for a handful of close vestries run by small groups of educated and progressive men. It was the enlightened improvement commissions, such as Manchester's, which offered the best prospect of efficient sanitary government in particular districts. Yet, ironically enough, it was these same improvement commissions which formed the major stumbling block to any comprehensive scheme. The explanation of the paradox lies in their *ad hoc* origin. All had been set up, as we have said, to tackle particular and individual problems – sewers, paving, lighting, cleansing, police, building and so on – without regard for co-ordination or reconciliation of functions. The consequence was endless overlapping and bickering. In one London area alone there were nineteen independent and hostile improvement commissions. In several provincial cities there were as many as half-a-dozen distinct bodies with powers over drainage. As we saw, the municipal reform act of 1835 did little to end the anarchy or reduce the autonomy of the multitudinous authorities. Only a handful of the reformed corporations took over the duties of the existing improvement commissions after 1835. Indeed we may say that so far from solving these problems, the 1835 act merely enlarged them by emphasizing the democratic and elective idea to the total exclusion of that of efficiency and order. On the one hand it tended to undermine the *ultra vires* exertions of the progressive and ambitious select vestries and improvement commissions by exposing them to popular attacks on the grounds of exorbitance and over-spending; on the other it generated a plethora of petty parliaments in the towns, which were bent on aping Westminster rather than tackling local problems. This was (as we shall see) particularly the case in London where the elected vestries became arenas for party conflict and developed a fierce spirit of radical independence and an absurd conceit.

Before the administrative problem could be tackled, however, there remained an engineering problem to be solved. As we saw, Chadwick had appeared to multiply the difficulties of the latter by insisting upon the interconnection of water supply and every aspect of sanitation. But an answer came almost miraculously to hand during the course of his investigations. It was the perfection by John Roe, a London engineer, of a new type of sewer: small, egg-shaped and strong, so constructed and laid out that water would rush through at great speed and force, carrying all matter with it irresistibly.[10] This of course provided a basis for the new system of interconnected services. Water could be harnessed to serve them all. The new type of house drainage could now be used without danger, for all filth would be borne rapidly and far away. Street cleansing could be linked with house drainage, for the same sewers would serve both purposes. Cesspools and the manual removal of refuse would no longer be necessary.

It is true that all this involved two new difficulties. First, arterial drainage demanded a constant supply of water on tap in the homes and streets. But the current practice of the privately owned water companies was to provide water only at certain hours in the day or week. Secondly, what was to become of the refuse? So vast a quantity could not be allowed to flow into the river from which the town drew its supply of drinking water. As to the first, Chadwick recognized that there was no other answer but a supply of water everywhere for twenty-four hours each day: whatever it implied, this would have to be ensured, and he had at least one example – the Trent water works which had been supplying 8,000 houses in Nottingham with unlimited piped water since 1830[11] – to draw on. As to the second, Chadwick's passion for economy eventually furnished a 'solution'. Liquid manure was at this time (just before artificial fertilizers became readily available) extremely valuable in agriculture. Accordingly, Chadwick proposed that the refuse be carried out into the countryside in closed sewers and there distributed, broadcast, into the fields.[12] Needless to say, this fantastic project would have involved immense technical difficulties of transport, distribution and accounting. But it provided so apparently neat and total a solution to the problem of the loose end, and promised so dazzling a financial reward, that Chadwick adhered to it through all discouragements.

Such a comprehensive system of arterial drainage based on Roe's new sewer formed the first part of Chadwick's recommendations in 1842. From it he went on to argue the 'necessary' administrative corollaries. Here, of course, he mainly repeated the concepts of his scheme of poor law government. First it was essential to sweep away the existing local authorities. They were unco-ordinated, too complex, corrupt, amateur and often elective. What was required was a single body with powers over all the hitherto divided duties of drainage, paving, street cleansing and water-supply. Moreover these powers should be exercised not over 'arbitrary' urban areas, but over natural physiographical areas, which meant in effect that the town or city together with its relevant hinterland was to be governed as a single unit. What form was the new body to take? Here Chadwick tried to avoid, as far as possible, the concessions to the representative principle which he had made in his poor law system. Some concessions there had to be. But he tried to minimize them by proposing the appointment of the chief officers of the town and poor law union (such as the mayor and the chairman of the board of guardians) *ex officio*. He obviously hoped that such dignitaries would be more politically robust and less liable to popular pressure than directly elected representatives. He also proposed a further counterbalancing of 'democracy' by the addition of crown-appointed members and by requiring that the new bodies work through professional men and experts only – duly qualified civil engineers and physicians. This was as near as he could get in the circumstances to his ideal of scientific government. He bolstered his arguments against elected authorities by pointing to the difficulties of financing the vast projects which would be involved. The only possible mode was long term borrowing on the security of the rates;[13] and what a field for corruption and selfish interest this would provide if the representative principle were in operation! One had only to look at current practices in London boroughs, which often 'out-Tammanied Tammany', to appreciate the power of this warning.

Such was the outline of Chadwick's *Sanitary report*. Its two most original features, the consolidation of all sanitary and water functions and unified arterial drainage, were to form the basis of all modern drainage. But it was one thing to propose the right type of solution in 1842; it was another to provide it. We must bear in mind the point made earlier that engineering and medicine were not yet fully experimental sciences. There were neither laboratories nor apparatus which could test adequately Roe's or any other technical innovation. The consequence was the development of various schools of thought in engineering which fought out their campaigns on paper and in a welter of abstract mathematical formulae. The equivalent was true of medicine: the atmospheric theory of infection was challenged by several others and the conflict conducted in the same *a priori* and apologetic manner. All this uncertainty was injurious to the *Report* in two respects. First the opponents of sanitary reform, or for that matter rival reformers, could count on the assistance of the schools of thought which were opposed to those backed by the *Report*. Secondly it led Chadwick and the Chadwickians into treating as certain something which had merely not been experimentally disproved. They got stuck, so to speak, at 1842. They were incapable of taking advantage of the very considerable advances in chemistry, medicine and engineering during the next fifteen years because the prevailing atmosphere of combat and assertion had committed them beforehand to particular dogma.

On publication, however the *Report* of 1842 scored an instantaneous success. It roused the middle classes generally to a realization of the conditions of their towns; it appealed to philanthropic and humanitarian sentiment; it seemed a response to the new birth of scientific discovery and scientific farming;[14] and it appeared to rise above party and class conflict. It was an issue on which politicians and citizens of all schools could unite, or so it was initially believed. Its date, 1842, was significant. This was the year in which chartism declined sharply, in which the economy began to settle after the alarming and disastrous booms and slumps of the preceding decade, in which Peel and Graham were searching about for some great measure to compensate the working classes for their successive failures, and in which Liebig's work on agricultural chemistry became widely known and blindly idolized in Great Britain. But it soon became clear (it should in fact have been clear from the beginning) that Chadwick's proposal would provoke powerful and dangerous opposition from the threatened vested interests – from all the local bodies which dealt with sanitation in any way, from the private water companies, from the urban landlords and from the schools of medical and engineering thought which were, so to speak, temporarily in opposition. Moreover Graham had begun to realize that many of the radical democrats would also be hostile, both because of the denial of elective principle in the administrative scheme and because of the heavy expenditure which would be inevitably involved. Finally, by this stage many would object to anything emanating from Chadwick, while others would object to the assumption that public authority could, let alone would, work more cheaply and efficiently than private enterprise.

Accordingly, Graham set up a royal commission on the health of towns in 1843,[15] ostensibly to pass judgment on Chadwick's *Sanitary report*. The commission worked after the same unscrupulous fashion of those of the 1830s. From behind the scenes Chadwick helped in the nomination of its members, the calling and questioning of witnesses, and even the writing of its reports. Not surprisingly these reports, published in 1844 and 1845, completely endorsed his recommendations. But they did more. The weight of distinguished scientific opinion on the commission gave them an aura of immense authority and impartiality; and the voluminous evidence, involving an exposure of the existing slum conditions, mortality, and administrative chaos and corruption in the fifty greatest towns of England apparently provided unanswerable arguments for wholesale interference and regulation. A further and very important consequence was the formation of a number of propagandist public health associations, particularly the health of towns association in 1844. The latter provided the sanitary reform movement generally with a very powerful pressure group; and for the first time in his career Chadwick had a body of organized opinion upon his side, organized with journals and propaganda substantially on the model of the anti-corn law league.[16] Still more significant, the new association cut across many old divisions. It included high whigs and tories, clericals and secularists, protectionists and free traders, humanitarians and Benthamite radicals. It also represented the first clear movement towards collectivist action on the part of middle class electorates.

The delay involved in setting up the royal commission had, however, deleterious effects upon the course of public health legislation. Not until 1845, when the commission issued its final report, could any major step be taken; and by then the corn law crisis had arrived. It is true that Peel permitted Lord Lincoln to introduce a very comprehensive bill along Chadwickian lines in 1845, but it was introduced only to be aired. Serious consideration of the measure was postponed until the following session, and by then such grave matters as the Irish famine and the break-up of the Tory party completely overshadowed public health. In 1847 the same factors, combined with a general election, a new poor law and a new factory act, led to further postponement. The interval, of course, enabled the health of towns association to spread its propaganda and investigations to the provinces. It also produced two ventures in self-help. The first was a disastrous attempt to set up a private company to provide an arterial drainage system for London on a profit-making basis. Strangely, Chadwick himself was involved in this, doubtless from impatience at the delay in state action and faith in 'the gold to be won from muck'.[17] The second was the adoption of arterial drainage and consolidated sanitation by a handful of the largest northern cities, including Manchester, Liverpool, Leeds and Newcastle. These were the cities with the best record for civic enlightenment, and they profited from the various sanitary reports by securing private acts of parliament to enable them to proceed along the recommended lines. But the interval between 1842 and 1847 also brought about the development and hardening of the opposition to sanitary reform, particularly in London. The first shock of the 1842 report gradually wore off while the conflicts in engineering and medical theory (which the threatened interests could use to their own advantage) grew more and more embittered and confused. Had it been possible to strike while the iron was hot, to take action in 1843, it seems likely that much more could have been carried through.

At last 1848 saw the appearance of a public health act,[18] introduced by Morpeth, the new whig home secretary. (A town improvement act[19] had been passed the year before, but this was for the most part a permissive and not a compulsory measure). Morpeth's original bill as compared with Chadwick's programme of 1842 made important concessions to the elective principle. There was to be a general board of health, rather like the reformed poor law board of 1847. But it was not to appoint the members of the local boards, as Chadwick had suggested. Instead, these were to consist of the corporations, as such, in the corporate towns, and of elected representatives in the non-corporate towns. Further, the initiative still partly rested with the locality. A local board would not be set up unless one-fiftieth of the inhabitants petitioned for it and a central inspector approved of their petition. On the other hand the general board had several important powers once the local board came into existence. It could consist on the appointment of a permanent official, the surveyor, who would be under its own control, and insist upon an ordnance survey and a sewage scheme. Local drainage projects and local borrowing for such projects required its sanction, and once the local board decided to adopt a sewage system it could not go back on its decision.

Thus this curious compromise tended to leave the first step to the discretion of the locality and to guarantee most localities the elective principle, while yet providing the general board with very considerable coercive powers once the locality had committed itself to action. Naturally the opposition to the bill – which consisted mainly of four great parliamentary interests: the water companies, the manufacturers, the corporations and most important of all the London members – concentrated upon whittling away the powers of the general board. By the time the bill had left the commons these had almost disappeared. Local boards could no longer be compelled to draw up sanitary schemes, or, once the schemes were sanctioned, compelled to put them into action; loans could now be raised without the sanction of the general board; and one-tenth instead of one-fiftieth of the inhabitants had to petition before a local board could be established. Chadwick was of course horror-stricken. It seemed as if the history of the poor law would repeat itself, with coercive power struck from the hands of the central authority and the measure reduced to a mere permissive one after all. The lords, however, came to the rescue at the eleventh hour and restored two of the three major amendments (an important consequence, incidentally, of the aristocratic patronage of sanitary reform). The general board regained its control over borrowing and was given the right to set up local boards arbitrarily wherever the death rate was 23 per thousand as against the national average of 21 per thousand.[20]

Thus the public health act of 1848 as it was eventually passed promised to be reasonably fair from the standpoint of the 1842 men. The essence of central and professional administration had been secured and the worst administrative weakness of the poor law of 1834 avoided. The general board of health had a proper link with parliament, it had regained its coercive financial and initiating powers, and (it might be hoped) sufficient play had been left for the elective principle to satisfy radical and local feeling. On the technical side also, the prospects seemed far from gloomy. The 'arterial drainage system' had been more or less sanctioned by the statute, and a great step towards realizing it had been taken in 1847 when earthenware pipes were baked at Chadwick's instance.[21] These proved strong, cheap and easy to replace – again, essentially the right type of answer whatever later improvements were still to come. Finally, the new general board consisted of Morpeth, Chadwick and Ashley (the last two, former antagonists over the factory acts), and all three worked in extraordinary harmony and co-operation – also in marked contrast to the poor law commission of 1834. Southwood Smith, who had been appointed chief medical officer, was also an easy and compliant colleague – in fact, a 'yes man'.

There were however two clouds on the horizon which were destined ultimately to overshadow all. The first was the arrival of cholera at the very moment when the act was passed. The epidemic lasted a full twelve months, until the winter of 1849, and produced an enormous death rate. In certain respects, of course, the outbreak worked to the advantage of the general board. It drove home in a most dramatic and terrifying way the necessity for strong precautionary measures. It also emphasized the contrast between the general board, whose members worked like slaves month after month during the epidemic and adopted emergency powers freely and fearlessly, and the existing local authorities, who proved themselves for the most part mean, heartless, slothful and cowardly throughout. There was however another aspect to the matter. First the habit of exorbitance and ruthless action, having been so early acquired, persisted right through the history of the board with very unfortunate consequences. Secondly and still more important, the board was diverted from its true work for eighteen fateful and decisive months. The explanation of this second point lies in the peculiar status of London. Early Victorian London was a sprawling agglomeration of boroughs drained and cleansed by over three hundred distinct and more or less autonomous bodies. It was unique in area, comprising over two million inhabitants already, and in the degree of corruption and the radical independence of its local government. It was also unique in its political power: the private water and burial companies, the vestries and the old city of London could command a most formidable influence in the commons.

From the beginning the problem of London bedevilled sanitary reform. Chadwick in his own report and through the medium of the royal commission of 1843–5 had insisted that the same solution of a single body with complete and comprehensive powers, a single physiographically determined drainage area and a single system of interconnected arterial drainage be applied as ruthlessly to London as to all other towns and cities. But this was obviously no easy task. The political power of the city's vested interests and the fierce pride of metropolitan radicalism on the one hand, and the physical problems of surveying London, deciding on a drainage area and disposing of so vast a quantity of refuse without polluting water on the other, barred the way. Ultimately it was decided to exclude London from the public health act of 1848 on the understanding that a special metropolitan measure would be passed when new surveys and inquiries had been completed. Meanwhile the multitudinous old commissions of sewers for London had come up for renewal in 1847 and at Morpeth's insistence they had been swept away, and a new single crown-appointed commission, packed with his own and

Chadwick's partisans, was set up in their place.²² This was the body conducting the surveys and inquiries. Morpeth himself had wished the new metropolitan commission to be a representative body like the local boards adumbrated in the act of 1848. He was undoubtedly right politically. The only hope of carrying sanitary reform in London was by concessions to radical and elective principle. But Chadwick (now thoroughly distrusting democracy and most of all, and with good reason, London democracy) had overborne him and secured an appointive body. Morpeth had then sought to reassure metropolitan opinion by nominating four members from the vestries, a fatal step in the event.

This then was the situation when cholera arrived in 1848. The general board dominated by Morpeth and Chadwick ran side by side with the new metropolitan commission of sewers, also dominated by Morpeth and Chadwick. No friction was expected. The commission would complete its work of investigation within two or three years and then in its own good time absorb all London within a single scheme and come to some amicable permanent administrative arrangements with the general board. The next eighteen months however produced a complete collapse of plans, a collapse in which the distraction of the cholera epidemic played a considerable part. The four London vestry representatives on the commission pursued so determined and harassing a policy of obstruction as to bring its work to a standstill and its bitter wrangling to the public notice. Here *The Times*, at one with the metropolitan members on the issue of the pollution of the Thames (long its King Charles's head), dealt the fatal blow by its constant and merciless exposures of the triumvirate's exorbitance and imperialism. The upshot was that the entire commission was dismissed in disgrace at the end of 1849 and a new one, free from both Chadwickians and London radicals and under the control of the Engineering Institute, was set up in its place.

During the next three years, 1850, 1851 and 1852, an extraordinary three-cornered fight for control of London developed. The Chadwickians had suffered a catastrophic loss but they still held the general board; and although as things turned out they had made the grave error of excluding London from the public health act, Chadwick and Ashley (now Lord Shaftesbury) struggled to regain control of the capital through their implicit powers over water and burials. They sought to build on and extend the emergency measures they had taken in these fields in London during the cholera epidemic. They were fiercely opposed in parliament by the metropolitan vested interests and the metropolitan radicals, who had now organized a very widespread opposition to 'centralization' and 'bureaucracy' in general, and to Chadwick and Shaftesbury in particular. They were also fiercely opposed by the reconstituted London commission of sewers – the engineers' commission. The new struggle between the general board and the commission derived partly from the engineers' natural desire to control London themselves and partly from the fact that the Engineering Institute was in the hands of a school of engineering which Chadwick had derided and attacked in his earlier anxiety to establish the practicability of arterial drainage. Finally there was a third and equally savage contest between the engineers' commission and the metropolitan radicals, whose power was threatened.

The whole affair proved disastrous for the general board. Its attempt to regain control of London through the back door of hygiene in water supply and burials was finally and ignominiously crushed at the close of 1852. The main consequences of the general board's monomania with winning back London were its failure to press on fully with furnishing provincial towns with arterial drainage; the growth and extension of the opposition to its centralization and exorbitance – for the delays permitted the organization of a provincial discontent and radicalism with which the London interests could and did make common cause; and the loss of most of the good will and public approbation with which the board had started out. In particular the board's preoccupation with London, from 1848 to 1852, was disastrous because it was due to come up for renewal in 1854. As *The Times* summed up the situation during the summer of 1852, the board

originally acquired unnatural licence from extraordinary circumstances of popular fear, but, instead of subsiding into sentiments of practical decorum as the public cooled down,

148

it foolishly pushed its notions and pretensions to a height more preposterous than before. ... In this unpopular position it asked for powers which a beleaguered community would hardly confide to a military dictator and it has suffered accordingly. It has paid the penalty, not of supineness, imbecility or discord but of immoderate scheming, outlandish fancies, and fanatical delusion.[23]

The question was whether it could regain sufficient prestige in its remaining eighteen months of statutory life to counterbalance its disgrace and the rising opposition. A heroic attempt was made. By 1854 almost three hundred towns had applied for a local board; in all almost two hundred local boards had actually been set up; and in two score or so, arterial drainage had been established and was working well. But it was of no avail. The engineering and the various hostile London interests, combined with the new provincial opposition which the procrastination had permitted to develop, secured their object in the end. Shaftesbury and Chadwick were dismissed. The two greatest – though often unwitting and indeed antagonistic – promoters of collectivization and centralization in the first half of the nineteenth century left office together, never to return. The board of health, weakened in scope, fell for a few years into the hands of their opponents and then in 1858 was finally disbanded and its duties apparently dispersed through various government departments. The mind and disposition of the exultant opposition – as well as the fact that it by no means constituted a mere knot of fools and knaves – may perhaps be discerned in the following 'obituary' composed in that year :

... a few doctrinaires, nursed in the narrow conceits of bureaucracy, scornful alike of popular knowledge and of popular government, seized upon the sanitary theory as a means of exercising a central power of domiciliary inspection and irresponsible interference with the conduct and property of Englishmen. The ready plea, of course, was the inherent right of every man to the enjoyment of the means necessary to health; and hence the duty incumbent upon the Government of making every man healthy. Well, if it could be shown that half a dozen men, constituting a board and sitting in a Government office, could so regulate the social and domestic conduct of the inhabitants of this country as to ensure to them the safe removal of all those causes which unnaturally impair their health, and shorten their lives, it might admit of an argument, whether, for the sake of the inestimable boon of health, it would not be desirable to surrender to such a board our most cherished political institutions. But this has not been proved. The contrary has been proved. For several years a Central Board of Health ruled with considerable activity and vigour, but with slender success. It is doubtful whether the notable Whig scheme of despatching those favourite Whig animals, briefless barristers of seven years' standing and crotchetty engineers, to scour the country as sanitary inspectors, has not resulted in causing more disease than it has cured. At any rate, no doubt can exist as to the unpopularity of this scheme. And no doubt can exist that any scheme which is unpopular in this country must fail. . . . The truth is, we do not like paternal governments. . . . This is another reason why the CHADWICKIAN sanitary *régime* so signally failed.[24]

The supreme irony was that the public health act of 1848 failed at precisely the moment when the essential correctness of its main principles was being established. The small earthenware sewer was substantially a success; the system of arterial drainage was a success and on the point of becoming really practicable through technical improvements. Both the northern cities outside the act and the towns which had adopted it provided ample testimony to this. Even the administrative mechanisms were comparatively successful, by and large. As we shall see, the new wave of public health legislation, represented by the public health statutes of 1866, 1871, 1872 and 1875, and a new royal commission in 1868,[25] largely confirmed and extended the recommendations of the commission of 1843 and the essential features of the act of 1848. The consolidation of all sanitary and water services into a single system, the use of constant water supply as the motive power of all, the small drain-pipe (earthenware and glazed), the central board with coercive powers over the localities and a professional service and inspectorate under its own control – all of these were substantially repeated. The only important changes were elaborations of the principles laid down in 1845 and a great increase in the authority and scope of the central board.

The whole campaign for sanitary reform from 1842 to 1854, and Chadwick's last rise and fall, are marked by several interesting and novel features. First he himself was using his concepts of centralization and 'expert government' for an avowedly collectivist purpose; we cannot say the same of his factory, poor law or police proposals. Secondly this campaign had behind it an organized and largely middle class body of opinion. The *avant garde* sanitarians joined hands with tory collectivists like the 'Young Englanders', with enlightened and progressive provincials, with humanitarians like Shaftesbury, with certain sections of the new professions (Lydgate in *Middlemarch* was spiritually a man of 1842–4 rather than of 1832–4 as in the novel), and with sentimental 'socialists' like Dickens or Kingsley. For the first time to many in the middle classes, collectivist action appeared to be in their own interest and the middle class sense of social responsibility, of scientific improvement and of local pride could be diverted along such channels. Thirdly the incompatibility of the efficient concept of local government and the radical and elective concept was thoroughly demonstrated. The municipal reforms of the 1830s and the new vested interests, tangible and intangible, which they had created, had come home to roost. Fourthly the difficulty of achieving collectivist and centralized reform within the old framework of politics and the old type of administration could be clearly seen. Once again we find that in a sense the cart was being put before the horse, as indeed was also the case with the introduction of administrative measures based on scientific discovery before the sciences had become fully experimental and demonstrable. Finally we see the last great 'victory' of the individualist principle and the beginning of the last great phase of dominant individualism, the later 1850s and the early 1860s. In certain fields the late 1840s proved a false dawn for collectivism, breeding as it inevitably did a violent reaction after the first shock of exposure. At the mid-century this reaction could still be sufficiently powerful to check even the great wave of sanitary improvement.

The terms 'formal' and 'public' should however be attached to any such phrase as the 'victory' of individualism. In many respects the check to collectivism was apparent, not real. The false dawn of the one in the late 1840s was to be succeeded by a false noon for the other a decade later. As with the medical elements in the poor law, *si naturam furca expellas tamen usque recurret* proved to be the case here. It was impossible to turn the clock back. Centralization, uniformity and concern for enforcement were by now irrepressible tendencies in public health. The events of 1858–9 were to show this clearly.

The débâcle of 1848–54 had contributed powerfully to two great waves of opinion which broke upon parliament in the mid-1850s. Pressure had long been building up for the re-assertion of local power – this was the first of the devolutionary moods to which Britain has been spasmodically subject in the past century and a half – and for the re-establishment of ministerial control over the central government departments, and of parliamentary control over the ministers. Patently the views and conduct epitomized by such a man as Chadwick had bred an angry reaction. So far as the present field of state action went, this duly received public expression after much confused struggle in the administration, the cabinet and the house of commons, in the local government act of 1858[26] and the public health acts of 1858 and 1859.[27] The fundamental intention of these enactments was to decentralize public health and to crush forever the over-mighty subjects who as public servants had domineered or sought to domineer the field. But it was not practicable simply to abolish and disband the general board of health by a single pen-stroke: certain functions performed by the board had to continue to be performed by someone. The two statutes of 1858 were meant to arrange for both the general winding-up and the disposition of the vestigial fragments.

The local government act of 1858 seemed to meet the demand for decentralization by empowering localities to set up their own sanitary authorities, where before these had been either awarded after application or forcibly established by the central power. The act also withdrew the compulsory powers hitherto exercisable by the now extinguished board. But the first change, although a showy expression and extension of the 'voluntary principle', did nothing to remove the need for central direction and co-ordination. As to the second, since, in the words of Dr Lambert, 'the compulsory powers now being so demonstratively abolished had scarcely been used by Chadwick and never by his successors, the legislature was simply ratifying old established administrative practice.'[28] Moreover all the other discretionary powers and duties of the former central board were retained, or in some cases even enlarged. Equally significant, the staff continued their old work in the same building. The change was merely one of name and bureaucratic appointment: they had re-emerged as a sub-department of the home office.

It was both desired and expected that the great majority of the activities of the officers of the former board (now members of the home office) should cease. But this was unrealistic. Ironically the demand for their assistance grew just as the supply was threatened. The need for services increased instead of diminishing as the new local sanitary authorities sought aid and guidance. Moreover the interior administrative momentum which had carried the board's officers forward before 1858 was sustained, or perhaps even grew in force. Contrary to anyone's intention (there were no over-mighty subjects in this sub-department) and unknown to and ignored by almost all, they steadily gathered power, eventually even coercive central powers of the widest range. For the local government act office, as the new sub-department was called, was the main repository of such experts and expertise as had emerged during, and survived from, the preceding decade. It was natural that it should be called upon for standards and direction; and from this it was a small step to co-ordination, uniformity and at last compulsion.[29]

The public health acts of 1858 and 1859 were much more a matter of accident and fortune. The first and most important antecedent accident was the appointment of John Simon as medical officer to the general board of health in 1855 in place of Southwood Smith. Simon, who had served with success and *éclat* as the original medical officer of the City of London from 1848 to 1855, was a master-bureaucrat of Chadwickian or Trevelyanesque stature. But his cast of mind was pragmatic, inductive and gradualist. His corresponding habits were mildness, persuasion, cautious response to evidence and a blessed blindness to ultimate implications at the time of acting. Characteristically, if undesignedly, he worked largely through private and personal influence upon the influential people. He was the very emollient and exactly the discreet conductor called for by the circumstances of 1855–65. He was a centralizer and an autonomizer, but neither in intent nor consciously, merely in effect.

In 1858 the preventive elements of central public health were given but a temporary respite. It seems as if the medical department of the privy council set up by the legislation of that year was meant to act as a sort of receiver in bankruptcy for the general board to arrange for the disengagement of the state as such from the whole business of preventive public health. At one stage in 1859 it looked as if the government would allow the new privy council medical office and the new post of medical officer (occupied of course by Simon) to lapse entirely at the end of the session, and with it all central responsibility even for vaccination and epidemical affairs. But in the end, chance and bureaucratic skill produced a very different conclusion in the public health act of 1859. The replacement of the conservative government of Derby by the liberals at a critical stage and Simon's lines of communication, first to the Prince Consort and then to the new vice-president of the privy council, Robert Lowe, greatly facilitated, if they did not actually occasion, what turned out to be not merely a renewing but also a remarkably centralizing statute.[30] Nonetheless the bill passed only because of its ambiguity. It was capable of an anti-centralizing and minimalist interpretation, and it was this interpretation which generally prevailed while it was being debated. The three crucial clauses were those which rendered the medical officership a permanent post, placed the vaccination service under his general direction and laid upon him both the right and the duty to investigate and report upon any aspect of preventive medicine which was deemed appropriate from time to time. Simon's position was thus absolutely secure and practically boundless in scope. Moreover the one successful venture into state medicine to that date – the first 'national, free and compulsory' health service which the vaccination legislation had produced [31] – was retained by the central power. Most important of all, the annual and occasional reports required of the office, while apparently advisory at most, opened the door to 'expert government' and to irresistible pressures for compulsion.

Thus after the storms of the mid-1850s had blown themselves out and the great oak had been uprooted, in some strange fashion two saplings had come to occupy its ground. Meanwhile in the course of the replacement the utmost administrative confusion had returned. In terms of central government the privy council now had direct powers over quarantine, vaccination and epidemical emergencies; the home office, over factories and burial grounds; the colonial office, over ocean passengers; the poor law board, over their workhouse infirmaries and (through their subordinate officers or bodies) over the actual administration of vaccination and the actual removal of nuisances; and the board of trade, over water companies and industrial waste. Nor was this the end of the proliferation. Even the war office and the admiralty, to go no further, possessed health sub-departments.

The hotch-potch at the centre was more than matched on the periphery. First came the local health authorities, which after 1858 required no central decision for their formation and were free of central control. Overlapping these or substituting for them were the old select vestries, water boards, improvement commissions, town councils and the rest. Moreover many places chose to work under their own local acts[32] and these statutes often created further and still more exotic administrative bodies. Finally a new layer of sewer authorities was imposed upon the existing maze by the sewage utilization act of 1865.[33] In many ways it was the 1760s returned again, but in a much more complex, busy and technically inclined form.

In these circumstances, Simon's office came gradually to occupy a commanding position. The medical department of the privy council was *faute de mieux* the overseer of the medley. Although formally powerless except for vaccination and its right to allow or disallow loans for large scale improvement projects, its indirect influence was immense. Its advice, which was sought by as well as proferred to the localities, inevitably worked for uniformity and government by scien-

tific 'certitude'. Its initiative, which took the form of an inspectorate spurring local bodies into action, was exercised individually and occasionally rather than collectively and systematically; it was, therefore, little resented or resisted. Its
national pressure, which operated through Simon's annual reports published as official papers, was powerful and cumulative because the medical officer was ostensibly dispassionate
and apparently moved to write by the findings of departmental
inquiries rather than by administrative imperialism, *a priori*
theory or partisanship. The department's essential strength was
the impression which it gave of possessing an ever open mind
and of waiting upon scientific and other tested evidence before,
cautiously and provisionally, pronouncing. Simon sincerely believed that this was how he and his officers proceeded, and the
world at large accepted him at his own valuation. It was this
above all which opened the door to power.

Gradually Simon's experience taught him, and in turn his
reports taught the public, that there were cardinal deficiencies
in the 'system' of the late 1850s and early 1860s. Three in
particular were distinguished: the lack of uniformity and uni-
versality in public health administration, its dependence upon
voluntarism and its restricted view of its area of operations.
Simon's annual reports of the mid-1860s, and especially those
of 1865 and 1866, brought matters to a head; and the sanitary
act which followed them represented a brave attempt to correct
the situation as it had been depicted in the accumulated findings of the department. According to this act of 1866,[34] the
sanitary powers granted to specific local boards of health under
the 1848 act were to be everywhere available and standard
in form; the authorities for the removal of nuisances were
enjoined instead of being merely allowed to carry out their
specified functions; and housing was included for the first time
in the definition of possible nuisance, with corresponding
powers to condemn, improve or destroy slum dwellings. It is
interesting to note in this last provision the return of housing
to the forefront of public health concern nearly a quarter of a
century after Chadwick had wrenched attention from it.

Although the sanitary bill had been amended during its passage through parliament, the changes were comparatively minor
and the support for its leading principles was bipartisan in

both houses. 'Seldom', commented *The Times*, 'has an enactment been received with more general approbation or milder
criticism.'[35] Considering the nature of its provisions, not to add
the fact that immediately after its introduction a conservative
government replaced Earl Russell's, a more extraordinary contrast with the struggles of a dozen years before can scarcely
be supposed. How are we to explain the turnabout? Three
factors appear to have been of high importance. First the
medical department's inquiries and reports over several years
had quietly worn down opposition. Secondly the cholera epidemic of 1866 produced a most opportune alarm. Finally the
localities had discovered, and in a gradual and unfrightening
fashion, that 'independence' in such a field was devoid of
meaning, value or profit. The first of the three factors, Simon's
Fabian scientism, was probably the most telling.

The sanitary act of 1866 was, like the Irish land act of 1870,
a most interesting piece of legislation, not because it settled
a major question but because it combined ineffectuality in
practice with revolution in principle. Although local authorities
were legally obliged to act after 1866 and central enforcement
was ultimately implicit in such an obligation, no attempt had
been made to co-ordinate either central or local government
or to settle the relationships between the two. Nor had any
attempt been made to require the establishment or reform of
local bodies where they were as yet unconstituted or administratively insufficient. In these circumstances the statute was,
to a considerable extent, unworkable. Coercion and centralization had been endorsed but without the tools which would
have enabled them to be effectively practised. It is not
surprising, therefore, that almost immediately after the coming
into force of the sanitary act of 1866, agitation for further
change got under way. A medical lobby, enthusiasts from other
professions and a new generation of sanitary reformers combined in a movement for a major inquiry into the entire
national condition of public health. The royal commission of
1868–71 on sanitation was at once the trophy and the vent
of the new movement, and broadly speaking its reports lived
up to the large expectations of the agitators.

The recommendations of the commission bore legislative
fruit in the four years following its final report. Together the

reforming statutes of 1871–5 sorted, selected from and re-arranged the work of forty years in the field of public health. They laid down the final high Victorian settlement of the great range of matters embraced under this head, and it was to last substantially for more than half a century. The local government board act of 1871 gathered the great majority of the central government's public health functions and officers into a new and distinctive ministry. The public health act of 1872 provided the equivalent consolidation in local government. A network of sanitary authorities, with specific obligations and sufficiently large to have their own medical and support staffs, was to cover the entire country. They were to form the petty pyramids within the gigantic one. These statutes of 1871 and 1872 dealt with administrative structures, manning and patterns of authority. The rationalization of powers, obligations and fields of action had to await the public health act of 1875, which represented a Napoleon-like codificaton of the great mass of unco-ordinated legislation of the preceding forty years and more. Finally, another statute of 1875, the artisans' dwellings act, extended the domain of public health more clearly and purposively to embrace the housing of the poor. By this measure local authorities were unambiguously empowered to destroy and replace insanitary dwellings.

The legislation of 1871–5 did not *formally* enlarge the area of state action very greatly, although *effectively* the opposite was the case. Except in mechanical and administrative terms it was not markedly innovative. The royal commission of 1868–71, from whose reports the legislation essentially derived, had been concerned to clarify and concentrate what the antecedent generation had devised and enacted rather than to build anew. But revolutions do not necessarily depend upon absolute novelty. Selecting and assembling the good pieces from amongst the mass and setting them into working order can also constitute radical change, and this (to put the matter very simply) is more or less what was done in the first half of the 1870s. The construction was faulty on many sides, yet sufficiently operable to endure with comparatively little alteration or additions for over sixty years. The next major revision in public health was made in 1936.

In one light the years 1830–70 may be regarded as a very lengthy period of gestation. In another they can be seen as furnishing object lessons in the achievement or otherwise of social reforms of large character, of manifold implications and of wide notoriety in early Victorian England – in other words they can be seen in political terms. The politics involved were neither parliamentary nor party to any significant degree. Who occupied a particular ministry was, as we have seen, occasionally important. Whether the liberals or conservatives were in office was, as we have seen, not always a matter of indifference. But over the entire sweep of events these were puny factors. The politics of the case were essentially governmental and bureaucratic.

Here at first sight the phases 1835–54 and 1855–75 seem to present the clearest of contrasts – between an 'age of Chadwick' and an 'age of Simon', between the 'closed mind' and the 'open', between the doctrinaire and the pragmatic habits of thought and action, between the deductive and the inductive, between the imposition of administrative change from above and its gradual upward growth, virtually untrained, and from the bottom. By no means should these antithesies be dismissed as entirely false or monstrously over-simplified. There is a considerable if unequal degree of reality behind each. The broad course of developments not only in this, but also in the other fields of 'intervention' which have been reviewed, amply confirm as much. Nor is it unfair to regard one set of forms as inherently more likely to achieve ends in the contemporary circumstances than the other.

Nonetheless sharp and absolute contrasts may be misleading. Certainly they are inappropriate in many ways. First the phase 1855–75 was to some degree the legatee of its precursor, 1835–54. Legislation, administrative structures, offices, practices and forms often survived despite the appearance – and for that matter the design – of a general collapse. The local government act office is a striking instance of this disguised or silent continuity. Secondly the fracas of 1845–54 had taught men many lessons. Various blind alleys and dangerous tracks had been clearly marked as such by an unhappy experience of others. In short, one half-generation was standing on the shoulders of its predecessor, and it would be unfair to apply a single standard of judgment to both. Thirdly, to contemporaries in England and Wales 1875 would have seemed little if any better than 1835 by the practical test of death rates. The general mortality of the quinquennial period 1841–5 was 21.4 per thousand persons and that of 1871–5, 22.0. In between it had never fallen below 21.8 (the figure for 1856–60), and in one half-decade it had reached 23.3. It is true that there were mitigating factors. A major cause of death in these years was infectious diseases, which were peculiarly deadly in mid-nineteenth-century urban conditions; and the population of England and Wales had risen by some 25 per cent, and their urban population by some 50 per cent in the forty years without significant changes in the death rates. It is arguable that this represented a species of negative achievement, part of which was surely attributable to the advances in public health administration.[36] Moreover 1875 marked the turning point. From then onwards general mortality fell quickly, down to 15.4 by the first decade of the present century. Nonetheless after all allowances are made we still find that by the simple yardstick of effect upon mortality – the truly meaningful yardstick in public health for contemporaries, at least – what is really striking about our two phases is not their difference but their virtual identity.

These last considerations, however, allow us to strike a more general balance, if only in the most simple terms. Infectious diseases accounted for fully one-third of the total deaths in the period 1835–75; they accounted for a much higher proportion of the infant, child and maternal deaths in the same years, and for a still higher proportion of the 'avoidable' mortality. They therefore constituted the critical element in the problem. But scientists still did not know in 1875 either the causes, or the mode of propagation, of the majority of these diseases. Thus whatever the form or the intensity of public health government, it was comparatively powerless to determine the issue. It had to await the advances in medical theory and practice in the late nineteenth century, which, while not entirely unconnected, were essentially proceeding independently. Moreover, although in certain aspects of social work (sanitation and housing are obvious instances), public health government could do much to stem the tide of death, other arrangements in society, which were altogether outside its sphere of action, kept up the high mortality; and changes in these, which lowered the death rate, were also proceeding independently. To take but a single instance from Lambert, the infectious disease which contributed most to infant deaths, summer diarrhoea, was spread by flies feeding on horse-dung; and as motor transport replaced horses in the city, so too this disease declined.[37]

Thus in some measure the success of state action in the field of public health depended on forces beyond the control of government or law. But it is no less true that the increase in medical knowledge would of itself have achieved little. It required a vast bureaucratic apparatus and bodies of appropriate legislation and orders and of men and women with laboriously acquired skills to effect truly significant changes in the national health. These were the real fruits of the great mid-nineteenth-century endeavours. Wasteful, ignorant, passionate and perverse as these endeavours often were, particularly in the first of our phases but to a degree in both, it was by them that the country felt its way towards a system capable of reaping, however clumsily, the late Victorian harvest in science and technology.

NINE

Law and public order

Early Victorian society was absorbed with law and public order partly because of their histrionic and spectacular facets and partly because of the widespread sense, before 1848, that the social floor separating civilization and chaos was thin and insecure. At the same time both, and in particular the legal system, were anachronistic, irrational, wasteful, anomalous and costly. They seemed easy targets for theory and common sense alike.

The eighteenth-century tradition of legal reform, pragmatic and humanitarian, had been carried over into the nineteenth century by Romilly and subsequently by Peel and Russell in their attempts to rationalize the application of the death penalty. In 1808, 1810 and 1811, Romilly successfully proposed bills for the abolition of capital punishment for certain particularly trivial or obscure crimes.[1] (He had failures, too, during the same years). Although he enjoyed both friendship with and stimulus from Bentham, Romilly should be regarded as a neo-classicist, a Beccarian in criminology rather than a Benthamite. The same might be said, with the usual allowances for anti-theory, of Peel in this particular field. Peel exempted more than one hundred felonies from the death penalty by his statutes of 1823;[2] this type of work was continued by Brougham during his chancellorship in the next decade, and by Russell in the later 1830s. In fact from an estimated two hundred in 1823 the number of offences subject to capital punishment had fallen to fourteen by 1839. But while these repeals were of course necessary, they were also largely formal,

the mere statutory recognition of changes in the general attitude to crimes which had come about many years before.
Further, it is arguable – at any rate, it has been argued – that
these particular 'reforms' were meant to increase the severity
of the criminal law by inducing juries to convict more often
now that the dread penalty could no longer be imposed. Although such a view may implicitly mislead, insofar as Romilly,
Peel, Brougham and Russell appear to have been moved mainly
here by decency and pity, it also implies another truth, that
the sum of human misery and degradation was not very materially diminished by these changes.

Of much more significance was Brougham's attempt to
codify English law and rationalize English legal procedure, to
some extent upon the lines advocated earlier by Bentham.
Brougham, the whig lord chancellor from 1830 to 1834, was
the prime representative of utility (or 'enlightenment' or
'reason' as he might have preferred) in the high politics of law
at this particular juncture. As Halevy put it, he fancied himself a second Bacon and he was accepted at his own valuation
for a time.[3] But by 1835 his vanity, pique and intemperance
had rendered him a liability rather than an advantage to the
cause which he had succeeded, largely, in identifying with
himself. This identification was maintained into the 1850s by
Brougham's steady retention of the presidency of the relevant
pressure group, the law reform association. He also kept the
direction of the association's organ, the *Law Review*, in his own
hands. The celebrated gibe, that 'if he had known a little law
he would have known a little of everything', evidences no
more perhaps than the professional lawyer's intolerance of
rationalistic or exterior change. But that it could have been
made at all, and busily circulated about England into the bargain, is indicative of the calamitously low standing of the
later Brougham in the world at large.

In the early 1830s, with his reputation still in the ascendant,
Brougham had initiated a number of royal commissions, packed
beforehand with orthodox utilitarians and radicals, to 'advise'
on a restructuring of English law and procedure. Brougham's
labours and the reports of the commissions bore some fruit.
The most important achievements of 1830–4 were, perhaps,
the substitution of fixed salaries for fees in several courts; the

abolition of the court of delegates and of many of the sinecures in the court of chancery; and the setting up of two new
courts of immense value, the bankruptcy court, and the central
criminal court in London, as well as the judicial committee of
the privy council. But even all this was merely nibbling at the
edge of the problem. Brougham was no more a legal Chadwick
than a second Bacon; and the lawyers' vested interest was extremely powerful in both the house of lords and the house of
commons. The essence of the structural problem, the multiplication of jurisdictions, was virtually untouched until the
judicature act of 1873.[4] The ever increasing technicality and
obscurity of law, and the expense, slowness and uncertainty
of legal actions, remained.

Two of Brougham's great failures are instructive : his attempt
to set up an office to investigate and record land-ownership in
England (originally a suggestion of Bentham's, and one which
was substantially realized in Ireland later),[5] and his attempt in
a bill of 1830[6] to institute local courts which would ease the
existing congestion by permitting specially appointed judges
to try certain offences without a jury. Both of these efforts at
rationalization came to grief. They were denounced as un-
English, inquisitorial and despotic because they seemed to
undermine the independence and the standing of the country
gentlemen – not to add, the livelihood of many lawyers. The
first of Brougham's proposals was supposed to menace, in the
long run, landed wealth. The second was regarded as a threat
to the unpaid jurisdiction of the justices of the peace.

It is remarkable how the institution of the non-stipendiary
magistracy (which also of course expressed landed power)
weathered the storm of the 1830s. The JPs were, of course,
losing administrative and financial power on various points. To
some extent the poor law of 1834 robbed them of both and the
modernization of government had, overall, the same general
effect. The new race of permanent officials to regulate factories
and prisons worked largely outside their control. Nevertheless
amateur government lingered on. Some of the new legislation
was originally left to them to enforce; more of it enlarged their
judicial sphere. For example the first passenger act, passed in
1803, required the attendance of a justice of the peace at the
muster of the passengers before a vessel might clear customs;

while that of 1842 placed the critical business of the licensing of passenger brokers in the justices' hands.[7] Within the fields with which we have been dealing directly, we might recall as instances that the attempt to deprive the justices of their partial control over highways failed, and that even the factory act of 1833 left them with a species of concurrent jurisdiction.[8] Moreover their cardinal function was untouched. They still supplied summary justice in the countryside, practically untouched by central interference or regulation.

Thus in this very important sphere no set of *a priori* legal principles or movement of legal reform made much headway in the 1830s, and as Russell observed in 1837,

the power of a Magistrate does not begin and end with sending a sheep-stealer to jail. The county purse is in a great degree under his control. ... The landed gentry are very respectable ... but they are certainly the class in this country most ignorant, prejudiced and narrow-minded of any.[9]

There was no rationalization here, no imposed uniformity of procedure, no paid and professional legal officers to deal with petty offences – except in London, where stipendiary magistrates had long been established, and in a handful of innovative or imitative provincial cities. For this failure it was ironically the popular wing of the radicals, the democrats, who were primarily responsible. They felt that they could not apply their sacred elective principle to a judiciary for obvious reasons; and they were equally opposed to state-appointed professionals because they feared that such an increase in state power would undermine individual, local and civil liberty. Hence the paradox that they were driven to support a generally tory and undemocratic institution. It is true that the institution (as a judicial body) was not quite unchanged. The new whig appointments in the town, occasioned by the 'democratizing' of town government, did introduce new attitudes, for better or worse, amongst the justices of the peace of many urban areas. But as an institution the magistracy survived the crisis of the 1830s. It was only in Ireland that the ideal of professional local justice was substantially secured; and there the first, although by no means the only or final, purpose of the stipendiary magistrates was to provide a more fearless and thorough repression.

The second wave of legal reform in this period (beginning in Peel's second administration of 1841–6, though still at that time largely directed by Brougham) at once presented a more serious challenge to the JPs and advanced significantly the cause of professional, uniform and centralized justice. Brougham's county courts act in 1846,[10] much on the lines of his local court bill of 1830, established local courts in each poor law union with jurisdiction in small debt and personal injury cases. The judges for these courts were to be barristers with at least seven years' experience, appointed (and removable) by the lord chancellor. The success of these courts was demonstrated by the fact that they heard an average of over 400,000 cases annually in the first five years of their existence. As with the poor law guardians in the field of local government, the role of the new courts was rapidly and regularly extended. Again, however, these changes were supplementary and modificatory rather than radical. The amateur magistracy was neither superseded nor emasculated. It was to last long enough and to remain sufficiently large and powerful to form an important constituent of the reconstituted English legal system of the present century.

The common law courts and chancery were also subjected to more thorough scrutiny in the mid-century than in the 1830s. A commission to inquire into the common law which sat throughout the 1850s, in fact to 1860, resulted in three pieces of legislation which produced significant changes in procedure, rules of evidence and jurisdiction. In some respects, they foreshadowed the judicature legislation of the 1870s. The court of chancery's procedures were similarly reformed, while the process started by Brougham of replacing official fees by salaries and of providing adequate staff to reduce delays was continued. The overall effect of these reforms was to diminish the obscurity and irrationality of the English legal system. But, in E. L. Woodward's mild words, it 'was still very far from an ideal code in which rights and remedies were clearly stated and simple processes ... could be carried out easily and cheaply'.[11] Battles had been won but not a war. Humanitarian reform had some trophies to show and rational reform still more. But the basic structures and pre-suppositions were little altered.

In early Victorian England the reform of police and public order was not absolutely distinguished from legal reform but rather regarded as its complement. The police systems obtaining in the first quarter of the nineteenth century were, broadly speaking, three-fold: the first depended on the parish, the second on the self-help or the self-interest of private individuals or businesses and the third on the agencies of local government in the towns. The first was a very ancient survival. In theory the parish constables were ordinary citizens appointed by the justices of the peace and serving their annual terms of office in turn. In practice they were quasi-professional (in the sense of semi-permanent), specific individuals paid as substitutes by those upon whom the office had temporarily fallen. It was generally, though not exclusively, in the towns that the second form, that springing from self-help and self-interest, operated. For this the reason was obvious. In a relatively static society it was only in the towns, with their aggregations of and changes in population, that crime normally demanded more than the parochial system. The towns developed a number of protective devices. One set consisted of the payment of watchmen or private companies of quasi-policemen by philanthropic individuals or groups, or more usually, by insurance companies or great trading interests such as that of the West India merchants. The third system derived from the corporations, vestries or improvement commissions which employed individuals or bodies of individuals for police purposes. London was naturally the pioneer in this last activity both because it vastly surpassed all other towns in population and property and because it was the seat of political power. But even so the very variety and multiplicity of unco-ordinated police organizations in the metropolis rendered them inefficient.

That this extraordinary chaos and want of direction survived so long is to be explained in part by the fact that, apart from London, cities were still relatively small, and modern urbanization only beginning to get under way; and in part by the very general prejudice, shared by rich and poor alike, against police action. Policing upon any considerable scale was glibly identified with Napoleonic or Bourbon despotism and presumed to be incompatible with British liberty. The *Annual Register* spoke for many when in 1822 it denounced large centrally controlled police forces as 'a species of *gens d'armerie* hitherto unknown to the laws or practice of a British parliament'.[12] Moreover professionalism in the field of public order was looked upon as a double threat to the ordinary justices of the peace. On the one hand it was generally supposed that the stipendiary magistrate, who was at this stage regarded as the normal accompaniment of the 'new' police, would inevitably supersede or dominate his unpaid fellows. On the other hand the JPs greatly valued the humble patronage of appointing or influencing the appointment of constables, and this would probably be lost in addition to their pride of station.

Yet the 1820s, when this resistance was hardening, were also marked by rising social alarm and more elaborate devices for social suppression, especially in London itself. The dangers of mob violence had been brought home to the government by working class agitation after Waterloo and by the Queen Caroline riots. But over and above the terror of popular revolution (with crowd perturbance standing for the first stage in a 1789-like sequence), there were ceaseless, nagging fears that the accepted order generally was disintegrating. These fears explain such legislation as the malicious trespass acts of 1820 and 1827, and the vagrancy act of 1824.[13] When statutes rendered such things as gaming in public places or damage to fruit and vegetables in gardens criminal offences, and when such indeterminate categories of people as the 'idle and disorderly' or 'reputed thieves' were subjected to possible imprisonment without any specific offence having been committed, the established classes were signalling their alarm and attempting to press people back into traditional moulds.

Although greater dangers to public order were more apparent in 1831–2 than at any time in the 1820s, the decisive step had been taken two years before 1830. In 1828 Peel, still not too far distanced from his experience of strong measures as Irish secretary, headed a select committee which investigated the metropolitan problem.[14] The committee's recommendations formed the basis for new legislation, in particular for Peel's metropolitan police act,[15] passed during the following session.

The metropolitan police act set up a central police department for London, to be directed by two commissioners and an assistant commissioner, subject to the control of the home office. The projected new force resembled closely the Irish peace preservation corps, which had been set up in 1814 during Peel's regime in Ireland and which later formed the model for both the Dublin metropolitan police and the Irish constabulary. Thus the London reform was probably much more a product of Irish experience than of police theorists such as Patrick Colquhoun or penal philosophers such as Bentham. The common factors in the Irish and English developments were, of course, Peel and his characteristic mode of administrative diagnosis. In Ireland he found the critical deficiencies to be an intimidated magistracy; ignorance and partisanship in the yeomanry and the existing baronial police; and 'over-kill' when, as often happened, the army was called in or the militia embodied. The answers were *seriatim* a professional magistracy; a professional, trained, numerous, specialized and centralized police force; and the abandonment, so far as practicable, of the use of the army or militia for peace enforcement.[16] When Peel went to the home office he found that the nine London police offices were ill-co-ordinated; that their police forces were ill-disciplined, ill-trained, tiny in number even when added together, and often corrupt; and that the directing magistrates concentrated their efforts upon capturing criminals and recovering stolen property rather than preventing crime, which appeared to be rapidly increasing. The one favourable circumstance was that all the forces were ultimately responsible to the home office: the door was open already for centralization.[17] Peel's answers, which were to a remarkable degree simply incorporated in the 1829 act (he was fortunate that the final political crisis of catholic emancipation coincided with its passage through parliament), were essentially the same as those which had been thrown up already in Ireland. The commissioners, who were also spoken of as stipendiary magistrates, were to be, respectively, 'a practical and efficient lawyer ... a soldier accustomed to discipline and capable of enforcing it ... [and] a man with legal training and business experience'.[18] Above them stood the home secretary; below, a corps of up to 3,000 men arranged in military hierarchy, specially recruited and trained for police work, uniform in conditions and subject ultimately to a single, central control and direction. In scale, structure, purpose and arrangements they were a repetition of the peace preservation corps, except for being unarmed and confined geographically to a particular place, and enjoying a more diversified and sophisticated pattern of immediate management.

The metropolitan police act of 1829 is not attributable, in any meaningful sense or measurable degree, to administrative Benthamism. Nonetheless the new statute generally conformed, in both scope and geographical definition, to the Benthamite ideas of central control and of a paid professional service. But Benthamism, at any rate as interpreted by Chadwick (who had worked on the same problem in 1829), was more positive and comprehensive in approach. For Chadwick, the police force was to be the executive arm which would enforce the artificial identification of private interests by the state, and the fundamental aim of policing should be not so much the punishment of crime as its eradication, and the forestalling of criminals. The primary purpose should be to strike at the causes of crime; only secondarily should the police be concerned with striking at the criminals themselves.[19] Chadwick's proposals formed an extraordinary amalgam of (in terms of the 1830s) progressive criminology and antique despotism – or, some might say, anticipated the 'innocent fascism' of many of the social reformers of the early twentieth century. On the one hand he proposed an attack upon the 'collateral causes' of crime: slum life, juvenile delinquency, want of religious and moral training, bad example and vagrancy. On the other he proposed a police regime so oppressive and omnicompetent as to aim at making crime impossible. 'Crime prevention' itself wore a double face. If it seemed to have 'humane' and 'progressive' objects on the one hand, it was also prospectively repressive upon the other. (Even the metropolitan police act of 1829 had extended police powers of arrest so widely as to include such 'offences' as attendance at an unlicensed theatre or flying kites in public places). Moreover the crudest of whig versions of English history was then rampant, and 'tyranny' correspondingly rebuked. When for example Chadwick interviewed a poor law physician and published an account of the meeting furnished by his own 'short-hand reporter', the *Lancet* called for the 'contemptuous rejection' of what had been 'obtained and published *under the sanction of A SPY*', and resistance to

> the insidious and blood-thirsty attacks of individuals whose character and practices bear a close resemblance to those of the OLIVERS and the CASTLES of a period of no remote date in the history of human delinquency and false-heartedness.[20]

Chadwick had had, of course, no influence upon Peel's act of 1829, but he engineered an opportunity for himself to intervene in 1836 when he persuaded Russell, then home secretary, to institute the familiar preparatory royal commission[21] with himself as chairman and Charles Rowan for colleague. Rowan was an Irishman, a peninsular veteran and currently commissioner of the metropolitan police. Between the three, he was very likely to have been *au fait* with all the innovations in policing in the United Kingdom over the preceding quarter of a century.

Chadwick had certain assets in beginning this fresh campaign. The metropolitan police act was generally supposed to have driven criminals increasingly away from London and into the provincial towns. Where these in their turn increased the efficiency of their own police services, the professional criminals tended to move to the smaller towns and even into the countryside. All this was, at any rate, widely believed in the 1830s, though it is difficult to say how well grounded the belief really was, since it was in the interest of the 'reformists' to extend it. Secondly industrial cities were growing prodigiously in the 1830s: a considerable number were now as large as only London had been a century before. Thirdly the new gigantic working class agitations were frightening almost all men of substance and property: there seemed an obvious danger that they might get out of hand and even turn to revolution in the absence of any civil force capable of maintaining public order. Fourthly the precedent of the metropolitan police was encouraging, so much so in fact that the municipal reform act of 1835 had empowered the corporate towns to imitate it if they so wished. Not only had the new system worked quite well in London, but the recent practice of sending groups of metropolitan police to reinforce temporarily and teach local constabularies elsewhere had accustomed several parts of the country to the ideas which it embodied.

On the other hand Chadwick was by now notorious, regarded with much justification as the personification of a new tyranny. Anything emanating from him was widely suspected of being autocratic and hostile to traditional liberty. Next there was the powerful vested interest of the justices of the peace, who would not readily forego any of their privileges within this field. Finally the working class and most other popular leaders believed from the start that Chadwick's immediate object was to secure an efficient instrument for enforcing the adoption of the new poor law, and recognized, more generally, that any forces which he designed would tend to serve the middle class aims of a free economy and security for property. By the time that the commission reported, 1839, working class opposition was a very formidable consideration. The anti-poor law agitation was at its height, trade depressed and the whig ministry in a perilous and nerveless condition.

In these circumstances Chadwick and Rowan prepared the report with the utmost care. They threw overboard, as impossible to carry, the ambitious project for attacking the collateral causes of crime and the elaborate mechanisms for forestalling and preventing crime which they had been devising. Instead they concentrated upon widening the scope of police duties and instituting a centralized, trained and professional force. While we do not know certainly, it seems quite likely that this meant that what was peculiarly Chadwick's work was shelved, while that to which Rowan contributed most came into prominence. Rowan would have known intimately not merely the London force, but also Drummond's recent Irish reforms which carried forward the ideas of organization which that embodied, and he may very well have been closely acquainted with the new Irish inspectors-general.[22]

In any case, the report prepared the way by the usual attempt to manipulate and stampede public opinion: here perhaps Chadwick's hand may be confidently detected. It first allowed that many would regard the proposals as inimical to liberty, and then argued that so far from destroying liberty, an effective police force was a *sine qua non* for its realization. This argument, commonplace now, was then comparatively novel and correspondingly potent. Next the report painted a very lurid picture of current crime, emphasizing repeatedly that the problem was a new one, arising from the very recent dispersal of criminals all through the countryside. Obviously it was hoped that the JPs and the smaller boroughs would be frightened into acquiescence by the supposed development. All this led up to the proposal that the metropolitan police system be adopted everywhere. Further, the new system should be, as far as possible, national and centralized. This followed the pattern of the Irish police reforms of 1836, whereby all forces in the country were reduced to three divisions, metropolitan, national and revenue, which were moreover tightly interknit. The report also argued that to diminish inefficiency and corruption the constabulary should be constantly translated from place to place. Once more this followed closely Irish reforms, although of an earlier period. Further, it was claimed that the necessary uniformity of discipline and policy would be impossible to secure without centralization. Again this repeated Irish arguments, preceding actual changes which had been effected in the 1820s.[23] Finally the new type of force, Chadwick and Rowan wrote, would be competent to take on novel and very desirable functions such as the preservation of public order, the regulation of traffic, the suppression of vagrancy and the management of crowds during fires, accidents and political meetings.

The difficulty in carrying the report into legislative effect was the opposition to be expected from the three major forces opposed to centralization, the JPs, the democratic radicals and the towns. With the first a compromise was suggested. The magistrates were to be given the right to set up a constabulary in their county area (note the administrative unit, a further attempted compromise) by calling in a body of metropolitan policemen to train up a force of their own. They should also retain the right to dismiss constables in their areas. On the other hand the discipline, training and even the distribution and transfers of the new policemen were to belong to a central authority in London. It may be significant that the 'compromise' was practically identical with that made in Ireland in 1822 when the county constabularies were established as a halfway house to the Irish constabulary of fourteen years later. But no concessions were made to radical opinion or to the towns, which last were to sink their identity in their respective counties.

But the new bill along these lines came before parliament at an inopportune time. Not only was serious working class discontent and agitation rife, but also a protracted cabinet crisis was currently paralysing the whig government. In the event the combined opposition of the JPs, the radicals and the boroughs carried the day. The local, traditional and democratic forces overcame the forces of centralization and efficiency. The act[24] in its final form was permissive, not compulsory, and it exempted the boroughs completely from its operation. Outside the towns the courts of quarter session had the discretion of raising a force for their county by appointing a chief constable who would then institute his own constabulary. The county was to be self-governing in the matter, paying for its own police out of its own pocket. There was to be no general or national board of control. The only concession to centralization was that the home secretary might ensure some degree of uniformity by drawing up a common scale of pay and rules of discipline. One interesting aspect of the county police act of 1839 is that we see once again the forces of democratic radicalism and the upholders of 'no local taxation without representation' fighting a battle (however unwittingly) for – or at least ranging themselves beside – the aristocratic and squirearchical country justices. The net result of the 1839 act was to leave the boroughs as they were and to increase rather than decrease the police powers of the local magistrates, with whom all initiative now resided. Meanwhile a second act of 1839[25] reorganized the London police system and made it still more effective and still further ahead of that in other areas.

The main statute had at least made possible the organization of a reasonable county police in rural areas. But this was by no means the same as bringing it about. From one reason or another, either from inertia, fears for liberty or reluctance to increase the rates, the justices of the peace in most counties refused to take advantage of the act. Even as late as 1853 only twenty-two out of the fifty-two counties had adopted the statute, although a few other counties had employed it for particular places within their jurisdiction; and as late as 1857 there were thirteen corporate towns which had still not acted upon their police powers under the municipal corporations act of 1835. For the benefit of the more conservative counties an attempt had been made in 1842 to revivify the archaic system of parish constables, but this was a hopeless undertaking.[26] Finally in 1856, as a consequence of an inquiry which had revealed the evils of having moderately effective county systems side by side with partial county systems or none at all and the folly of not co-ordinating the various constabularies, the county and borough police act,[27] commonly known as 'the obligatory act', was passed. This made the setting up of borough and county constabularies compulsory, and thus for the first time every part of England and Wales was to be provided with a stipendiary and professional police. Further the act insisted on co-ordination and gave the home office increased powers of discipline over local forces as well as the right to set up a central inspectorate to see that its edicts were enforced.

Thus to a considerable degree was Chadwick's administrative method eventually vindicated – although, as we have seen from this field, he had by no means exclusive or proprietary rights in it. We must not allow ourselves to be over-prejudiced by his unscrupulous behaviour as a royal commissioner, by his immediate desire to crush working class resistance to the factory system and his own despotic poor law legislation, or by his failure to see or care for the dangers to liberty involved in his ultimate plan for a preventive, forestalling and inquisitorial police based on what he conceived to be the French and Prussian models. His leading concepts of centralization, professionalism, expert training and a powerful inspectorate, which form the hard core of all his social planning, were the right ones to secure the sort of government demanded by the new, vast, complex, urbanized and mobile society. His grasp of the importance of getting beneath the surface of a problem, of searching through patient and informed inquiry into the fundamental causes of poverty or crime, is very striking in the context of his time. Granted that he never worked out fully these ideas; granted that his own investigations were usually neither impartial nor exhaustive; granted (as again the field of public order demonstrates) that others adopted the same approaches, if only from simple clarity of mind and purpose – and all the more effectually perhaps because no abstractions were blazoned on their banners – granted, too, that 'there was,' as *Blackwood's* put it in 1859, 'an autocratism about him which the people of this country will bear neither from rank nor wealth, and which they showed in his case that they will not bear from talent';[28] nonetheless Chadwick was laying down, well ahead, many lines of future exploration. He was the towering specifier and generalizer of his administrative age. Finally his prophecies of the evil consequences of leaving the police forces under the independent control of amateur local government, whether that elected by ratepayers or that furnished by justices of the peace, were completely upheld by the findings of the inquiry which preceded the 'obligatory act' of 1856. Conversely we should note that the local framework was not entirely destroyed in England. There was to be no national police force moved constantly from place to place as was already the case in Ireland, once more the home of a purer form of national administration and order – not to add coercion. Here is yet another example of the importance of the survival of older forms of government for long enough to be embodied in a modern system.

This completes our survey of the reforms of the 1830s: other fields, of which there are many, lie outside the main line of development which I am trying to trace. It will be clear at once that these reforms were generally the work of the democratic principle, or of the class interest of new and rising groups struggling to establish or aggrandize themselves within society. As we saw, the reformers by no means fully achieved their objects. Occasionally, in fact, their efforts resulted in the strengthening of aristocratic powers and institutions. But whether they succeeded or failed, they did not aim at producing any form of administrative revolution; if thoughts of such a kind had entered their heads at all, the Reformation, with its restoration of pristine purity, simplicity and earnestness, would have seemed a more pleasing analogy. Incidentally they may, sometimes and in the long run, have facilitated development of modern government by the reduction of the number of clogging, archaic institutions, for example, or by their stimulus to the two-party system, or by their desire to reduce public spending (the latter being a two-edged sword, however). But to the main pillars of the early and mid-twentieth-century state, the collectivist and the centralizing ideas, they were fundamentally opposed. Self-help, freedom from restraint, universal suffrage and tight democratic control over elected bodies – these were the formulae to which they were committed. In a vague way it was assumed that radical political devices would automatically resolve all problems of rule and management. Correspondingly the new type of bureaucracy was misconceived. The democratic radicals commonly regarded it as a retreat into the old type of privileged, authoritarian and parasitic state which would deprive them of the control over local matters and the freedom for private enterprise, so recently and so hardly won, by restoring the eighteenth-century system of government-through-venality and -nepotism. They failed to see that what was being proposed (even if the proposers were often disingenuous) was something novel: a permanent and expert public service divorced from party politics and from special interests alike.

TEN

Ireland

It is not only fair, it is probably necessary to include Ireland in even a general survey of early Victorian government. Britain and Ireland (and more particularly for our present purposes, England and Wales and Ireland) constituted a single kingdom with the same law-making agency and a common pool of political and professional administrators at the highest level. The force of example and precedent constantly worked below the surface; and even overhead the Irish apprenticeship of so many British statesmen, from Peel and Stanley at one end of the century to Campbell-Bannerman and Balfour at the other, enlarged the administrative horizons of the homeland. More important still if even more difficult to quantify was the slow corrosion of a basic presupposition of mid-Victorian Britain: that she herself represented a norm in government and economic organization to which other advanced states would gradually approximate. Over time the Irish experience revealed to British opinion how exceptional, curious and merely prescriptive so many of the systems obtaining in Great Britain really were. In part the process was one of self-revelation. Dr Stokes' observation about another dependency is equally pertinent to Ireland: 'British rule in India was not a disconnected fragment of English history but even from the most insular standpoint it holds a mirror up to nature, reflecting the English mind and character in a way that often escapes the Englishman confined in his domestic setting.'[1]

It may be significant that Dr Stokes uses the terms 'England' and 'English' rather than 'Britain' and 'British' in speaking of Indian influences on and administrative traffic with the 'mother-country'. Certainly such a usage would have significance in the case of Ireland, as, formally, Irish law, administrative structures and procedures and local government were virtually replicas of England's. Unlike Scotland the indigenous systems in Ireland were obliterated and replaced there entirely by English models. Whereas after 1707 Scotland continued to be *sui generis* in many respects, Ireland was by then another England, legally and governmentally. It is for this reason that Irish developments are peculiarly relevant to our subject. Mechanically speaking, they were readily transferable to the parent system (and of course the converse was equally true); and where they were not so transferred, they raised challenging and penetrating questions. This was the case throughout the eighteenth century but it was much accentuated by the act of union of 1801 which swept all regions of the British Isles under a single parliamentary rule and apparently opened the door to single and uniform government.

In several ways the union had advanced administratively by the opening of our period. For example, 'of the twenty-two Irish departments existing at the time of the union, eighteen had disappeared either by abolition or absorption'[2] by 1835; and the armed forces, the revenue departments (in 1816), and the postal services (in 1831) of Great Britain and Ireland had been effectively amalgamated. The amalgamation of the two treasuries was probably the most significant of all the changes. Apart from an overall power of determining questions of public finance, this gave the British treasury direct rule over certain Irish departments, such as the reconstituted board of works. Moreover 'treasury control' from Whitehall extended to all branches of the Irish government, and it was applied quite rigorously from a comparatively early stage. This, imbued as it was with the current British orthodoxy on the proper limits of state action and state spending – indeed, applied with extraordinary vigour because of Ireland's reputation in Whitehall as a land of jobbery and extravagance – held back appropriate social and economic reform in Ireland, particularly after 1840. Thenceforward the emphasis was on eliminating corruption and 'waste' in, and if possible reducing absolutely, state expenditure, not on stimulating economic

growth or creating new employment. From his famine experiences in 1846-7, Trevelyan, who became critically important in this field when he was appointed assistant secretary
to the treasury in January 1840, was to learn something of
Irish needs: 'In England for the business of private society to
be done by private society is the rule, and for the government
to do that business is the exception. ... In Ireland for the
government to do this class of work is the rule.'³ But before
1845 Trevelyan and his acolytes at the treasury saw Ireland
in terms of the English norms. Even thereafter they still struggled to make English norms apply. Although they did not win
every battle with recalcitrant Irish circumstances, they won
many.

About 1830, as we have seen, a new sort of state activity
was being born in Great Britain. Central regulation of certain
aspects of economic and social organization through inspectorates quite suddenly got under way. In most cases this new
activity was based from the start upon the United Kingdom
as a single administrative unit. Ireland might have its own
inspector or inspectors, but only in the same way as Yorkshire
or East Anglia. Thus the factory and the mines inspectors and
the emigration officers, for example, were responsible directly
to the home office and colonial office respectively. Even in the
case of so vast and localized an undertaking as the Irish poor
law of 1838, it was down to 1847 ultimately managed by a
parent body in London with a member of the English board
acting as the resident Irish commissioner, and with four of
the first eight Irish poor law inspectors appointed from the English service. Again, this represented an advance (albeit in the
particular instance a short-lived one) for the administrative
union, and a further inroad upon Ireland's administrative
autonomy.

But it would be misleading to suggest that all the forces at
work in the 1830s and 1840s were working for governmental
uniformity within the United Kingdom or for Whitehall over-
lordship. On the contrary, it is doubtful whether, for all their
advances, they predominated over the forces of administrative
idiosyncrasy in Ireland. In the fields of education, economic
development, police, prisons and public health (to take but
leading examples) the state intervened in our period to a de-

gree and in a fashion scarcely conceivable in contemporary England. As Nassau Senior told de Tocqueville, 'Experiments are made in that country [Ireland] on so large a scale, and pushed to their extreme consequences with such a disregard to the sufferings which they inflict, that they give us results as precious as those of Majendie [the eminent contemporary physiologist].'⁴ 'Experiments' is probably a misleading term; improvisations would be closer to the truth. But certainly Senior's observations on the scale, immoderation and olympianism of the Irish administrative undertakings hit many nails on their heads. For centralized authoritarianism and national uniformity had long been characteristics of Irish government at all levels, including local.

Why? One reason was that the Irish ruling class was too few and too scattered to govern individually or in small groups as in England, and that Ireland was too poor for so small a unit as the parish to be administratively self-sufficient. Another was that the Irish ruling caste, alien in religion, language, interest and habit to the mass of their fellow-countrymen, bound themselves together on national rather than parish, county or even regional lines: their primary identification was with their own order spread thinly across the entire country, not with a particular place or neighbourhood. Hence necessity and natural inclination alike had throughout the eighteenth century predisposed them to centralized and common forms of government under the surveillance of or directed from and supported by Dublin, in a fashion altogether foreign to their English counterparts. Even by 1850, as we have seen, the English JPs and parishes had lost comparatively few functions to the central government; possibly on balance they had gained. In Ireland it was otherwise. By 1850 the local authorities had been shorn of very many of even their surviving powers and replaced by national and centralized organizations. Whereas the first stage in administrative reform in English local government represented an attempt to broaden electorates and break anglican and squirearchial monopolies, the equivalent phase in Ireland was marked by the passage of some of the old and almost all of the new functions of government from local to central control.

A third reason for the differentiation was that the Irish

G

system of local government was being 'democratized', even if to a still more limited degree than that of England and Wales, in the 1830s. Any step in this direction meant, over most of Ireland, an admission of catholics and nationalists to some share in power. Faced with this possibility, Irish protestants, who broadly speaking constituted the ruling class to this date, acquiesced in centralization. On the whole it seemed to them to offer better security for their material interests in much the same fashion as they had come to prefer the act of union to the dangers of active catholic participation in a domestic political system. The British governments of the 1830s and 1840s had corresponding reasons for working in the same direction. They saw each step towards democratization in Irish local government as also enlarging the arena for agitation and factional and sectarian conflict. The first they feared; the second they were already beginning to approach in the spirit of a district commissioner faced with tribalism. On both counts it seemed desirable to minimize self-government. To these considerations should of course be added the general poverty and disorder in Irish life and the consequent traditions of both state intervention and central regulation, and of government's almost automatic assumption of tutelary and manipulatory roles. The experience of the 1830s and 1840s did nothing to weaken such tendencies amongst those in power. These strains are well illustrated by much of the social and economic reform extended or initiated in our period. It is perhaps more illuminating to regard these reforms as contributions to the Irish polity and institutional framework rather than to Irish social and economic development as such. In the long run of course, the latter was deeply influenced by the changes. But in the middle quarters of the century the ills of Irish society and the economy alike were so deep and widespread that the meliorative measures undertaken scarcely counted one way or other.

A prime illustration of these generalizations was the new board of works set up in 1831.[5] It was innovatory in degree rather than kind. It was also more significant institutionally than materially during much of the nineteenth century. The new commission superseded a number of late eighteenth-century and early nineteenth-century bodies, including an earlier board of works. But its direct administrative forebear was a central loan fund for Irish public undertakings, charged upon the imperial revenue, which had been established in 1817. The advances from this fund were not confined to public buildings, roads and bridges; fisheries, mines and even communal re-settlement projects were beneficiaries. The new Irish foundation (or re-foundation) of 1831 presented an interesting contrast to the contemporaneous establishment of an English commission of public works. Though its grant was much larger, the English commission was charged only with organizing *ad hoc* relief projects to cope with current economic distress. Characteristically, however, the Irish board was intended to be permanent. Equally significant, its works were to be reproductive and part of a national plan. The Irish commissioners had, also, much more comprehensive powers; as Thomas Spring Rice, the leading Irish Whig of the day put it, 'their function was both deliberative and executive where the role of their English counterparts was deliberative only.'[6] This neatly captures the differences in the respective concepts of state activity and national need.

The new Irish board, with a national inspectorate of engineers (mainly drawn from that great pool of executive talent, the Royal Engineers), presents a remarkable instance of formal governmental growth in our period. At first its major work was in the field of road communications and port and harbour development, and here the inspectors were often directly involved in the construction with all the concomitant practical 'interventions' which this implied. But in the later 1830s their activities quickly extended to railway building and planning, inland navigation, coastal fisheries and land reclamation and drainage. The board itself supplied the majority of the members, and largely determined the conclusions of the successive commissions and committees which enquired into these various subjects of possible state interference. In the theoretical sense at least, its most striking 'success' was the report of the Irish railway commission of 1838. This issued in 1839 in a bill outlined to the house of commons by Morpeth which proposed to provide over £2.5 million from imperial funds for the construction by the board of works of the trunk lines of an Irish national railway system.[7] Permission to raise the money was granted, although the bill was eventually dropped by the government[8] with the upper house hostile and their own retention of power uncertain at that particular juncture. To have come even as close as this, however, to establishing a pattern of state built and managed railways in Ireland in the 1830s was an extraordinary achievement.

Concrete though more modest attainment in the other new fields was marked by the Shannon navigation act of 1839[9] and by the Irish fisheries and drainage acts of 1842.[10] The first ended the much – and long – divided responsibility for the Shannon river and its estuary and tributaries and placed all of them under the autocratic control of a new commission, which was in fact a creature of the board of works – one might almost say, the board wearing another hat. The whigs fell from office before the report of the fisheries commission could be translated into a statute and Peel approached state action in Ireland with the sourness and scepticism engraved on him by his earlier Irish experiences. Everyone in Ireland, he once wrote 'instead of setting about improvement as people elsewhere do, pester[s] government about boards and public aid. Why cannot people in Ireland fish without a board if fishing be, as Lord Glengall [the current applicant for support] declares it to be, so profitable?'[11] Nonetheless, the conservatives did carry through the earlier fisheries recommendations which gave the board of works considerable powers and responsiblity in the development and organization of both the river and the sea fishing industries.

The drainage act of 1842 was significant constitutionally as well as practically; for not only did it charge the board with, in some senses, the regulation of land use, but it also empowered it to levy compulsory charges on the 'beneficiaries' of drainage schemes, even if they had opposed them, provided that two-thirds of the landowners affected were in agreement with the board.

Apart from road construction, where its impact was immediate and powerful – 'even small portions of these roads were scarcely out of the engineers' hands before they were covered with the carts of small farmers', it was observed in 1838[12] – the board prepared for the future rather than altered the present during the pre-famine years in Ireland. It had spent just over £1 million in grants as well as loans by 1845. But this was trivial in terms of Irish need. Nonetheless, not merely was the board being geared, unwittingly, for the impending crisis of the great famine, when the arrangement and management of gigantic schemes of relief was thrust upon it, but it was also adumbrating a new form and philosophy of government – indeed, a revolutionary view of society.[13] The inspectorate, as was not uncommonly the case, tended to produce uniformity and coherence in administration and to initiate an unanticipated cycle of governmental expansion. Centralization and the needs of supervision meant some degree of planning, if only to establish priorities in expenditure. In time the corps developed its own expertise and the largeness of their task led them into some very distant fields. For example, they had virtually to determine the wage rates in areas – and there were many of these – where there was little or no cash employment outside the public works. This in turn forced them into the realm of wage policy and economic theorizing. Again, the railway commission was as much concerned with job-provision as with traffic, and the debate on drainage largely circled round the increase in land resources. The ideas that the building of an economic infra-structure was the state's responsibility, that a national economy needed to be continually primed and steered and that the critical decisions should come from experts and from above were all unfolding here.

A second example of the same phenomenon, of the very early development of collectivist structures in society, lay in public health and its associated fields. In public health Ireland may have been *formally* one of the most advanced of European countries during the second quarter of the nineteenth century. As early as 1805 provision had been made for Irish public dispensaries, half the cost of which was to be met by the local authorities.[14] In theory the dispensaries furnished free medicine and free medical attention to the sick poor. They spread rapidly: by 1845 over 650 had been established. The quality and effectiveness of this facility may have been, probably was, very bad; and since each foundation depended on local initiative, their distribution was haphazard. They sometimes originated in a desire merely to supplement a physician's income or to secure his residence. But at least an organization and a principle, which England was to lack for several decades, had been established; and both the network of dispensaries and the experience of conducting this sort of medical outdoor relief were necessary forerunners of the wholly public system set up in Ireland in 1851.

Moreover every Irish county and county borough inherited from the eighteenth century at least one infirmary and one fever hospital maintained largely by public funds; and by 1830 all appointments to these seventy-four institutions were being made by public authorities. Even the so-called private hospitals were semi-state establishments in Dublin, being supported by initial or recurrent grants from the central government. In our period, apart from the 'poor law' hospitals, another seven in Dublin continued to receive annual grants despite many efforts at Westminster to stop the payments upon the ground that no other hospitals in the entire British empire were state-supported. Again Ireland possessed throughout our years not only elaborate emergency organizations like the general board of health set up in the cholera epidemic of 1832, but a permanent board of health which had been constituted in 1820.[15] The permanent board was meant to provide the Irish government with information and advice upon public health, in particular upon epidemics and the institution of local boards, while also providing the local boards and local authorities with instructions and financial supervision. Thus, so far as Great Britain was concerned, not only the idea but even the institution of a co-ordinating, centralized authority in public health was anticipated here by, substantially, a generation.

One aspect of Irish medicine, the treatment of insanity, was marked by two very interesting developments, one of which culminated and one of which burgeoned in our period. The first was the grouping together of adjacent counties for the establishment of large regional mental hospitals. This was virtually complete by 1835. It represented a startling break with the conventional divisions of local government, and also marked the entry of quantitative 'rationalization' upon the administrative scene. The second innovation was a centralized, national system of control and inspection to ensure uniformity in the treatment of mental illness. The preparations for this development lay in the institution of a general board for the super-

vision of district asylums in 1817, and in the duty laid upon
the national inspectors of prisons in 1826 of inspecting all mental hospitals. In 1843 the board of works took over the supervisory tasks of the general board so far as building and similar
matters were concerned, while a year earlier a licensing system
for private asylums was set up to be administered by the prison
inspectors. In 1845 a special Irish lunacy inspectorate was
established, while a little later the state took the care of criminal lunatics entirely into its own hands. In all of this the contrast with English heterogeneity, localism and *laissez-faire* is
once more arresting.

These developments may also illustrate a more general
governmental tendency of the day, the occasional dichotomy
of formal and substantial progress, for it may well be that the
bureaucratization of the treatment of the insane in Ireland
worked against the patient's immediate interests.[16] Nonetheless
is it true that if one takes public policy and structures as the
criteria, Ireland had one of the most advanced health services
in Europe in the first half of the nineteenth century. It was to
a large degree state-supported, uniform and centralized. It
aimed, if waveringly, at providing the poor (which was in this
case the huge bulk of the population) with some measure of
security against illness. Its course was one of rationalizing
and specializing the hospital services: twenty-one of the thirty
Dublin hospitals in 1840, for example, concentrated on one
branch or other of medicine. It is of course impossible to gauge
the efficiency of this system, especially at so early a stage of
modern medical science; and however efficacious it cannot
possibly have sufficed to meet the ills of poverty in what was
mainly a subsistence economy. Nevertheless the very mechanics of the system and the ideas which, consciously or un-
consciously, it embodied were remarkably sophisticated. It
cannot have been altogether a coincidence that the years
1830–50 constituted a Golden Age of Irish medicine and medical discovery and research, the age of Colles, Graves, Corrigan
and Wilde.[17]

At first sight it might seem sinister that so much of the
lunacy administration came within the orbit of the prison
inspectorate, but such an impression would be misleading. The
early nineteenth-century government of Irish prisons was by

contemporary standards positive and humane – at any rate in declared intention and apparent endeavour. In addition the history of Irish prisons exhibited the now familiar pattern of rapid centralization and country-wide organization. A national inspector-general had been appointed as early as 1786 by the lord lieutenant;[18] and he set out (having virtually written his own terms of office) not only to improve the standards of decency and health in the forty-one county and county borough prisons throughout Ireland, but also to establish uniform regulations and procedures. The system was reorganized in the 1820s with two inspectors-general now charged with promoting the segregation of prisons both according to sex and according to which of five specified causes of incarceration had led to the prisoner being gaoled. The inspectors were also directed at this time to ensure that all prisoners were provided with a prescribed diet and prescribed furniture and bedding, and to report the misconduct of prison officers.

Thus by 1830 a characteristically hybrid and closely regulated system had developed in Ireland. The bulk of the costs of prisons and much of their day-to-day administration were local authority matters. But state intervention and control were steadily increasing. The declared general policy of the inspectors was to render the system as reformatory (as opposed to punitive) as practicable: hence their emphasis upon penitentiaries and the segregation of the classes of criminal. 'Prisoners', they wrote in one annual report, 'have not forfeited their claims on society.'[19] On returning to the world they would be better or worse men according to the use made of their imprisonment. In 1830, however, they complained that local magistrates and authorities generally were still deaf to such a penal philosophy.[20] This was in part presumably because the philosophy made high demands upon the local resources: penitentiaries and segregation demanded new and more expensive buildings and a more numerous staff. Still, prison reform progressed. Throughout 1830–60 more and more county prisons were either rebuilt or 'improved' to meet the new desiderata. Moreover there were areas of prison administration where the inspectors could innovate independently of the local authorities. In 1830, for example, the important step of withdrawing military guards from the Irish gaols was

taken; up till his death in 1837, the medical inspector of convicts (yet another state officer) worked with some success to
improve their health and abate the inhumanity of their treatment; in 1838 a national penitentiary for female convicts was
opened in Grangegorman; and in 1845 an act was passed en-
abling the lord lieutenant to build a central criminal lunatic
asylum.[21] Thus, here too state power and responsibility steadily
advanced.

As the ultimate linkages of public health and prison reform
indicate, it is not really easy to draw the apparently sharp
distinction between ostensibly ameliorative and ostensibly
coercive state machinery. Certainly police reform was complex
in both its administrative and political implications.[22] In 1830
Ireland had travelled, mainly in recent years, half the way
towards the establishment of modern centralized police forces.
The lord lieutenant already appointed two-thirds of the Dublin
police magistrates and nominated the chief magistrate, and
to that extent Dublin Castle indirectly controlled the metropolitan force of some 700. Outside the capital, the barony, and
not (as in England) the much smaller unit of the parish, was
the organizational base down to 1822. Thereafter the scale
was enlarged to county bodies. The baronial and county police
forces, over 7,000 strong, were recruited and, after recruitment,
maintained locally. But they were equipped from government
stores; and from 1825 on the lord lieutenant appointed inspectors-general who were to work towards common standards
of discipline and conduct over the entire country. The lord
lieutenant was also empowered from this date onwards to
move constables out of their own counties. The Irish revenue
police, who dealt with smuggling and illicit distillation, formed
a separate force. They were 'hired' by the various senior
revenue officers and commanded by army lieutenants commissioned as excisemen for the purpose. This curious administrative arrangement defies exact categorization: 'quasi-
official' and 'semi-central' are perhaps the least misleading
terms. Finally there was a second essentially national force,
the peace preservation corps, which had been established by
Peel in 1814. This was a mobile, para-military body, approxi-
mately a thousand in number, detachments of which might
be sent to any district proclaimed by the lord lieutenant. The

peace preservation corps (which formed, as we have seen, a substantial model for the later London metropolitan police) possessed a hierarchical military-like structure and was governed by stipendiary police magistrates with the powers of JPs.

Apart from the corps, the Irish police forces were poorly organized, badly paid, untrained and ill-educated. The revenue police were said to have been 'without discipline and without instruction of any kind', the majority of the Dublin bobbies to have been 'decrepit, worn-out old men',[23] and the baronial forces to have been mere partisans pandering to their selectors and masters, the local magistrates. 'They speak', wrote Thomas Drummond, the new Irish under-secretary, in 1835, 'of loyal inhabitants meaning thereby protestant inhabitants.'[24] For in Ireland administrative reform could rarely be disentangled altogether from power-sharing and the promotion of civil parity, and one important feature of the police and related reforms of 1835–6 is that they contributed more perhaps than any other single venture before the land acts of 1881–1903 to the diminution of protestant ascendancy. 'In 1833,' Lecky wrote, four years after catholic emancipation –

> there was not in Ireland a single Catholic judge or stipendiary magistrate. All the high sheriffs with one exception, the overwhelming majority of the unpaid magistrates and of the grand jurors, the five inspectors-general, and the thirty-two sub-inspectors of police, were Protestant.[25]

The centrepiece of the profound change in this regard, which took place in Ireland over 1835–41, was the constabulary legislation of 1836. Strangely enough, this constabulary reform had not ranked high on the repealers' programme, nor was it to prove another victim of the lords' powers of (substantially speaking) legislative veto. Rather it grew out from the new British strains (for Irish application) of administrative rationalization and supra-factional government.

Immediately and in detail, the reform was Drummond's work; and it is noteworthy that Drummond, like the men who actually carried out the Irish police reorganizations of the 1830s, Shaw Kennedy, Brereton and McGregor, was a

former army officer. The three policemen were in fact Peninsular veterans, as indeed Rowan of the London metropolitan
police had also been. The general political implications of the
1836 acts do not appear to have been appreciated by any
party of the day. The tory acquiescence (for although the bills
were delayed in the upper house, they were neither strenuously resisted nor materially amended) is perhaps explicable
in terms of police reform implying for many conservatives
merely more potent and efficient instruments of authority.
The repealers' lack of interest may be explained in much the
same fashion. Habit and experience might have led them
loosely to associate Irish constabularies of all kinds with
political repression. Moreover, where radical or liberal viewpoints co-existed with nationalistic, the usual prejudices against
'French' or 'Austrian' modes of social control would have
aggravated this sort of feeling. As for men like Morpeth and
Drummond, they would doubtless have assumed that the elimination, or balancing, of partisanship in any element of the
state machine was itself a non-partisan activity. Anyhow for
one reason or another the profound immediate political consequences of the police reforms were largely unforeseen.

The major measure of 1836 amalgamated the county and
peace preservation forces into a single centralized police responsible for order over the entire country, Dublin, Belfast
and Derry apart. A second measure produced the equivalent
reforms in a new Dublin constabulary and a third provided
for the reorganization of the revenue police on the same principles. The new forces together amounted to some 10,000
men, with the Irish constabulary (later the Royal Irish constabulary) accounting for nearly 80 per cent of the whole.
The essential novelties of the new police were their complete
centralization and co-ordination, their professionalism and
mobility, and their quasi-military organization and discipline.
To some extent these structures and features had been foreshadowed in the peace preservation corps, and the increasing
involvement of the Irish executive in the recruitment and
management of the county forces had represented a further
stage in the same development. However, the 1836 acts brought
all Irish police under an ultimately united command with an
autonomous national inspectorate to enforce, as the original

recommendation put it, 'one uniform system of rules and regulations for the entire Irish police establishment',[26] and with a single, large training depot in Dublin to serve the whole body. Thus Ireland came to possess a coherent, stratified, paramilitary police at a time when the lonely, untrained village constable was still the instrument of law enforcement over most of rural England.

Initially at least, police reform worked against the traditional ascendencies. The new forces were carefully selected, and comparatively well paid and drilled; and they acted with quite unprecedented impartiality: they were even 'popular', Drummond concluded in 1839.[27] They were supported in this drive towards state neutrality by a further extension, under the constabulary act of 1836, of the Irish stipendiary magistracy, which had always been relatively more numerous and influential than its English counterpart. The permanent professional magistrates were at this juncture markedly less partisan and ignorant legally than the ordinary JPs. The extension of their numbers and operations was a corollary of the new form of police action. The whig government further redressed the imbalance between the conflicting sections of Irish society by wholesale revisions of the ordinary magistracy (particularly in 1838), whereby more than one-third of the existing JPs were removed from the list. Most of those dismissed were Church of Ireland clergymen, squireens, absentees or land agents.

The police reforms of 1836 could, however, turn in a repressive as well as a conciliatory direction. They provided the Irish executive with an instrument of law – and policy – enforcement of rare efficiency in terms of the Europe of its day. It happened that initially it was state policy to treat the nationalist and popular movements with unwonted mildness, and their opposites with unwonted severity. But a full-scale liberal alliance was not, to say the least of it, a permanent condition in Anglo-Irish relations; and in different circumstances the power and omnipresence of the Irish constabulary wore a very different mien in the eyes of the populace. Moreover its mode of officer-recruitment, on a caste basis like that of the armed services, led as it was bound to lead in time to a considerable measure of identification between the bias of the police and the interests of the gentry. Nonetheless, it would be quite wrong to regard the Irish constabulary simply as the oppressive engine of a police state *à la* Metternich, or to suppose that it ever degenerated into either the gross partisanship or the disarray which had characterized the early nineteenth century.

Moreover its work and significance were by no means exclusively political. Possibly the most important consequence of the police reforms was the provision of a modern underpinning for nineteenth-century Irish society. Agricultural data was collected as well as political information. Local censuses were managed as well as the registration of fire-arms. It was not only political violence which was repressed : faction fighting and a host of other contemporary manifestations of brutality were slowly worn down. A vast range of day-to-day duties, such as enforcing the current regulations on slaughterhouses or weights and measures or poison schedules, imperceptibly established a new and more sophisticated and responsible form of social organization. Not least remarkable, as with so many of the administrative improvisations of our period, was the speed and thoroughness with which a highly articulated and nationally extensive system was set up. Here, as in several of the other areas, much must be attributed to the extraordinary number of military and naval officers whose administrative abilities had emerged in the forcing house of the Napoleonic campaigns, but who, in the 1820s and 1830s, could be called on to use their organizational skills in creating a novel form of civilized order.

Institutional change faltered and even fell back, however, whenever self-government was involved. If Irish police reform was perhaps the most striking success, Irish municipal reform was perhaps the most striking failure of the liberal-Irish alliance of the 1830s. The civic government of Ireland in 1830 was at once scandalous and damaging to whig, liberal and catholic interests alike. The sixty-odd corporations which had survived in Ireland were aggressively and almost exclusively protestant and Tory in attitude, inefficient and corrupt in the comparatively rare cases where they possessed enough resources to make corruption worthwhile. They ensured a dozen tory seats before 1832 and bloated tory influence in the other parliamentary boroughs. Most were small self-perpetuating oligarchies, 'in many instances of no service to the community; in others injurious; in all, insufficient', to quote the hostile report of the commissioners of inquiry of 1835.[28] Yet in addition to their influence over parliamentary representation, the Irish corporations also dispensed patronage, mercantile and other privileges, and local justice upon a large scale and a sectarian basis. They represented an area in which catholic emancipation and the substitution of a liberal for a conservative government had proved totally ineffectual in producing change in the early 1830s. They seemed an obvious and easy target for assault by the liberals and repealers.

Things turned out differently. In the years 1830–5 O'Connell was generally concerned to achieve power-sharing in the corporations rather than to change them structurally, or to modernize them as instruments of local government: at one stage, indeed, he tried to bargain with the Irish tories on dividing the political and other spoils involved.[29] The whig government on the other hand, was committed to rendering the corporations more representative and more 'efficient' (often a euphemism for cheaper). But they were driven to such an approach by radical prodding rather than natural inclination, and they saw little advantage at this juncture in substituting an O'Connellite for a tory monopoly – for this they saw as the net effect of democratizing the municipal franchise – in the majority of Irish cities and towns.

With these cross-purposes and much double shuffling, the matter never really came to an issue before 1835. In that year, however, the situation changed in two important respects. Firstly the English municipal reform act was passed and there was now a model for the Irish to aspire to. Secondly it was part of O'Connell's new compact with the whigs that they should introduce an Irish municipal reform bill along the lines of the English measure. The English model appealed particularly to O'Connell. With a £5 household franchise as its centrepiece, it was essentially political in character, aimed at destroying anglican and conservative power bases. This was precisely what he himself wished to do at home. Moreover it was now possible for him to argue the Irish case for reform on the favourable ground of parity within the United Kingdom. With his usual optimism he looked forward at once, when an

Irish bill substantially along the English lines was introduced in July 1835, to nationalist majorities and catholic and liberal office-holding in most municipalities, and to each Irish corporation serving as 'a Normal school for teaching the science of peaceful political agitation'.[30]

But the conservatives countered the bill, not only by their now-normal practice of voting the whigs' Irish measures down in the house of lords, but also by producing the alternative 'reform' of simply abolishing all Irish corporations and substituting for them the much more limited and humble boards of commissioners, available under an act of 1828 to provide for urban 'lighting, cleansing and watching'.[31] The conservative counter-proposal was defeated on several occasions in the later 1830s in the house of commons, but it lent respectability to the lords' resistance and provided the tories with something to bargain with over and above their phalanx of diehard peers. Four sessions were to pass before a bill was finally enacted, after successive emasculations.[32] Overall the Irish municipal reform act of 1840 represented a victory for the house of lords. Only ten Irish corporations survived and even these had their judicial, financial and administrative functions much reduced. A £10 householder franchise and high property qualifications for election were meant to ensure an upper and middle class combination.

The struggle and the result showed again the supremacy of politics over efficacy in local government reform, with Irish circumstances inducing British ministries both to leave much less power in the localities and to render the local franchise much more exclusive than in England. Irish protestants faced with sharing power with catholics, with their share probably diminishing in time and with factional struggles likely to develop in the representative institutions, acquiesced in the centralization and the loss of self-government. On the other hand the episode also showed that the popular pressures could not be altogether held back. The gains here were very disappointing. But in terms of O'Connell's objects, gains there were. Most of the surviving corporations were nationalist, and much of the corporations' activity was political even in a narrow party sense. But the negative gains seemed almost as important: an 'orange' monopoly had been broken, and even if much of the old 'orange' power went not to nationalists but to central government, it nonetheless diminished the redoubts of the ascendancy. Perhaps, after all, it was the sharing rather than the power which was being sought throughout.

In terms of our interests, however, the most striking single feature of the municipal debate was perhaps the general silence upon the substance of civic government. Sanitation, arterial drainage, housing, roads, gas lighting and similar affairs critical to the comfort and even tolerability of urban life were practically ignored. Yet these were the subjects of rapid change in both theory and practice, of challenge and conflict, elsewhere in Europe throughout 1835–60. Here, certainly, in Ireland, politicization was the enemy not only of reform but even of reality. People dwell, wash, walk, play, live noisomely or not, live in light or dark, die young or old, as well as struggle for vicarious power or snatch at tokens. The daily banalities did not enter much into the Irish administrative polemics of our period. Fortunately, though to no one's credit in particular apart from a handful of Drummonds, Burgoynes and subordinate inspectors, they found some lodgment in various of the institutional innovations.

Thus three of the four examples chosen for a consideration of Irish government – public works, public health and public order – show clearly its inherent tendency towards centralization, rationality, autocracy and expert rule; and these, innocent of theory, had their roots deep in humdrum eighteenth-century administrative practice and were continuously impelled further forwards by diverse Irish necessities. The fourth example, local government, illustrates other sorts of Irish idiosyncrasy, if we assume England to be the norm: first that the surrender or loss of local power to central government carried with it a parallel surrender of local initiative, especially in fields of social reform; and secondly that even with social reforms, the criteria for judgment of the surrounding populace tended to be factional and denominational rather than substantive. The question of precedents apart, it is far from a simple matter of awarding palms, but rather one of discerning and counting implications.

ELEVEN

The civil service

The last major field of reform or attempted reform within the years 1830–70 was the civil service itself. Curiously though not surprisingly, radical reform after 1840 was directed at changing central government rather than local. We have seen already what a stumbling block to effective change the old concept of central administration, and the old relationship of central administration to politics, formed in the two decades before 1850. Fear for further patronage, extravagance and incompetence was one of the stock, and perhaps the most influential of the objections to increased state action. Fear of patronage also drove men like Chadwick and his fellow-bureaucrats to fatal demands for 'independent status' for the new departments of administration. The failure to recognize thoroughly the growing divorce between party politics, which ebbed and flowed, and a professional public service, which was permanent and conducted a continuous state policy, was at the bottom of the many defeats and partial defeats inflicted upon incipient collectivism and centralization during the 1830s and 1840s. Up to a point the attempt to modernize government before eradicating the remnants of the eighteenth-century civil service was putting the cart before the horse.

The eighteenth-century form of politics which depended on patronage to secure day-to-day majorities in the house of commons was in ruins by the 1820s. But it is a mistake to suppose that Burke's economical reform marked even the beginning of the end of the *ancien régime* in administration. It is true that the evils of the nineteenth century did not take the same form as the evils of the eighteenth. The old type of sinecure, the open sale of offices, the inheritance of offices and the making of profit from office were all disappearing or had disappeared. 'A placeman is in these days an odious animal,' Charles Greville wrote plaintively in 1830, 'and as a double placeman I am doubly odious.'[1] But the root cause of these abuses – the recruitment of the civil service through political patronage – still remained. The peculiar direction which this took in the early nineteenth century was the systematization of patronage for all the lower branches of the civil service, and the vesting of patronage in the private member whose constituency was concerned, rather than government as such. By the closing years of the Napoleonic wars the ministerial whips were already complaining of these tendencies. In 1823 Lord John Russell observed that customs and post and stamp office patronage had become highly systematized and almost automatic: the treasury had taken to writing directly to the local member for his nomination. Six years later Wellington deplored the fact that the government was steadily losing control of patronage to the private member, even where that member belonged to the opposition party.[2] This development was probably a consequence of the new type of politics which tended to be based upon legislative policies and programmes rather than the fruits of office. Ironically it was accompanied by, and ultimately linked with an opposite trend in legislation itself, whereby the private member was rapidly losing ground to the government as the proposer of measures.

But though after 1832 a government could no longer buy support or base its existence upon bought support, the system of civil service recruitment originally designed to serve this end remained to serve others; namely, provision for the families, friends and clients of ministers and private members (still a highly intermarried and interconnected class); the satisfaction of MPs' sense of power; and their capacity to exercise cheap benevolence. It also nurtured the buccaneering type of member, especially of borough member who used his influence to build up support for himself in contradistinction to whichever party he might at the moment patronize. There were early Victorian Horatio Bottomleys, even 'born gentlemen' swashbucklers like Nathaniel Sowerby in *Framley Parsonage*. Thus patronage had tended to box the compass in its political effects. It now bolstered aristocratic influence and connection rather than ministries, and personal rather than party politics. It was a prop for social privilege and a clog upon the emergent independent electorate and opinion. As Trevelyan, the permanent secretary of the treasury, expressed these points in letters to Delane (the editor of *The Times*) and Gladstone, respectively: 'our high Aristocracy has been accustomed to employ the Civil Establishment as a means of providing for the Waifs and Strays of their Families';[3] and, 'The Government Patronage is habitually employed in influencing, or according to a stricter morality, corrupting Representatives and Electors at the expense both of their independence and of the public interest.'[4]

What of the public service thus recruited? Trevelyan produced a terrible indictment in 1849 which was confirmed and repeated in his and Northcote's report on the civil service of 1853. He found that 'admission into the civil service is indeed eagerly sought after, but it is for the unambitious and the indolent or incapable that it is chiefly desired'.[5] It was the last refuge, not of the scoundrels exactly, but of those who had failed in all other professions, who were delicate in health or undistinguished in intellect yet sufficiently fortunate as to have a string which could be pulled on their behalf. There was no examination whatever for some departments; for the rest, the examination was the merest formality. Just how farcical it might be may be gauged from Trollope's account of his own recruitment by the post office in his *Autobiography*, or of Charley Tudor's examination in *The Three Clerks* where the successful applicant re-transcribed a passage from a newspaper leader, which was never read. The treasury had made one attempt in 1840 to ensure that the clerks for the main departments should at least know the principles of double bookkeeping, but their circular had been ignored by most offices and was soon neglected by the remainder. There was, moreover, no age limit for the service, so that a boy could make the rounds of many jobs before coming at last to what Trevelyan caustically named his 'secure asylum'. For it was scarcely possible to fail in the civil service: only a handful ever plumbed the depths of incompetence necessary to secure dismissal.

The consequence was a general undifferentiated mass of drones and mediocrity with the corollary that work degenerated into meaningless routine and promotion into a mechanical movement according to seniority. The vicious circle was complete. There were no incentives to work or to make administration more efficient because of the type of official who was recruited, and scarcely anyone of ability would attempt to enter because of the hopelessness of the prospects for merit and the general dreariness of the barren routine. Of course with the comparatively large numbers involved there were exceptions to these general rules. The regular methods of recruitment did occasionally throw up men of marked ability; Trollope and Edward Yates at the post office, for example, or T. F. Elliot and T. W. C. Murdoch at the colonial office. But such men were sports and comparatively rare.

Needless to say, even early nineteenth-century England could not be governed solely by routineers and ancient methods. The picture of malignancy and systematic inaction which Dickens painted with his Circumlocution Office in *Litle Dorrit* bore little relation to actuality. (One cannot help wondering at times whether Dickens was not counter-productive as a social reformer, with the intemperance and absurdity of his depictions leaving no base for caricature to work from.) The vast new social problems, the new energy of ideas, the new political developments, all demanded fresh expedients. The two most important of these expedients were, firstly, the filling of leading positions in the service by men who had distinguished themselves in other walks of life; and secondly, the new race of executive officers. As to the former, almost all the great Victorian civil servants were recruited from without – Trevelyan himself, Kay Shuttleworth, James Stephen, Chadwick, Simon, Senior, Jebb, Rawlinson, Burgoyne, Porter, Hill, Merivale, Taylor, Farrer, Southwood Smith. Some were lawyers; others, physicians; others, dons; others, businessmen, chemists or engineers. So far, so good: the practice did produce chief administrators of the highest class. But it also produced crusading, war-lording and empire-building within the service, and to a grievous extent, exorbitance and excursions into politics. Here Chadwick and Trevelyan were prime, but far from sole offenders. The very system bred 'statesmen in disguise'. And its effect upon the ordinary civil service was wholly bad. The rank and file felt all the more certainly and irrevocably condemned to their servile status when the plums of office seemed reserved for the world outside. Once again a vicious circle operated. 'The permanent Civil Servants are habitually superseded because they are inefficient and they are inefficient because they are habitually superseded.'[6]

To a lesser extent the same weaknesses were discernible in the latter expedient, the new field administrators – inspectors, assistant commissioners, surveyors, engineers and medical officers – working directly under the new type of board. They too were almost invariably recruited from outside, from the ranks of half-pay naval and army officers, physicians, chemists, surveyors, engineers and barristers. Again the practice did supply, as the regular service certainly could not have done, the sudden demand for scores of men of initiative, inventiveness, energy and professional or quasi-professional training for the new fields of state action, factory, labour, poor law, public health and police regulation. It would be difficult to over-emphasize their merits *en masse* – their general aptness for the work, their devotion and (in all the circumstances) their extraordinary efficiency and zeal. We must also recognize, however, that in the circumstances of the time, the new model had its limitations.

First it did nothing to improve the old civil establishments. The inspectorates (to use the most convenient corporate term) were concentrated in the novel fields of state activity. The core of the civil service was untouched. In a sense the innovation resembled the eighteenth-century device of the improvement commission, whereby new *ad hoc* agencies were tagged on to an unreformed system without regard to consistency or co-ordination. Secondly the ill-defined status of the inspectors aggravated the exaggerated and often injurious degree of administrative independence which marked so many of the new ventures of the 1830s. The history of the poor law administration between 1834 and 1847 provides many examples of this weakness. Arbitrariness and intransigence naturally produced widespread opposition, and opposition naturally hardened in time into a self-conscious individualist reaction, often obscuring the essential issues. Thirdly a supreme merit of the new order was that it vested the power to make appointments in the central board, not the political head of a department, nor the minister in parliament. A further incidental advantage was that the very nature of the new branches of administration often demanded subordinates with some measure of technical qualification, medical, engineering or chemical, thus *ipso facto* guaranteeing a certain competence. But who was to guard the guardians? How were the central boards themselves to be removed from the hands of the political families? Here again, the history of the poor law commission, and for that matter of several other of the early central boards, shows how powerfully they attracted the hereditary master-class once the stipends reached £1500 or even £1000 per annum. In consequence subordinate executive officers tended often to be more intelligent, independent and (in our sense of the word) professional than their own superiors. Finally the attempt to set up a series of autonomous administrative bodies, the usual setting for the new type of field inspector, was in many respects beginning the wrong way round. Ideally the convention of a permanent, professional and expert civil service carrying out a continuous state policy without political interference should have been first established. The failure to establish this principle initially goes far towards explaining the defeats and the consequent cross purposes and confusions of this era. It was insufficient to invent the right type of administrative technique without arranging simultaneously the right sort of relationship to party politics.

In the event the reform of the civil service was promoted by the middle classes, rather than by utilitarian or any other high theoretical pressures. It was significant that the first major external move came from Gladstone, as chancellor of the exchequer in Aberdeen's coalition. For by 1853 he was already the supreme surviving representative in ministerial ranks of the Peelite tradition of fiscal and financial reform, and already beginning his return to the political milieu of his childhood. What were his objects in setting up the Northcote-Trevelyan inquiry into the civil service in 1853? First to reduce the cost of administration: he expected that reform would produce efficiency and business methods in government, which would in turn automatically produce so many savings. Here, of course, he was at one with the middle class reformers of the 1830s. Their demand for the abolition of sinecures and the reduction of the number of offices, and part, at least, of their opposition to the creation of new departments, sprang from their simple passion to save money and to get good value from what was still being spent. A second purpose was to reduce the extent of state activity – at least to rationalize, consolidate and simplify existing state activity and to eliminate redundancy and overlapping. This attitude rested upon the premise that state spending (to use Gladstone's own words) was inherently 'sterile' as against the 'fructification' which money underwent in the pockets of citizens.

Gladstone was also inspired by the idea, which powerfully impelled middle class radicals, of formal civil equality. The civil service (even more than the universities and almost as much as the armed services, which were also under attack) was a stronghold of the aristocracy. As his fellow conspirator, Trevelyan, wrote privately to him at the time, 'The old established political families habitually batten on the public patronage – their sons legitimate and illegitimate, their relatives and dependants of every degree, are provided for by the score.'[7] This too was Gladstone's secret sentiment, as is evident from his confidential correspondence at the time. Finally Gladstone himself described his efforts as 'my contribution to *parliamentary reform*.'[8] 'Parliamentary' may sound a surprising adjective in this context but it was in fact most apt. Administrative reform, or at least the attempt to produce it, was a logical follow-through to the reform act of 1832. 'Besides the adventuring disreputable class of member of parliament,' wrote Trevelyan, 'who make God knows what use of patronage, a large number of borough members are mainly dependent upon it for their seats.'[9] The maintenance of the patronage system did much to counteract the representative principle in politics, to bolster up client politics, to burke the free expression of political opinion in the boroughs and to negate the placing of a portion of political power in middle class hands, which the reform act had seemed to promise. Gash's *Politics in the age of Peel*[10] amply demonstrates the political significance of this survival.

Thus the prime aim of Gladstonian reform was not to produce a 'modern' type of administration or even an 'efficient' administration in the mechanical sense – although, of course, such a reform was a necessary preliminary if either of the two were to be absolutely and comfortably established. Gladstone's aims were rather those of fiscal, civil and political reform according to the Peelite and Manchester traditions. These were also the aims and traditions which impregnated Trevelyan's earlier work, the Northcote-Trevelyan report of 1853, and indeed the whole administrative reform agitation which developed in the 1850s. The 'movement' for administrative reform dated, of course, from the late eighteenth century, and since 1830 it had been carried forward successively by the Humeites and Cobdenites. But the true originator of the effective campaign with which we are concerned was Trevelyan himself. In character, stature and ability Trevelyan resembled Chadwick. He was a man of unfailing energy and organizing power, unscrupulous in pursuing what he assumed to be the public good and not over-scrupulous in pursuing even private and family advantage. While he was the hammer of patronage, he was far from opposed to the Trevelyans themselves being patronized.[11] Needless to add perhaps, he was a doctrinaire, but his doctrines were semi-popular: the McCulloch, Hume and Cobden varieties, instead of the pseudo-systematic construct of the philosophical radicals. Trevelyan's appointment as permanent secretary to the treasury (and in effect head of the civil service) had placed him in a commanding situation, and this was raised to the level of golden opportunity when in 1848 (after his return from the herculean though disastrous labour of directing Irish famine relief) he was commissioned to conduct an inquiry into his own department. The report of this commission opened the way for widespread change, for it adumbrated two of the principles on which all subsequent reform was built: the separation of clerks into classes, and recruitment by examination instead of by nomination.

While Trevelyan shared fully the purposes ascribed to Gladstone, he cast them in his own particular mould. His further objectives were the control of the entire public service by the treasury and the use of open competition for recruitment and promotion, for reward and punishment. In the first place, Trevelyan was ever a treasury man, profoundly disturbed by

the ineffectiveness and weakness of the treasury's control of
public finance and of other departments in the first half of the
nineteenth century. 'Yet at the Treasury alone', he wrote, 'could
a comprehensive view be taken of the taxation of the
country';[12] and again, 'the real check of simple intelligible
accounts, rendered at short intervals and examined and certi-
fied by independent Auditors [should be substituted] for the
sham check of the Exchequer.'[13] Step by step in the five years
from 1849 to 1854, Trevelyan and his assistants at the treasury
virtually secured the desired control by establishing a more
modern system of forward accounting and budgeting and the
need to win antecedent treasury consent for all possible public
spending. The audit act of 1866[14] capped these developments
by facilitating direction and checks from the centre.

As to the second and more general reform, Trevelyan's
opportunity came, as we have seen, in 1853, and came essentially through Gladstone who provided the indispensable link
with high politics. From the start the new chancellor accepted
eagerly Trevelyan's objects – entry by merit, promotion by
merit, dismissal for incompetence, and division of the service
into 'intellectual' and 'mechanical' grades – and Gladstone's
former secretary, Northcote, rounded off the connection. In
March 1853 Trevelyan and Northcote were commissioned to
undertake an official inquiry into the board of trade, and this
was followed up by inquiries into seven other departments.
These inquiries and their due train of reports produced important extensions and elaborations of the principles of the classi-
fication of clerks, promotion by merit and recruitment by
examination. But now another factor entered the equation.
Gladstone was concurrently involved in two royal commissions, on the condition of Oxford University and the state of
the public schools; and Northcote himself sat on the Oxford
commission as well as that on the reorganization of the civil
service. Mysteriously the three movements began to blend and
intertwine. In particular, the Oxford reformers, Jowett of
Balliol and the Dean of Hertford College, took a hand in the
reform of the public service. In concrete terms this interming-
ling of university, public school and administrative reform produced not only the proposal of a permanent commission of
examiners for all appointments to the civil service – a revolu-

tionary and far-reaching step in the long term – but also, and still more important, the grounding of the civil service of the future upon a caste drawn from the reformed public schools and universities and judged by the curricula of these institutions. More or less simultaneously the domination of classics and mathematics in these curricula was confirmed, and the public schools began to increase rapidly in number.

In certain ways this imposed interconnection of school, university and administrative reform seems quite perverse. As R. R. W. Lingen, secretary to the privy council education office, put it at the time, 'It appears to me to be quite beside the question to discuss the organization of the Civil Service as if it existed for the sake of the general education of the country.'[15] But there is good reason to suspect that nothing less was aimed at than the exclusive preservation of the vital sphere of civil administration for the educated upper and upper middle classes, while there was still time to beat the oncoming democracy to the gun. 'In an age when the shadow of democracy was already looming on the horizon,' writes Asa Briggs, 'men like Vaughan, Jowett and Trevelyan realized the need for a plentiful supply of informed gentlemen.'[16] How far the anti-democratic purpose (if such it was) of administrative reorganization was realized I shall not attempt to say. But certainly a link between the higher civil service and a humanities education of the type provided by the older universities was forged. It was to endure for a century. Perhaps to a degree it endures today.

We must now return to the actual Northcote-Trevelyan report itself. The major recommendation of Trevelyan and Northcote was the abolition of patronage in all forms since this was the source of every evil. Instead, the civil service should be entered only through competitive examinations conducted periodically by an independent board; there should be an age limit for candidates and a medical examination and a strict period of probation for those who were successful. The commissioners also suggested that a division be made in the service, with corresponding examinations and scales between the 'mechanical and the intellectual type of labour'. Their objects and expectations were defined as, first, reduction in numbers and greater efficiency of operation; secondly, considerable savings in the cost of administration; and thirdly, the raising of the standards of the public schools and universities. Open competition and promotion by merit within the service was expected to increase its prestige sufficiently to have a marked effect upon public school and university teaching. Underlying all is much of the old middle class competitive principle. The best was to be secured by rewarding energy and intelligence by the very highest prospects with the corollary of destroying security for those unfit to survive. It was in its own way a rather simple application of the open labour market concept to the field of professional government.

A measure along the lines of the commissioners' report was promised in the speech from the throne at the beginning of the session of 1854. But the political crisis which ultimately brought about the downfall of Aberdeen's coalition government was already developing by the time that this promise was made public, and as a consequence the bill was shelved. In February 1855 the whigs came to power. Patronage had no more ardent defenders than these oligarchs. A record discovered by Professor Edward Hughes of the voting on the cabinet decision for the bill for 'free examination' taken on 26 January 1854 ran as follows: in favour, Aberdeen, Newcastle, Graham, Herbert, Gladstone, Granville and Molesworth – six Peelites and one radical; against, Russell, Lansdowne, Clarendon, Wood and Cranworth – every one of them a whig.[17] The closely intermarried whig 'Cousinhood' regarded the higher (or more exactly the highest) public service as its peculiar province, as the whig administrations from 1830 to 1841 and 1846 to 1852 clearly show. One of them said frankly, 'The more the civil service is recruited from the lower classes, the less will it be sought after by the higher, until at last the aristocracy will be altogether dissociated from the permanent civil service of the country.'[18] Lord John Russell was obstinately opposed to any change on the extraordinary ground that it would lead directly to republicanism. Even Palmerston, who had seen to it as early as the 1830s that his own department, the foreign office, was made tolerably efficient, was still sufficient of a whig to reject the Northcote-Trevelyan recommendations as sinister.[19] Hence the paradox that, essentially upon class grounds, the ostensibly progressive party refused to carry through the reforming proposals of its Peelite one-time-tory colleagues.

Something had to be done, however, even by the new, purely whig government of Palmerston, in the light of the devastating report of 1853. But it was done by an order in council of 21 May 1855, not by statute. This procedure not only by-passed the house of commons and thus forestalled the radicals, but it also re-emphasized the old idea that the civil service was a subject for the royal prerogative, that it belonged to the executive and not the political domain. The order gave the shadow of reform without the substance. It set up a permanent commission of three to conduct examinations for what it called 'junior situations in the Civil Establishment'; and for these posts it required a certificate from the commission as to the age, health, character and ability to carry out the relevant duties, of the candidates. But it neither insisted on competition for posts nor interfered in any way with the rights of nomination of political patronage. As the royal commission of 1912 summed it up: 'The actual effects were (a) to limit the commissioners' certificate to the junior stations; (b) to make competition a permissive but not a compulsory method of selection for such certificates; and (c) to leave the power of appointment in all cases where it had previously rested – with the political heads of the department.'[20] The only important principle established by the order in council was that for the lower grades of the civil service only those who were pronounced competent by an authority other than that which was appointing them could be recruited.

Palmerston's government, however, did not get away scot-free with its manoeuvre. This was the juncture at which the Crimean disasters and the tragi-comic findings of administrative inefficiency by the Sebastopol Committee were rousing public opinion to indignation – particularly against the war office. In June 1855, Layard, a private member, proposed a resolution condemning the 'party and family influences' and 'blind adherence to routine' which were disgracing the civil service:[21] the mode of recruitment and the intellectual and moral quality of the recruited were alike assailed. Although the motion was lost, it was debated for three days and received most impressive support in the house of commons. Gladstone and the Manchester radicals were among its warm supporters, and the conservative Northcote, who had served with Trevelyan, denounced the order in council as a fraud, and warned the house that so long as the civil service commission could do no more than impose a mere qualifying test, it would be a 'Board for stereotyping mediocrity or concealing bad appointments', utterly powerless to resist patronage.[22] Meanwhile outside parliament an administrative reform association had been set up very much on the lines of the earlier health of towns association, and this pressure group managed to get a resolution in favour of open competition carried in the commons in 1857. But so long as the whigs (or for that matter the protectionists) were still in power, nothing happened. It was not until Gladstone returned to the exchequer in 1860 that the next blow was struck. A select committee secured by him in that year found that although a few abuses had been checked since 1855, on the whole the new examinations were 'a delusion to the public and a fertile source of abuse',[23] and that the immense numbers rejected by the commission at the preliminary stage showed how irresponsible the nominators had always been. Not that the infant commission was severe. Preston-Thomas, a poor law inspector, later recalled:

It was towards the end of the year 1859 that, fresh from Marlborough, I distinguished myself by gaining the first place in a competition held by the Civil Service Commissioners for a clerkship in the Privy Council Office. Frankness compels me to add that the two other nominees (required by the regulations to make up the prescribed number of three) may possibly have been the special couple known as the 'Treasury Idiots', who could never pass anything, and were sent again and again to give a walk-over to any Minister's protégé able to reach the standard of minimum qualifications. At any rate, they could barely read or write, and so I found myself entitled to a desk in Downing Street.[24]

The select committee of 1860 agreed that open competition was the answer. But it was afraid to recommend it unreservedly because of vested interests and the conservative state of opinion. Instead it put forward a compromise in the hope of really securing a lesser gain. What it proposed was a real though limited competition. Candidates were still to be nominated, but within this closed group competition for places was to be open, determined by merit as revealed by written examination. The compromise was gradually accepted by the departments during the 1860s and bore some fruit in the decade of its operation. In 1870 during Gladstone's first and great reforming administration, in the course of which the possible opening of the ancient universities, the armed forces and the established church to competition and merit was attempted, a decisive step in administrative reform was taken with the famous order in council of 4 June 1870. The extent of this reform is often exaggerated. The order swept away the nomination system and rendered competition full and open. It was, however, a more limited measure than is commonly supposed. One major qualification was that it applied only to certain specified departments; another, that even in those departments certain posts and offices were exempt. On the other hand, the war office act of 1870 marked an extension of the new principles to yet another area.

Before Gladstone left office in 1874 the next step in the reforming process had been taken with the appointment of the Playfair commission,[25] a second general review of civil service recruitment and manpower of the Northcote-Trevelyan type. Sir Lyon Playfair, by now a sort of stock scientific and educational adviser to governments, was a typical Gladstonian liberal in these matters; and the commission's report inevitably stressed how much remained to be done before Trevelyanism was universally applied, and smoothed the way for its further and speedier application. In the later 1870s the competitive system was gradually extended in the service, and by the early 1880s its cumulative effects were becoming more clearly apparent. The division between the grades was also penetrating deeply by now. It had taken more than two decades to displace the old order over the majority of the public service. Yet again under Gladstone's aegis, another assault on the remnants of the *ancien régime* was launched with the establishment of the Ridley commission[26] (a renewal, in effect, of the Playfair) in 1886. After its report and the subsequent implementation, only a small area of the service remained outside the ring of Trevelyanism. Only the foreign office, the most senior posts in the other ministries and ministerial secretaries were still exempt. Even these final outposts fell after the MacDonnell commission of 1912, which represented the ultimate and universal triumph of orthodox Gladstonian liberalism in this field. All was now swept into the arena of competition.

Thus like the decline of crown influence three-quarters of a century earlier, the decline of patronage in the civil service was a gradual process stretching over fifty years. Again like the earlier process, it is impossible to state precisely when the decline in patronage reached such a point that the new order predominated quantitatively. But just as somewhere in the decade 1800–10 crown influence ceased to be an effective part of the general political system, so also somewhere in the decade 1875–85 the centre of gravity shifted within the public service and the products and fruits of patronage ceased to form the preponderant element within the system. Of course the two movements were related. In the very broad view they may be regarded as manifestations of the same radical reforming tendency. Trevelyanism aimed at formal civil equality in the sense of opening careers to talent (or what was so regarded in terms of the pre-ordained tests); at contributing towards the destruction of the traditional political and social systems; at rationalization, quantification and uniformity; at effective controls of both public labour and public expenditure; and at establishing more firmly ministerial accountability and answerability. All this was in the mainstream of British radicalism. Such a drive was conceived of by many as both democratic and egalitarian in tendency, although the moving forces for the principal authors of the reform, Trevelyan and Gladstone, were rather power-hunger, efficiency and economy, in the first case, and the Athenian ethics of public service and private self-fulfilment through duty in the second. But the democracy applied only to the upper one-tenth of society, and the equality was circumscribed by a syllabus based on a set 'humane' and 'gentlemanly' interpretation of education.

The merits of the reformed public service need no emphasis. It is not a myth, it is the simple truth that its integrity, laboriousness, devotion to the public interest and general level of intelligence rendered it a cynosure and pattern for many other governments. At the same time the social and economic costs of such a system may have been very high. The Gladstonian assumptions that public expenditure tended to be the enemy of social reform, that it was the chancellor's business to ensure that it absorbed as small a portion of the national income as practicable and that, unless jealously overseen, departments would spend more than they need, were all inimical to state action. Treasury control not only facilitated the achievement of these objectives but also produced an official climate hostile to new ideas, fresh undertakings, administrative experiment and forward or creative planning. Treasury conservatism applied even in its own parish : there was no major innovation in public finance from 1850 until the introduction of PAYE in 1940. Moreover the higher civil service, in ordinary times, tended to be drawn from a very narrow band of society in educational as well as class terms. Its recruits were almost without exception lacking in scientific, mechanical, technological or commercial training or experience. Scarcely any were men who had earlier practised another profession. The Oxford and Cambridge, general and humanities, type of man predominated. The novice tended to be stereotyped despite the boasts that the gymnasia of classics and mathematics fitted one for almost any subsequent occupation, and most certainly that of rule. On the contrary the cumulative consequence was excessive formalism, rigidity and timorousness and a sort of 'lay priesthood' raised from initiation to respect the 'order'. Hence the critical importance of the waves of new energy, exterior experience and experimental and positive dispositions infused into the service by the success of certain social reforming agitations of 1890–1910, as well as by the two world wars. As with the innovations of 1830–50, they set loose in the public domain a host of mature men, often used to commanding and deciding, to thinking in other fashions and creating things anew. But all that is another story.

There is perhaps a final irony to be noted : that the radical ideals of open competition and selection of the fittest by examination contests should have been interlinked with the reactionary ideal of education as an experience and an exercise rather than the acquisition of particular skills or knowledge, or being graded according to intellectual attainment. Newman's

Idea of a University, published almost contemporaneously with the Northcote-Trevelyan report, was in every sense the classical expression of the eighteenth-century view that the young educated one another and should be neither taught nor examined formally at universities. Newman's was in effect a defence of the *ancien régime*, of the system of effortless privilege against which the Oxford reformers and Trevelyan and his supporters went to war. But the result of the battle – *à la* 1832 – was to enlarge and rebuild, not to destroy or even weaken the exclusive elite. The ancient universities and all their associated network of institutions did not lose their masses of mediocrity to whom the world, mysteriously, owed a living. Instead the currency was now backed by a new sort of gold standard[27] – the small percentage of working, writing, striving and achieving people who carried off the prizes and the ribands, who won the mortal garlands of formal scholarship, not without dust and heat.

Notes and References

CHAPTER ONE: THE FAVOURING AND RESISTING FORCES

1. H. J. Grierson, ed., *Letters of Sir Walter Scott* (Centenary edition, London, 1934), vol. vi, p. 190.
2. J. F. Rees, *A social and industrial history of England, 1815–1918* (London, 1920), p. 87.
3. E. Halevy, *The age of Peel and Cobden* (London, 1947), p. 20.
4. A. V. Dicey, *Law and public opinion in England* (London, 1905), pp. 39–40.
5. S. E. Finer, *The life and times of Sir Edwin Chadwick* (London, 1952), p. 21.
6. A. Smith, *An inquiry into the nature and causes of the wealth of nations* (Cannan edition, London, 1904), vol. 1, p. 123.
7. J. Morley, *The life of William Ewart Gladstone* (London, 1903), vol. ii, p. 53.
8. In March 1837, Nassau Senior assured Poulett Thomson that according to his calculations 'the whole net profit was derived from the last hour ... a ten-hour bill would be utterly ruinous. And I do not think that any restriction of the present hours of work could safely be made'. J. T. Ward, *The factory movement 1830–1855* (London, 1962), p. 170.

CHAPTER TWO: EARLY FACTORY LEGISLATION

1. 42 Geo. III, c.73.
2. Section 9.

3. It might be more correct to speak of the amendment bill as Owen's, for he had first composed the draft, and Peel's alterations to it were comparatively few. M. Cole, *Robert Owen* (London, 1953), pp. 96–8.

4. *Report of evidence on the state of children employed in manufactories,* 167, 1816 (397), iii (evidence of Adam Bogle).

5. *Bills and papers,* 735, 1814–15 (364), ii.

6. The measure was passed as 59 Geo. III, c.66.

7. The 1833 report on child labour in factories stressed the long hours of labour and consequent gross overwork and physical deterioration as the chief of all the evils of the system. *First report of the commissioners on employment of children in factories,* 25–29, 1833 (450), xx.

8. 6 Geo. IV, c.63 and 1 & 2 Will. IV, c.39.

9. *Hansard,* 2nd, xiii, 421.

10. W. R. Greg, *An enquiry into the state of the manufacturing population* (London, 1831), p. 30; quoted by M. W. Thomas, *The early factory legislation* (Leigh-on-Sea, 1948), p. 32.

11. Ward, op. cit., p. 156.

12. O. MacDonagh, *A pattern of government growth: the passenger acts and their enforcement, 1800–60* (London, 1961), pp. 68–72.

13. *Hansard,* 2nd, xiii, 647.

14. *Ibid.,* 3rd, xl, 388.

15. *Report of the select committee on factory children's labour,* 19, 1831–2 (706), xv (evidence of Abraham Whitehead).

16. *Ibid.,* 102 (evidence of Thomas Bennett).

17. *First report of the commissioners, on employment of children in factories,* 20, 23, 1833 (450), xx.

18. *Bills and papers,* 263, 1833 (48), ii.

19. J. Bentham, *Works,* ed. J. Bowring (Edinburgh, 1843–59), vol xi, p. 20.

20. E. Halvey, *The growth of philosophical radicalism* (2nd ed. London, 1934), pp. 75–85.

21. Dicey, op. cit., pp. 136–8; W. Harrison, introduction to Blackwell's Political Texts, *A fragment on govern-*

ment and *An introduction to the principles of morals and legislation* (Oxford, 1948), pp. xvii–xix.

22. Dicey, op. cit., pp. 130–1.
23. Halevy, *Philosophical radicalism*, op. cit., p. 487.
24. Finer, op. cit., pp. 14–19.
25. L. Stephen, *The English utilitarians* (London, 1900), i, p. 30.
26. J. S. Mill, *Autobiography* (World's Classics edition, Oxford, 1924), p. 89.

CHAPTER THREE : THE FACTORY ACT OF 1833

1. For the opposition to the commission, see Ward, op. cit., pp. 94–9; Thomas, op. cit., pp. 48–50.
2. *First report of the commissioners on employment of children in factories*, 52–3, 1833 (450), xx.
3. Chadwick, whose work in the field of life assurance also persuaded him in this direction, prevailed on Lyndhurst in 1836 to introduce in the house of lords a bill instituting the registrarship-general of births; M. Marston, *Sir Edwin Chadwick, 1800–1890* (London, 1925), p. 26. The bill was passed as 6 & 7 Will. IV, c.86, and after amendment came into force on 30 June 1837.
4. 3 & 4 Will. IV, c.103.
5. 'Alfred', *The history of the factory movement from the year 1802* (London, 1857), i, p. 65. 'Alfred' was the pseudonym of Samuel Kydd.
6. The inspector for the northwestern district of England and northern Wales had initially little short of 3,000 factories, manned by more than one quarter of a million workers in his jurisdiction. Thomas, op. cit., p. 98.
7. Ibid., p. 96, n. 9.
8. See below pp. 168–70.
9. L. Horner, *On the employment of children in factories* (London, 1840), pp. 1–2.
10. Ibid., p. 2.

CHAPTER FOUR : LATER FACTORY REFORM

1. K. M. Lyell, *Memoir of Leonard Horner* (London, 1890) vol. i, p. 287.

2. *Hansard*, 3rd, lv, 788. It was Fielden who read this letter aloud in the house of commons when moving for a select committee to inquire into the government's use of the factory inspectors and superintendents as 'political spies'.

3. *Report of factory inspectors*, 100, 1849, [1017], xxii, Horner and Saunders made similar confessions.

4. Horner had served as one of the commissioners of inquiry for the west. He was then forty-eight years of age and his latest occupation had been the wardenship of the newly founded London University between 1829 and 1831.

5. *Report of factory inspectors*, 70, 1834 (596), xliii.

6. It is a measure of the early administrative haziness in factory law enforcement that it was not firmly and finally located at the home office until the later 1830s.

7. *The Times*, 11 May 1836.

8. Thomas, op. cit., pp. 146–8.

9. For the inspector's minute of the occasion, see ibid., p. 157; for Russell's announcement, see *Hansard*, 3rd, xlix, 914.

10. Ibid., lii, 860.

11. *Report select committee on factory regulation act*, 1, 1841, sess. I, (56), ix.

12. E. Hodder, *The life and work of the seventh earl of Shaftesbury* (London, 1893), vol. i, p. 180.

13. Russell and Fox Maule, and even to a degree Peel and Ashley, defended the government's action, but none attempted to deny that the inspectors were being used to gather political intelligence. *Hansard*, 3rd, lv, 785–802.

14. Cf. Horner, op. cit., pp. 15–19.

15. *Report, select committee on factory regulation act*, 29, 1841, sess. I, (56), ix.

16. *The Times*, 11 May 1836.

17. *Second report children's employment commission*, 1843 [430], xiii.

18. Halevy, *Age of Peel and Cobden*, op. cit., p. 54.

19. *Hansard*, 3rd, lxvii, 422–4.

20. D. H. Akenson, *The Irish education experiment: the*

national system of education in the nineteenth century (London, 1970), pp. 102–22.

21. 'Lost time' might no longer be made up in any factories except those in which the machinery was powered by water (a small minority by now), and even in those the maximum addition was one hour on any particular day, and might only be added after the superintendent had been given due notice, sections 33–5.

22. *Report select committee on factory regulation act*, 12, 1841, sess. I, (56), ix.

23. 7 & 8 Vic., c. 15.

24. The basic salary of a superintendent was raised from £250 p.a. to £450 p.a., and he was re-named 'sub-inspector'. The objection to his having free access to the mills had hitherto been that (presumably) because of his comparative poverty and low status he might be tempted to sell trade secrets to manufacturing rivals.

25. F. E. Mineka, ed., *The collected works of J. S. Mill: the earlier letters, 1812 to 1848* (Toronto, 1963), vol. xiii, pp. 716–17.

26. 10 & 11 Vic., c. 29.

27. The test case was *Ryder v. Mills*, judgment in which was delivered by Mr Baron Parke on 8 February 1850.

28. *Hansard*, 3rd, cxxviii, 1268.

29. Thomas, op. cit., p. 326.

30. 8 & 9 Vic., c. 29.

31. J. S. Mill, *Principles of political economy with some of their applications to social philosophy* (Ashley edition, London, 1909), pp. 953–65. Mill allows other exceptions or partial exceptions in such matters as public works, public charities and public utilities; but these are not relevant to the present argument.

32. Ibid., p. 959. Mill is primarily concerned to argue that women should have 'as absolute a control as men have over their own persons and their own patrimony, and acquisitions'. He regards factory women as freer than other women of their social class because they choose their employment, and he seems to suggest that restrictions on their selling their labour would reduce their

opportunities to attain such 'freedom'.

33. T. B. Macaulay, *History of England*, (London, 1850), vol. i, p. 417.

CHAPTER FIVE : COAL MINING

1. This chapter is largely drawn from 'Coal mines regulation: the first decade 1842–1852', in R. Robson ed., *Ideas and institutions of Victorian England* (London, 1967), pp. 58–86; for permission to use which I am indebted to Dr Robson and Messrs G. Bell & Sons.
2. *Report, select committee on accidents in mines*, 1835 (603), v.
3. 5 & 6 Vic., c. 99.
4. James Wyld, MP, reported in *Newcastle Chronicle*, 21 September 1849.
5. *Hansard*, 3rd, lxiii, 196, 198.
6. Ibid., 1336–7.
7. Ibid., 1357–9.
8. Ibid., 1347.
9. *The Times*, 8 August 1842.
10. For an account of Tremenheere's appointment, character and some of his work, see R. K. Webb, 'A whig inspector', *Journal of modern history*, vol. xxvii, pp. 352–64.
11. H.O./O.S. 1490, Tremenheere to Sir George Grey, 31 December 1846.
12. *Fourth report, commissioner appointed under 5 & 6 Vic., c. 99*, 1847 [844], xvi.
13. *Hansard*, 3rd, cvi, 1336.
14. Ibid., xciii, 1076.
15. Ibid., 1077.
16. *Report, lords select committee on accidents in coal mines*, vii, 1849 (613), vii.
17. Ibid., viii.
18. *Report on ventilation of mines by J. Kenyon Blackwell*, 1850 [1214], xxiii; *Report on ventilation of mines by John Phillips*, 1850 [1222], xxiii.
19. 13 & 14 Vic., c. 100.
20. Meanwhile in 1852 the number of inspectors had been

increased to six, H.O. 45/O.S. 3790, Grey: Treasury, 15 December 1851. When the corps was increased again, to 24 in 1873, the number of districts remained the same and each inspector was given an assistant.

21. *Report select committee on coal mines*, iii–x, 1852, (509), v.

22. The penalty proposed for failure to perform in such matters as fencing and the production of plans was £1 per day during the delay. The inspectors also proposed that coroners should give at least six days' notice, instead of forty-eight hours, of their intention to hold an inquest on a fatal colliery accident, and that notice should be sent to a district inspector as well as the secretary of state. There were several other minor recommendations.

23. Further light is thrown on the inspectors' views at this time in the evidence of two of them, Mackworth and Dickinson, before the 1852 and 1853 select committees on mining accidents, especially *Report, select committee on coal mines*, 42–3, 48, 59, 64, 1852 (509), v; *First report, select committee on mines accidents*, 6–48, 55, 1852–3 (691), xx.

24. 18 & 19 Vic., c. 108; 23 & 24 Vic., c. 151; and 25 & 26 Vic., c. 79.

25. R. N. Boyd, *Coal mines inspection: its history and results* (London, 1879), p. 156.

26. *Reports of Messrs Dunn, Dickinson and Morton, Inspectors*, 37, 1851 [1422], xxiii.

27. *Reports inspectors of mines*, vii, 1875 [c. 1216], xvi; vii, 33, 1876 [c. 1499], xvii; Boyd, op. cit., pp. 237–40.

28. Boyd, op. cit., p. 184.

CHAPTER SIX: THE POOR LAW

1. See *Report, select committee on poor laws*, 1817 (462), vi, and *Report, select committee on labourers' wages*, 1824 (392), vi.

2. For a fuller discussion of the old poor laws, see S. G. and E. O. A. Checkland, eds., *The poor law report of 1834* (London, 1974), pp. 11–19.

3. 'It is likely, however, that the same Speenhamland was elevated into a false notoriety by Sir Frederick Eden, a writer on Poor Law affairs who in 1797 blamed the original Speenhamland decision [to supplement deficient wages on a scale based on the price of bread] for many of the evils he discovered. ... Common problems produce common solutions, and it is not surprising that, faced with chronic low wages temporarily below subsistence level, Poor Law authorities all over England should resort to some form of supplementing wages.' D. Fraser, *The evolution of the British Welfare State* (London, 1973), p. 33.

4. N. Senior, *Remarks on the opposition to the poor law amendment act* (London, 1841), p. 11.

5. Finer, op. cit., pp. 105–11.

6. 13 & 14 Ch. II, c. 12 and 8 & 9 Will. III, c. 30.

7. Finer, op. cit., pp. 48–9.

8. Ibid., pp. 44, 46. Finer observes, 'A very large part of Chadwick's success was due to his early conversion of Nassau Senior'.

9. Cf. ibid., pp. 90–2.

10. *Report, royal commission on poor laws and relief of distress*, 94, 1909 [Cd. 4499], xxxvii.

11. Finer, op. cit., pp. 110–11.

12. Nicholls substantially repeated the approach and administrative devices of Chadwick in advising on a poor law for Ireland in 1836, *Report of G. Nicholls on poor laws in Ireland*, 1837 [69], li; G. Nicholls, *A history of the Irish poor law*, (London, 1856), pp. 160–88.

13. Finer, op. cit., pp. 92–4.

14. S. G. and E. O. A. Checkland, op. cit., pp. 29–33.

15. 'Bonaparte', Chadwick once wrote, 'in his extreme avidity for power, did with respect to his civil administration what he would have done for his Military Government if he had ordered that none of the operations ... should be performed except with the sanction of the commander-in-chief on a written memorial duly presented.' Quoted by Finer, op. cit., p. 92.

16. I.e., members of the Indian civil service.

17. Salisbury's minute, dated 20 April 1875, is quoted in an

unpublished paper of Professor E. Stokes entitled 'Land revenue systems in the North West Province and the Bombay Deccan 1830–60: Ideology and the official mind'.

18. Finer, op. cit., p. 92.
19. M. E. Rose, *The English poor law 1780–1930* (Newton Abbot, 1971), pp. 140–1.
20. 10 & 11 Vic., c. 109.
21. For public dispensaries and medical clubs generally, see R. G. Hodgkinson, *The origins of the national health service* (London, 1967), pp. 205–36.
22. Fraser, op. cit., p. 84.
23. *Seventh report, poor law commissioners*, 11, 1841 sess. I, [327], xi.
24. 3 & 4 Vic., c. 29.
25. 4 & 5 Vic., c. 32.
26. 16 & 17 Vic., c. 100. See also R. J. Lambert, 'A Victorian national health service: state vaccination 1855–71', in *Historical Journal*, 1962, no. 1, pp. 2–3.
27. Fraser, op. cit., p. 84.
28. Ibid., pp. 86–7.
29. R. Pinker, *English hospital statistics 1861–1938* (London, 1966), table ix, p. 62.
30. *Hansard*, 3rd, clxxxv, 150–175, in particular 163. Gathorne Hardy was president of the poor law board in Disraeli's first ministry.
31. 30 Vic., c. 6.
32. Fraser, op. cit., p. 85.
33. 48 & 49 Vic., c. 46.

CHAPTER SEVEN: LOCAL GOVERNMENT

1. 5 & 6 Will. IV, c. 76.
2. *First report, commissioners on municipal corporations*, 32–49, 1835 (116), xxiii.
3. Idem.
4. 9 Geo. IV, c. 17.
5. 59 Geo. III, c. 85. This statute amended a vestry act of the previous year, 58 Geo. III, c. 69.
6. 1 & 2 Will. IV, c. 60.

7. See the preamble and schedules annexed to the act.
8. *Hansard*, 3rd, xxxi, 98.
9. R. Russell, ed., *The early correspondence of Lord John Russell* (London, 1913), vol. ii, pp. 138–9.
10. See Chapter 8.
11. 5 & 6 Will. IV, c. 50.
12. J. W. Probyn, ed., *Local government and taxation in the United Kingdom* (London, 1882), pp. 122–3.
13. Ibid., p. 122.
14. 45 & 46 Vic., c. 50; 51 & 52 Vic., c. 41; 56 & 57 Vic., c. 73; and 62 & 63 Vic., c. 14.
15. 35 & 36 Vic., c. 74.
16. 38 & 39 Vic., c. 36.
17. 38 & 39 Vic., c. 55.

CHAPTER EIGHT: PUBLIC HEALTH AND SANITATION

1. R. A. Lewis, *Edwin Chadwick and the public health movement* (London, 1952), p. 150.
2. Ibid., pp. 42–3. R. J. Lambert, *Sir John Simon 1816–1904 and English social administration* (London, 1963), p. 59.
3. Lewis, op. cit., pp. 34–6.
4. Lambert, *Simon*, op. cit., pp.58–9; Finer, op. cit., pp. 212–16.
5. Finer, op. cit., pp. 162–3; Lewis, op. cit., pp. 37–8.
6. See Chapter 9.
7. It was entitled *The sanitary condition of the labouring classes, by Edwin Chadwick, published by the poor law commission.*
8. Finer, op. cit., p. 210. This was by now a well-tried publicity technique; in 1839, Chadwick caused 7000 copies of the *Sanitary report* of that year and over 3000 copies of his *Constabulary report* to be distributed amongst the influential. Ibid., pp.162, 172.
9. Lewis, op. cit., pp. 55–6.
10. Roe, surveyor to the Holborn sewers commission since 1820, had been experimenting with flushing and cleansing methods for many years; ibid., pp. 53–4. Later Chad-

wick came to regard him as old-fashioned, although Roe remained loyal to Chadwick to the end.

11. Ibid., pp. 91–2.
12. E. Chadwick, *Sanitary report*, pp. 50–1.
13. Ibid., pp. 223–4. See also Finer, op. cit., pp. 226–7.
14. O. MacDonagh, 'Government, industry and science in nineteenth-century Britain: a particular study', *Historical Studies*, 1975, vol. xvi, p. 507.
15. See *Reports of the commissioners of inquiry into the state of large towns and populous districts*, 1844 [572], xvii; 1845 [602], xviii.
16. Finer, op. cit., pp.237–9.
17. Ibid., p. 300.
18. 11 & 12 Vic., c. 63.
19. 10 & 11 Vic., c. 34. One of its provisions was, however, mandatory, and another absolute.
20. In fact this was more favourable to the general board than was apparent at the time. Although the death rate in the early 1840s had been 21.4 per thousand, it averaged 23 during 1846–55.
21. Finer, op. cit., p. 298.
22. Lewis, op. cit., pp. 152–7.
23. *The Times*, 21 June 1852.
24. *Lancet*, 13 February 1858.
25. See *First report of the royal sanitary commission*, 1868–9 [4218], xxxii. This commission was appointed in April 1869 to replace a similar commission of 1868 which was abandoned when the senior commissioner resigned.
26. 21 & 22 Vic., c. 98.
27. 21 & 22 Vic., c. 97 and 22 & 23 Vic., c. 3.
28. Lambert, *Simon*, op. cit., p. 271.
29. Ibid., pp. 271–2, 396, 421–3. In 1870 Simon in effect subordinated the office (with its own consent) to his department.
30. Ibid., pp. 276–84.
31. Lambert, 'State vaccination 1855–71', op. cit., p. 1.
32. Fraser, op. cit., pp.67–8.
33. 28 & 29 Vic., c. 75.
34. 29 & 30 Vic., c. 90.

35. *The Times*, 11 August 1866.
36. Lambert, *Simon*, op. cit., pp. 597–603.
37. Ibid., pp. 599–600.

CHAPTER NINE : LAW AND PUBLIC ORDER

1. Amongst them stealing from the person, stealing from bleaching grounds and (for the armed forces) being found vagrant without a pass. He failed to carry similar proposals with respect to shoplifting and theft from dwelling houses.
2. 4 Geo. IV, cc. 46, 48, 52–4. See also N. Gash, *Mr Secretary Peel: the life of Sir Robert Peel to 1830* (London, 1961), pp. 326–31.
3. E. Halevy, *The triumph of reform, 1830–41* (2nd ed., London, 1954), p. 102.
4. 36 & 37 Vic., c. 66.
5. In 1891–2 a central registry and local registries were set up in Ireland for the registration of land titles.
6. *Bills and papers*, 123, 1830 (568), i; 167, 1830 (569), i.
7. MacDonagh, *Pattern of government growth*, op. cit., pp. 58, 149.
8. See especially clauses 11–12, 30–1, 34–5 and 43.
9. Russell, op. cit., pp. 143–4.
10. 9 & 10 Vic., c. 95.
11. E. L. Woodward, *The age of reform* (2nd ed., Oxford, 1962), p. 473.
12. *Annual register*, 1822, p. 45.
13. 1 Geo. IV, c. 56; 5 Geo. IV, c. 83; 7 & 8 Geo. IV, c. 30.
14. See *Report, select committee on police of the metropolis*, 1828 (533), vi.
15. 10 Geo. IV, c. 44.
16. G. Broeker, *Rural disorder and police reform in Ireland* (London, 1970), Ch. 2–4; Gash, op. cit., pp. 176–85.
17. Gash, op. cit., pp. 489–90.
18. Ibid., p. 498.
19. Finer, op. cit., pp. 165–6. The pioneer in Great Britain of the concept of a preventive and regulatory police was Patrick Colquhoun, a Middlesex stipendiary magis-

trate, who published his classic *Treatise on the police of the metropolis* in 1795.

20. *Lancet*, 5 November, 1836.
21. See *First report, commissioners on establishing an efficient constabulary*, 1839 [169], xix.
22. Rowan was a Peninsular veteran and so too were the three men who created the new Irish police forces, Shaw Kennedy, Brereton and McGregor. It is not improbable that they knew each other for many years. Rowan was, besides, an Irishman himself.
23. Broeker, op. cit., pp. 142–6. See also R. B. McDowell, 'Ireland on the eve of the famine'; R. D. Edwards and T. D. Williams, eds., *The great famine* (Dublin, 1956), pp. 28–30.
24. 2 & 3 Vic., c. 93.
25. 2 & 3 Vic., c. 47.
26. 5 & 6 Vic., c. 109. This statute is worth study as a corrective to over-emphasis on the modernization of government in these years. It breathes the very spirit of Elizabethan administration and social organization.
27. 19 & 20 Vic., c. 69. See also the metropolitan police act of the same year, 19 & 20 Vic., c. 2.
28. *Blackwood's Magazine*, February 1859, vol. lxxxv, p. 233.

CHAPTER TEN: IRELAND

1. E. Stokes, *The English utilitarians and India* (Oxford, 1959), p. vii.
2. R. B. McDowell, *The Irish administration 1801–1914* (London, 1964), p. 23.
3. Trevelyan was also convinced 'that it was necessary to force the Irish midde classes to undertake their own administration'. A. R. G. Griffiths, 'The Irish board of works in the famine years', *Historical Journal*, 1970, no. 4, p. 647.
4. M. C. M. Simpson, ed., *Correspondence and conversations of A. de Tocqueville with Nassau Senior* (London, 1872), vol. i, p. 52.
5. McDowell, op. cit., pp. 203–4.
6. *Hansard*, 3rd, v, 387.

7. Ibid., xlv, 1060–85.
8. R. B. McDowell, *Public opinion and government policy in Ireland* (London, 1952), p. 197.
9. 2 & 3 Vic., c. 61.
10. 5 & 6 Vic., c. 106; 5 & 6 Vic., c. 89.
11. Quoted by McDowell, *Public opinion*, op. cit., p. 211.
12. Quoted by L. M. Cullen, *Life in Ireland* (London, 1968), p. 132.
13. O. MacDonagh, *Ireland* (Englewood Cliffs, 1968), pp. 29–30; see also Griffiths, op. cit. p. 647.
14. McDowell, *Irish administration*, op. cit., p. 166.
15. Ibid., pp. 167–9.
16. A. P. Williamson, 'The origins of the Irish mental hospital service' (Unpublished thesis, University of Dublin, 1970), pp. 179–80.
17. MacDonagh, *Ireland*, op. cit., pp. 26–7; McDowell, 'Ireland on the eve of the famine', op. cit., pp. 34–5.
18. Under 26 Geo. III, c. 27 (Ire.) which authorized such appointment.
19. *Seventeenth report, inspectors-general of prisons, Ireland* appendix, 33, 1839 (91), xx.
20. *Eighth report inspectors general of prisons, Ireland, 6*, 1830 (48), xxiv.
21. McDowell, *Irish administration*, op. cit., p. 174.
22. See Broeker, op. cit., especially chs. 2 and 3.
23. *Select committee on constabulary, Ireland, 6*, 1854 (53), x; *Select committee on state of Ireland*, 1002, 1839 (486), xii.
24. McDowell, *Public opinion*, op. cit., p. 185.
25. W. E. H. Lecky, *Leaders of public opinion in Ireland* (London, 1912), vol. ii, pp. 99–100.
26. 6 & 7 Will. IV, c. 13 and c. 29.
27. McDowell, *Public opinion*, op. cit., p. 185, citing Castle Howard MSS.
28. *First report of the commissioners of inquiry into municipal corporations, Ireland, 39*, 1835, xxvii.
29. McDowell, *Public opinion*, op. cit., p. 156.
30. *Hansard*, 3rd, xxxi, 98.
31. 9 Geo. IV, c. 82.

32. A. MacIntyre, *The Liberator: Daniel O'Connell and the Irish party* (London, 1965), pp. 236–59.

CHAPTER ELEVEN: THE CIVIL SERVICE

1. C. C. G. Greville, *Memoirs* (London, 1874), vol. ii, p. 382.
2. *Fourth report of the royal commission on civil service*, 5, 1914 [Cd 7338], xvi.
3. Gladstone papers, British Museum Additional MSS 44333/138, quoted in E. Hughes, 'Sir Charles Trevelyan and civil service reform 1853–5', in *English Historical Review*, 1949, no. lxiv, p. 84.
4. Ibid., 44333/65, quoted in Hughes, op. cit., p. 68.
5. *Report on the organization of the civil service*, 4, 1854 [1713], xxvii.
6. *Fourth report of the royal commission on the civil service*, 6, 1914 [Cd 7338], xvi.
7. Gladstone papers, B. M. Add. MSS, 44333/216, quoted in Hughes, op. cit., p. 210.
8. Morley, op. cit., i, p. 511.
9. Gladstone papers, B. M. Add. MSS, 44333/216, quoted in Hughes, op. cit., p. 210.
10. N. Gash, *Politics in the age of Peel* (London, 1953), p. 10.
11. J. Hart, 'Sir Charles Trevelyan at the treasury', in *English Historical Review*, 1960, no. lxxv, pp. 97–8.
12. Gladstone papers, B. M. Add. MSS, 44333/198, quoted in Hughes, op. cit., p. 54.
13. Ibid., 44334/206, quoted in Hughes, op. cit., p. 232.
14. The full title of the statute (29 & 30 Vic., c. 39) is 'The exchequer and audit departments act'.
15. Hughes, op. cit., p. 62.
16. A. Briggs, *Victorian people* (Pelican edition, London, 1965), p. 169.
17. Hughes, op. cit., p. 62.
18. *Hansard*, 3rd, cxxxviii, 2070. Layard was quoting Romilly, presumably John Romilly, Master of the Rolls and later the first Lord Romilly.
19. In 1860 Palmerston observed 'that the present system is most consistent with the public interest – namely, that those who are at the heads of different departments

should make a selection of the young men who are to be examined. . . .' *Hansard*, 3, clvi, 1197.

20. *Fourth report, royal commission on the civil service*, 8, 1914 [Cd 7338], xvi.
21. *Hansard*, 3rd, cxxxviii, 2040–79.
22. Ibid., 2089.
23. *Report of the select committee on civil service appointments*, xiii, 1860, (440), ix.
24. H. Preston-Thomas, *The work and play of a government inspector* (London, 1909), pp. 1–2.
25. See *Reports of the civil service inquiry commission*, 1875 [c. 1113], [c. 1226] and [c. 1317], xxiii.
26. See *First report of the royal commission to inquire into the civil establishments of different offices*, 1887, [c. 5226], xix.
27. I am indebted for this image to R. Knox, *Let dons delight* (London, 1938).

Suggested
additional reading

This brief bibliography is neither comprehensive nor general but comprises those books and articles which the author considers most immediately useful as additional reading on the specific topics which make up the chapters of the book. In several cases the work referred to is, of course, of value in more than one context; but each is listed only once, where it appears to have most relevance. Unless otherwise stated, the place of publication is London.

For a wider survey of the contemporary and pre-1960 literature of all kinds, and in particular that concerning the departments and inspectorates, the reader is recommended to consult the bibliographical essay in D. Roberts, *Victorian origins of the British welfare state* (New Haven, 1959).

CHAPTERS 2, 3, AND 4: FACTORY LEGISLATION

'Alfred', *The history of the factory movement from the year 1802* (1857). ('Alfred' was the pseudonym of Samuel Kydd.)

Best, G. F. A., *Lord Shaftesbury* (1956).

Butt, J. (ed.), *Robert Owen : aspects of his life and work* (New York, 1971).

Cole, M., *Robert Owen* (1953).

Driver, C., *Tory radical : the life of Richard Oastler* (New York, 1946).

Hodder, E., *The life and work of the seventh earl of Shaftesbury*, 3 vols. (1886).

Horner, L., *On the employment of children in factories* (1840, reprinted Shannon, 1971).

Hutchins, B. L., and Harrison, A., *A history of factory legislation* (1903).

Lyall, K. M., *Memoir of Leonard Horner*, 2 vols. (1890).

Thomas, M. W., *The early factory legislation* (Leigh-on-Sea, 1948).

Ward, J. T., *The factory movement* (1962).

——, *The factory system*, 2 vols. (1970).

CHAPTER 5 : COAL MINING

Boyd, R. N., *Coal mines inspection : its history and results* (1879).

Edmonds, E. L. and O. P. (eds.), *I was there : the memoirs of H. S. Tremenheere* (Eton-Windsor, 1965).

MacDonagh, O., 'Coal mines regulation: the first decade, 1842–1852' in R. Robson (ed.), *Ideas and institutions of Victorian Britain : essays in honour of George Kitson Clark* (London, 1967).

Webb, R. K., 'A whig inspector', *Journal of Modern History*, xxvii (1955).

CHAPTER 6 : THE POOR LAW

Checkland, S. G. & E. O. A. (eds.), *The poor law report of 1834* (1974).

Edsell, N. C., *The anti-poor law movement 1834–44* (Manchester, 1971).

Finer, S. E., *The life and times of Sir Edwin Chadwick* (1952).

Hodgkinson, R. G., *The origins of the national health service* (1967).

Poynter, J. R., *Society and pauperism* (1969).

Rose, M. E. (ed.), *The English poor law 1780–1930* (Newton Abbot, 1971).

Webb, S. and B., *The development of English local government 1689–1835*, 11 vols. (1907, reprinted 1963), volume vii.

Blaug, M., 'The myth of the old poor law and the making of the new', *Journal of Economic History*, xxiii, 1963.

Blaug, M., 'The poor law report re-examined', *Journal of Economic History*, xxiv, 1964.

Lambert, R. J., 'A Victorian national health service: state vaccination 1855–71', *Historical Journal*, v, 1962.

Suggested additional reading

CHAPTER 7: LOCAL GOVERNMENT

Hennock, E. P., *Fit and proper persons : ideal and reality in nineteenth-century urban government* (1973).

Lubennow, W. C., *The politics of government growth* (Newton Abbot, 1971).

Redlich, J., *Local government in England* (1903).

Smellie, K. B., *A history of local government* (1946).

Webb, S. and B., *The development of English local government*, vols. v and vi.

CHAPTER 8: PUBLIC HEALTH

Chadwick, (Sir) E., *Sanitary report, 1842* (1842, reprinted Edinburgh, 1965).

Cullen, M. J., *The statistical movement in Early Victorian Britain : the foundations of empirical social research* (New York, 1975).

Lambert, R. J., *Sir John Simon 1816–1904 and English social administration* (1963).

Lewis, R. A., *Edwin Chadwick and the public health movement 1832–54* (1952).

Midwinter, E. C., *Social administration in Lancashire, 1820–1860* (1968).

Macleod, R. M., *Treasury control and social administration* (1968).

Simon, (Sir) J., *English sanitary institutions* (1890; reprinted 1970).

CHAPTER 9: LAW AND ORDER

Hart, J. M., *The British police* (1951).

Parris, H., *Constitutional bureaucracy* (1969).

Radzinowitz, L., *A history of English criminal law*, 3 vols. (1948–56).

Hart, J. M., 'Reform of the borough police, 1833–56', *English Historical Review*, ixx, 1955.

Parris, H., 'The home office and the provincial police in England and Wales, 1856–1870', *Public Law*, 1961.

CHAPTER 10: IRELAND

Akenson, D. H., *The Irish education experiment : the national system of education in the nineteenth century* (1970).

Suggested additional reading

Broeker, G., *Rural disorder and police reform in Ireland* (1970).
MacDonagh, O., *Ireland* (Englewood Cliffs, 1968).
McDowell, R. B., *Public opinion and government policy in Ireland 1801–1846* (1952).
Nicholls, (Sir) G., *A history of the Irish poor law in connexion with the condition of the people* (London, 1856).
Griffiths, A. R. G., 'The Irish board of works in the famine years', *Historical Journal*, xiii, 1970.

CHAPTER 11 : *The Civil Service*

Cohen, E., *The growth of the British civil service* (1941).
Wright, M., *Treasury control of the civil service 1854–1874* (Oxford 1969).
Clark, G. Kitson, 'Statesmen in disguise: reflexions on the history of the neutrality of the civil srvice', *Historical Journal*, ii, 1959.
Hart, J., 'Sir Charles Trevelyan at the treasury', *English Historical Review*, 1960, lxxv.
Hughes, E., 'Sir Charles Trevelyan and civil service reform 1853–55, parts i and ii', *English Historical Review*, lxiv, 1949.

Index

235

Index